As a 20th century giant of faith, Ted Engstr̶ world, touching multitudes with spiritual li̶ ̶a̶n̶d̶ ̶h̶e̶a̶l̶t̶h̶ and influencing the evangelical movement with practical dynamics. His influence was, in ways, very much as Simon Peter's, whose shadow was a God-ordained extension of His divine love and power. His writings are worth the while of us all, as new and successive generations of believers will profit from them through this volume.

JACK W. HAYFORD, PRESIDENT, INTERNATIONAL FOURSQUARE CHURCHES
CHANCELLOR, THE KING'S SEMINARY-LOS ANGELES
FOUNDING PASTOR, THE CHURCH ON THE WAY

For more than 15 years, I had the privilege to meet with Ted Engstrom on a regular basis and ask him questions about life and ministry. Much of who I am today as a Christ-follower in leadership is because of his transparency, truth telling, and candor. I encourage you to use *The Essential Engstrom* as I will. Keep it front and center on your desk and when you need insight, wisdom or strategy, open it and be reminded of this man's great and insightful wisdom. May you be strengthened in your courage, committed to God-honoring excellence, protected by integrity, and inspired by visionary leadership. I know I will.

JON R. WALLACE, PRESIDENT, AZUSA PACIFIC UNIVERSITY

The best of leaders stand taller when standing on the shoulders of yesterday's leaders. *The Essential Engstrom* gives the leaders of today and tomorrow some very broad shoulders to stand on.

LEITH ANDERSON, PRESIDENT, NATIONAL ASSOCIATION OF
EVANGELICALS AND AUTHOR OF *LEADERSHIP THAT WORKS*

By his personal example, Ted Engstrom taught many of us what it means to be a Christian leader. He is no longer with us, but fortunately he wrote down many wise thoughts that can still inspire and instruct us. *The Essential Engstrom* is a wonderful gift to all who care about effective Kingdom service!

RICHARD J. MOUW, PRESIDENT AND PROFESSOR OF
CHRISTIAN PHILOSOPHY, FULLER THEOLOGICAL SEMINARY

Ted Engstrom literally wrote the book on Christian leadership, modeling how to lead, then telling us how he did it. This collection lets busy leaders cut to the chase and learn what made Ted tick, so they too can become a leader well-pleasing to God.

REX M. ROGERS, PH.D., PRESIDENT, CORNERSTONE UNIVERSITY

Having worked in an organization under the leadership of Dr. Engstrom, not only can I recommend the principles of this excellent book on leadership, but I can also testify to the practical implications contained within. The theory and the examples in this compendium are both sensible and helpful. If you are looking for answers to leadership questions, you will probably find them here. Happy reading for even better leading!

MARY DAILEY BROWN, PRESIDENT, SOWHOPE

Dr. Ted Engstrom's wisdom and leadership have impacted countless Christian leaders and organizations. Over the course of more than 60 years of servant leadership, Dr. Ted gained invaluable experience and insight, which he collected in the 55 books he wrote. This anthology captures the best of those books and will serve as an essential resource and reference. Even as Dr. Ted has passed on, we all can continue to benefit from his legacy.

DEAN HIRSCH, PRESIDENT, WORLD VISION INTERNATIONAL

Ted Engstrom was a role model, encourager, mentor, and leader for more than sixty years. Because he stood so tall in our sector, the Christian Management Association has established the Engstrom Institute to carry on his legacy of excellence in governance, leadership, and management. This book is a wonderful tribute to this remarkable man of God.

FRANK LOFARO, PRESIDENT, CHRISTIAN MANAGEMENT ASSOCIATION

Ted was a mentor and friend, whose service on 40 boards, authorship of more than 50 books, and both formal and informal leadership in so many ministries leaves us breathless. Lessons from Ted continue to challenge us. Thank you Tim Beals for a book of Ted's best that should be read by every board member and manager in Kingdom work.

ROBERT C. ANDRINGA, PH.D., PRESIDENT EMERITUS, COUNCIL FOR CHRISTIAN COLLEGES & UNIVERSITIES, CHAIRMAN, CEO DIALOGUES, INC.

If I could choose one quality for any person it would be wisdom. Ted Engstrom lived a life of wisdom and was clearly one of the wisest men I ever knew. My dear friend's wisdom flows through the pages of this great work. Let Ted teach you in print what he taught me and other leaders over the years . . . how to live and lead wisely.

DR. RON JENSON, CHAIRMAN, LIFE COACH FOUNDATION AND CO-AUTHOR, WITH TED W. ENGSTROM, OF *THE MAKING OF A MENTOR*

On behalf of the Engstrom family, we are so honored and pleased that *The Essential Engstrom* has been compiled. Our father's commitment to excellence, to furthering the kingdom of Christ, and to higher education and life-long learning has played an essential part in developing our walk with Christ. We are so pleased to have a book that will honor Dad's commitment to serving his Lord and Savior. Thank you Mr. Beals for working so diligently to pay a tribute of this kind to our father, Dr. Ted W. Engstom. May your life be transformed and enriched and may you gain a strong walk with Christ as you read about our Dad.

JO ANN ENGSTROM BENGEL, TED W. ENGSTROM'S DAUGHTER

Dr. Ted was a pioneer in teaching and modeling the art of Christian leadership. He was an inspiration and mentor to many of us for several decades as we prepared to take on leadership roles in the wonderful Christian agencies that were coming of age in the late 20th and early 21st century. *The Essential Engstrom* is exactly that—essential. It is essential as a reminder to those of us who have been in the saddle for many years and essential as a beacon to the new generation soon to follow. "For many are called, but few are chosen"—truly Dr. Ted was chosen to lead us and to guide us as we follow our Lord into a life of service.

JOHN REID, EXECUTIVE DIRECTOR, CHILDHELP

Aspiring leaders and seasoned veterans alike will want to keep this engaging volume close at hand. *The Essential Engstrom* abounds with invaluable inspiration and advice from someone who had a profound positive impact on my life for more than 30 years. In many ways, Tim Beals has compiled "the best of the best" by Dr. Ted W. Engstrom. Highly recommended!

DAVID SANFORD, PRESIDENT, SANFORD COMMUNICATIONS, INC.

Over the last forty years, I have read dozens of leadership books and hundreds of articles on the topic of leadership. *The Essential Engstrom* reminds us that while basic leadership ideas are often simply explained, their implementation is usually a complex art. This book confirms in multiple ways the gift God gave the church when He gave us Ted Engstrom. An excellent read. I highly recommend it.

EUGENE B. HABECKER, PRESIDENT, TAYLOR UNIVERSITY

The
Essential
ENGSTROM

The
Essential
ENGSTROM

Proven Principles of Leadership

TED W. ENGSTROM

edited by TIMOTHY J. BEALS

Authentic

COLORADO SPRINGS · LONDON · HYDERABAD

Authentic Publishing
We welcome your questions and comments.

USA	1820 Jet Stream Drive, Colorado Springs, CO 80921 www.authenticbooks.com
UK	9 Holdom Avenue, Bletchley, Milton Keynes, Bucks, MK1 1QR
	www.authenticmedia.co.uk
India	Logos Bhavan, Medchal Road, Jeedimetla Village, Secunderabad 500 055, A.P.

The Essential Engstrom
ISBN-13: 978-1-934068-06-9
ISBN-10: 1-934068-06-3

Published in association with the literary agency of
Credo Communications, LLC, Grand Rapids, MI 49525.

Cover design: Paul Lewis
Interior design: Angela Lewis
Editorial team: Credo Communications, Megan Kassebaum

Printed in the United States of America

Contents

A Man of Vision

The first time I met Dr. Ted, he told me a story. Several years before, Billy Graham and Bill Bright and Ted Engstrom met to reflect on the past and plan for the future. Near the end of their time together, they made a solemn commitment to one another: to finish well. They agreed to hold each other accountable and to pray for one another, that each one would stay true to his marriage vows, to his kingdom call, to the God he loved and served. And they did!

In a recent tribute to Dr. Ted W. Engstrom, *Christianity Today* said that he "has had a profound impact on generations of leaders." This was due in part because Ted was a man of action. He modeled what he learned from others and from his many years of leadership experience. But Ted was also a man of thought and passion. He mentored others through the written and spoken word. Ted was a friend to many, and a leader to all. What you hold in your hand is the essence of what Ted knew, practiced, and taught about leadership.

He came to leadership early. In the late 1930s, as a newly minted journalism major from Taylor University, Ted joined the fledgling Zondervan publishing company, accepting the post as the company's first editor and general manager, working directly under founders Pat and Bernie Zondervan. He never got over his love of books, and he would go on to write an average of one new book a year for the next half century.

He left Zondervan after a decade of service to join another upstart organization in the late-1940s, Youth for Christ, where he served first as executive director in Grand Rapids, Michigan, and then as president of the international youth ministry in Wheaton, Illinois. There he honed his leadership skills and nurtured two of his great passions: young people and world evangelism. It was at Youth for Christ that he would meet and minister with another young giant, Billy Graham, a life-long friend.

Ted was then called to World Vision in the early 1960s by its founder, Bob Pierce. A growing but floundering Christian aid organization based in Southern California, World Vision would be the place he would serve for the rest of his life. During the early years, Ted provided much-needed leadership as vice president and finally as president of the organization that would, under his leadership, become the largest Christian humanitarian aid organization in the world.

Until his final days at age 90, Ted served as president emeritus, going into the office several hours every day at World Vision International's headquarters in Monrovia, California. There he would meet and encourage visitors from around the world, correspond with his many friends and colleagues, and continue his book-writing ministry. Ted's mind and heart were never very far from those in need around the world, and he often prayed, not to be a great leader, but a faithful follower: "Make me, Lord, to be a more worthy follower off Him who cared for the poor and the oppressed, and could never see disease without seeking to heal it or any kind of human need without turning aside to help."

Throughout his more than 60 years of service to God and His people around the globe, Ted served on the boards of dozens of church, educational, and non-profit ministries, and at one point he served on 22 boards simultaneously. He also had an ongoing commitment to one-on-one mentoring and leadership development. I was just one of many who benefited from his generosity, encouragement, and tireless enthusiasm for leaders and the work God was doing in them around the world.

A Man of Words

His love for leadership and for leaders spilled over into every chapel talk, board presentation, conference message, and personal conversation. He lived and led well. And he shared freely what he had learned along the way. The following pages contain all of Dr. Ted's essential lessons about compassionate leadership and effective management. They also reflect his priorities for leaders present and future: the biblical foundation, the theory and practice, and the essential role of prayer, excellence, enthusiasm, and the family in the life of leaders.

Part One provides a lasting definition of the role and responsibilities of the godly leader, whether in a corporate setting, in the local church, in educational institutions, or in non-profit ministry. The biblical mandate and the many biblical examples of effective leadership are explored in *Part Two*.

In *Part Three*, the theoretical foundations for leaders is examined, and in *Part Four*, Ted looks at the importance of excellence in every endeavor. The entire text of Ted's most popular book, *The Pursuit of Excellence*, is presented there. *Part Five* tackles the critical issue of leadership integrity, culled from another of Ted's wildly popular title, *Integrity*.

Part Six and *Part Seven* cover the many facets of good management and successful decision making, respectively. Nearly every subject important to leaders in their day-to-day management is detailed in these chapters. *Part Eight* looks at the contribution of young leaders and the preparation of established leaders for the next step in the journey. *Part Nine* considers the important role of the leader outside of the workplace—at home and in the community. And the *Epilogue*—written a dozen years before the new millennium!—provides a fitting conclusion to the collection: it takes a prophetic look at the issues that will confront leaders in the twenty-first century, and it issues a fresh challenge to leaders like you.

In all, forty chapters summarize the convictions, experience, and wisdom of one of the most important thinkers and leaders of our day. Ted W. Engstrom's is a legacy to celebrate and a life to emulate. Let's get started.

Timothy J. Beals
May 2007

Part One

LEADERSHIP DEFINED

CHAPTER 1

What Is Leadership?

A friend of mine once visited a friend of his in a little church in Connecticut. He had been there for many years, preaching to a handful of people. My friend said to him one day, when he saw the minister washing the church windows, "What in the world are you doing?" He was occupied with every menial task in the church—many tasks that could have been turned over to high-school students or men and women in the church. His answer appeared pious and commendable—actually it was tragic. He said, "I do everything myself [to demonstrate his self-sacrificing]. I run off my own bulletins. I wash the windows in the church, as you can see. I put out the hymnbooks. I do everything . . . this way I know it's done properly." Was that minister a leader in the best sense?

Well, what is leadership? Everyone knows what it is. Or do they? No one seems really to be sure. We are able to define what managers do, but the closest we seem able to come to a broadly acceptable definition of leadership is, it is what leaders do. Then when we try to define leaders, about all the agreement we get is that leaders lead.

Frankly, leadership is an elusive quality, if in fact it is a quality at all. Sociologists and psychologists have examined individuals' leadership traits, far too often with meager results. The fairly recent enthusiasm for group sociometrics has proved to be somewhat more rewarding, but still leaves much in doubt.

Why should we be concerned? Because, as stated in the preface, leadership development is the key to meaningful development of modern society and the effective future of the Christian church in the world. We must take a closer look, because true leadership is a quality found in far too few individuals.

Making Things Happen

Nicholas Murray Butler, a former president of Columbia University, said, "There are three kinds of people in the world—those who don't know what's happening, those who watch what's happening, and those who make things happen."

Though leadership may be hard to define, the one characteristic common to all leaders is the ability to make things happen—to act in order to help others work in an environment within which each individual serving under him finds himself encouraged and stimulated to a point where he is helped to realize his fullest potential to contribute meaningfully.

Outstanding results cannot be forced out of people. They occur only when individuals collaborate under a leader's stimulation and inspiration in striving toward a worthy common goal. Action is the key, because the leader and manager types are not mutually exclusive. The leader usually is a good manager, but a good manager is not necessarily a good leader because he may be weak in terms of motivating action in others.

When all the facts are in, swift and clear decision is a mark of true leadership. Leaders will resist the temptation to procrastinate in reaching a decision, and they will not vacillate after it has been made.

We might say, then, that leadership is an *act* or behavior required by a group to meet its goals, rather than a condition. It is an act by either word or deed to influence behavior toward a desired end. A leader usually leads in many directions. We often identify people as leaders by virtue of their occupying a position, possessing recognized skill, knowledge, or prestige, holding a certain social status, or having certain compelling personal characteristics. However, they still may not be included in our definition because of the inability to motivate people and act decisively to accomplish this. Complete is the one who can meet *every* act requirement in all situations. Few there are.

Never Passive Puppets

Men of faith have always been men of action. It is an impossibility for active men to serve in a passive role. This implies that such people are decisive in nature. Leadership action demands faith. The setting of and striving for goals is an act of faith.

Richard Wolfe in his excellent book, *Man at the Top,* points out that when God creates a leader he is given a volition for action. It is in this way that God works in people (Philippians 2:13). Wolfe further states that prayer is not a substitute for action which flows from decision.[1]

That Christ motivates leaders for action does not mean that human beings are merely passive puppets. This is unbiblical. Paul admitted that God worked in him (1 Corinthians 15:10), but he never disclaimed his active part in getting results in his ministry. This is a part of the tension always evident in leadership action. The apostle was able toward the end of his life to say, "I have fought a good fight" (2 Timothy 4:7 KJV), meaning that he recognized the need and effectiveness of grace, but he did not underestimate the attributes that made him an active agent in leadership.

Performance Too

For many years the World Olympic Committee had to wrestle with Communist nations over their sending professional athletes to the Olympic games. Distinctions were sharply drawn, especially by non-Communist countries. The basic difference between professionals and amateurs is that professionals earn their living or are paid.

We need to enlarge the definition of leadership to mean that professionals are also the best at what they do and get results. This means they are professionals because of their ability, not only to act, but to perform at a high efficiency level. Such would be true of all fields and vocations. Persons are where they are because of prescribed study and credentials. But more than that: they perform competently. If not, they soon lose their right to practice through competition.

For Best Results

If a leader is to act decisively to get results, he must follow certain principles. We will examine these in depth later on. But here are some of the major considerations to achieve the best results:

1. *Determining your objectives:* Determine the important end results you want to attain and when. State them in writing—accurately, briefly, and clearly.

2. *Planning necessary activities:* Decide what major activities must be performed to achieve your objectives: general objectives; specific objectives; long-range, intermediate, and immediate objectives. Question every proposed activity: Is it necessary? Is it important? Why?

3. *Organizing your program:* Make a checklist of all *important* things that must be done. Remember that urgent things are not necessarily important. Dwight D. Eisenhower said, "The important is seldom urgent, and the urgent is seldom important." Arrange these in an order of priorities. Make a breakdown of each activity. Identify essential steps in sequence of importance. Question every step: *What* is its purpose? *Why* is it necessary? *Where* should it be done? *When* should it be done? *Who* should do it? *How* should it be done?

4. *Preparing a timetable:* Prepare a work schedule. Set a time limit for the completion of each step in your program. Stick to your schedule—or reset it. Don't let time slip by without definite action. Follow through.

5. *Establishing control points:* Determine where and when you will review progress in relation to objectives. Establish bench marks. Make necessary adjustments. Determine remedial action as required.

6. *Clarifying responsibilities and accountability:* Clarify all delegated responsibilities, authorities, and relationships, and see to it that they are *coordinated* and *controlled.*

7. *Maintaining channels of communication:* Keep your associates (superiors, assistants, subordinates, and others affected) fully informed. Make it easy for them to keep you advised on all pertinent matters essential to successful operations.

8. *Developing cooperation:* Successful achievement largely depends upon groups of people working together. Clarify results to be accomplished; identify what is expected of every individual affected. Otherwise, lost motion, misunderstandings, and frictions are almost certain to delay progress.

9. *Resolving problems:* Group thinking multiplies individual thinking and coordinates capacities of members of the group. Build morale through participation. An operating problem is any interference with desired end results.

    a. Spot the problem; clarify it. Tackle one specific problem at a time. Analyze underlying causes and contributing conditions.

    b. Develop possible solutions; select the best solution.

    c. Determine a plan of action; put it into effect.

     d.   Check results in terms of improvements and objectives. Acquire: Explore: Sort: Assimilate: Utilize: Test: Act—Follow through.

10. *Giving credit where credit is due:* Recognize and give due acknowledgment and credit to all who assist in the successful attainment of your objectives. The *law of recognition* is as fundamental as the *law of action and reaction.*

There Is a Difference

Because leadership is an attitude as well as an action it must be distinguished from management. While there are certain functional similarities in both leadership and management, leadership has distinctive characteristics. It is unfortunate that so often little attention is given to these distinctives in developing organizational philosophy and in training an organization's executive personnel. Christian organizations are no exception.

What then are some of these distinctives? Comparison may be helpful at this point. My friend Olan Hendrix has made the following distinctions (with some personal modifications):

1. Leadership is a quality;
   management is a science and an art.

2. Leadership provides vision;
   management supplies realistic perspectives.

3. Leadership deals with concepts;
   management relates to functions.

4. Leadership exercises faith;
   management has to do with fact.

5. Leadership seeks for effectiveness;
   management strives for efficiency.

6. Leadership is an influence for good among potential resources;
   management is the coordination of available resources organized for maximum accomplishment.

7. Leadership provides direction;
   management is concerned about control.

8. Leadership thrives on finding opportunity;
   management succeeds on accomplishment.

Not So Easy

Sometimes one might see a leader effectively managing a group of people, and he is apt to think, "That looks easy. Let me at it. I can do that."

A friend of mine told me about friends who visited him in the East. My friend took two sons and two of his visitor's sons water skiing. One was about fifteen years old; he said, "I'd like to ski, too."

"Do you know how, Jim?"

"Oh, yeah, yeah, sure."

My friend agreed to let him try it. As the pilot pulled the rope taut, the boy's skis were very unsteady. When it seemed the boy was ready, the pilot raced the engine and began to pull the skis; legs and arms went all over the place! The pilot pulled back around, harnessed the boy again, and tried once more. Again legs and arms and skis went in all directions. After the fourth time my friend asked, "Jim, are you sure you know how to ski?"

"Sure, I know how to ski."

My friend thought better of the question and asked, "Jim, have you ever skied?"

"Well, maybe not, but it looks so easy."

That's the way it is with leaders. We stand a few feet back and watch a person leading effectively and think, "Oh, that's easy." So we smile, say a few words, write letters, and lead meetings. We can give orders and receive reports, and it's great . . . until we really try. Then we discover that the leadership function is not that simple. Most fail because they do not possess the inherent capacity to take the necessary and right actions.

To summarize, the concept of *leader* in this book means one who guides activities of others and who himself acts and performs to bring those activities about. He is capable of performing acts that will guide a group in achieving objectives. He takes the capacities of vision and faith, has the ability to be concerned and to comprehend, exercises action through effective and personal influence in the direction of an enterprise and the development of the potential into the practical and/or profitable means.

To accomplish this, a true leader must have a strong drive to take the initiative to act—a kind of initial stirring that causes people and an organization to use their best abilities to accomplish a desired end.

CHAPTER 2

Leadership Style

Perhaps in despair over defining leadership, management theorists have attempted to picture it in terms of *style*. In using such a broad term they are attempting to describe how the person operates, rather than what he is. If you think about a number of leaders that you know personally, you can probably come up with your own summation of their style: "He's a player/coach kind of guy," or "she's a prima donna," or "he's a one-man show." In other words, we tend to characterize a leader on the way he leads by our personal perception of him or her. It follows that one person may feel differently than another about a leader's style. "Style" turns out to be the summation of how the leader goes about carrying out his leadership function and how he is perceived by those he is attempting to lead or those who may be observing from the sidelines.

What Leadership Styles Are There?

Since leadership style includes how a person operates within the context of his organization, it is easiest to discuss different kinds of style by describing the type of organization or situation that either results from or is appropriate for a particular style. Our concern for the moment is with those who are in positions of leadership already, rather than those who are pondering their potential skills. We will discuss five leadership styles: Bureaucratic, permissive, laissez-faire, participative, and autocratic. We will look at each one of these in terms of how the leader operates *within the organization.*

Bureaucratic—This is a style marked by a continual reference to organization rules and regulations. It is assumed that somehow difficulties can be ironed out if everyone will abide by the rules. Decisions are made by parliamentary procedures. The leader is a diplomat and learns how to use the majority rule as a way to get people to perform. Compromise is a way of life because in order to have one decision accepted by the majority it is often necessary to give in on another one.

Permissive—Here the desire is to keep everyone in the group satisfied. Keeping people happy is the name of the game. It is assumed that if people feel good about themselves and others that the organization will function, and thus the job will get done. Coordination often suffers with this style.

Laissez-faire—This is practically no leadership at all and allows everything to run its own course. The leader simply performs a maintenance function. For example, a pastor may act as a figurehead as far as the leadership of the organization is concerned and concern himself only with his preaching while others are left to work out the details of how the organization should operate. This style is sometimes used by leaders who are away a great deal or who have been temporarily put in charge.

Participative—This is used by those who believe the way to motivate others is to involve them in the decision-making process. This hopefully creates goal ownership and a feeling of shared purpose. Here the problem is the delay in action in times of crisis.

Autocratic—This is marked by reliance upon authority and usually assumes that people will not do anything unless told to. It discourages innovation. The leader sees himself as indispensable. Decisions can be made quickly.

What Do These Styles Assume?

Notice that each one of these styles depends to a large extent on one's view of people and what motivates them. Since the function of leadership is to lead, getting people to follow is of primary importance. The *bureaucratic leader* believes that everyone can agree on the best way to do things and that there is some system outside of human relationships that can be used as a guide. Hence rules and regulations.

The *permissive leader* wants everyone (including himself) to feel good. Internal stress is viewed as being bad for the organization (and perhaps even unchristian).

The *laissez-faire leader* either assumes that the organization is running so well that he can't add to it, or he assumes that organizations really don't need a focal point of leadership.

The *partcipative leader* usually enjoys solving problems and working with others. He assumes that others feel the same way, and therefore, the most will be accomplished by working together and sharing all decisions and goals.

The *autocratic leader* assumes that people will only do what they are told to do and/or that he knows what is best. In other words, he may appear to be a dictator. (But he can also be a benevolent dictator.)

Which Style Is Best?

Leaders are different. But so are followers! Which is another way of saying that some situations demand one style of leadership, while others demand a different one. At any given time the leadership needs of an organization may vary from another time. Since organizations have difficulty continually changing their leaders, it follows that those leaders will need *different styles* at *different times*. The appropriate style depends a great deal on the task of the organization, the phase of life at the organization, and the needs of the moment.

What might be some examples of how the *task of the organization* affects leadership style? A fire department cannot perform without at least some autocratic leadership. When the time comes for the organization to perform, to do what it was designed to do, autocratic leadership is a must. There is no time to sit down and discuss how to attack the fire. One trained person has to decide for the group, and the group must abide by his decision. Later on there may be more free discussion on which way will be best next time.

An autocratic style may even be needed in a Christian organization! In times of crisis, such as the evacuation of mission personnel, or the need to radically reduce costs, the leader often must act unilaterally.

Organizations go through different *phases in their corporate lives*. During periods of rapid growth and expansion, autocratic leadership may work very well. For example, the founder of a new Christian organization, or the founding pastor of a church, is often a charismatic figure who knows intuitively what is to be done and how to do it. Since the vision is his, he is best able to impart it to others without discussion. But during periods of slow growth or consolidation, the organization needs to be much more reflective to attempt to be more efficient. Participative leadership may be the order of the day.

Both of these considerations need to be tempered by the *needs of the moment*. Using autocratic leadership may work well for fire fighting (either real or figurative), but it will probably be less than successful in dealing with a personal problem. An emergency in the medical group may demand that someone assume (autocratic) leadership.

Fitting Style to Organization

It follows that ideally a leader should have many different styles. He should be a man for all seasons, shifting from the permissiveness of summer to the demands of winter.

Looking at it from the side of the organization, the organization needs to adopt a *strategy for effectiveness,* taking into account its needs and its "product." Most voluntary organizations and not-for-profit organizations are founded on the assumption of a common vision and shared goals. They have a strategy of *seeking success* (reaching their goals). When the organization is young, the founder can depend on his strength of vision to attract others who share his goals. However, as the organization is successful other means of maintaining a common vision will be needed. If the leadership style is not modified to include participative sharing of goals, too often the organization will adopt the strategy of *avoiding failure.* When the organization reaches a size where an autocratic style will no longer work, if the leader is unable to switch to a participative style, many times he is forced (and perhaps unknowingly) to adopt a laissez-faire style. Meanwhile the second level of leadership (which is now forced to run the organization) is most likely to adopt a bureaucratic style.

Where Are You?

What is your leadership style? A cursory examination of some of the management literature will help you discover that. Hopefully you will discover that you have exercised different types of leadership style at different times. Do you have evidence that you *can* change your style as needed? Or, as you think of the decisions that have been made in the past six months do you discover that they were always made the same way (by you, by others, together, or by the bureaucracy)?

Where Is Your Organization?

What kind of leadership does your organization need at this time? What is its task? What phase of organizational growth are you in? What are the different needs of this moment? Analyze this with help from your board, leadership team, members, etc. Are different styles of leadership needed for different areas of organizational life?

Where Do You Go from Here?

Review your calendar of meetings for the past two weeks. What happened in those meetings? Did you go to meetings just to announce your own decision (autocratic style)? Did you go to the meeting expecting to work with the group to arrive at a decision (participative style)? Did you go expecting to sit back and let others worry about the problem (permissive style)? Or, did you go intending to use the parliamentary procedures to make sure that the ship stayed on an even keel (bureaucratic style)? Perhaps you didn't go at all (laissez-faire)!

If you discovered that you handled each meeting in the same way, you are probably locked into one style and should consider intentionally setting about to modify your style as a function of the situation that you are in. By deciding before the meeting the style you will adopt, you will give yourself the advantage of being able to observe the response of the other members of the meeting.

If you have been limiting yourself to one style, sudden changes will often result in confusion in others. It may be necessary for you to very clearly spell out the ground rules as to how you are anticipating the decision-making process will work.

CHAPTER 3

The Price of Leadership[2]

True leadership, even when it is practiced by the most mature and emotionally stable person, always exacts a toll on the individual. In our world it seems to be axiomatic that the greater the achievement, the higher the price to be paid. The same is true of leadership. Jesus himself seemed to have this thought in mind when he said, "Whoever wants to save his life will lose it, but whoever loses his life for me will save it" (Luke 9:24).

It is so very true that any worthwhile accomplishment has a price tag. The issue reduces itself to one basic question: how much are you really willing to pay—in hard work and sweat, in patience, in faith and endurance—to obtain it?

Ted Williams—baseball superstar of the forties and fifties—was once asked about his natural ability and immediately replied, "There is no such thing as a natural born hitter. I became a good hitter because I paid the price of constant practice, constant practice." Likewise, professional excellence in leadership doesn't just happen; it comes only through persistent effort.

Criticism

Criticism is a great price paid by leaders. If one cannot handle criticism, it means that basically he or she is emotionally immature. This defect will eventually show up and impede the leader's and the group's progress toward the common goal. Every leader has to expect some criticism.

The mature leader is able to handle this and makes the needed adjustments and corrections. He or she is able to say, in essence, "Thank you for your criticism of my life. It has led to a deeper self-examination, which I needed."

Fatigue

Someone has said that the world is run by tired men. There is probably real substance in the statement, for genuine leaders must be willing to rise early and study longer than their contemporaries.

A wise leader will try to find a balance, a change of pace to reduce stress. You have no doubt heard the cliché, "I'd rather burn out for God than rust out for the devil." That sounds noble and pious, and a person's dedication must come close to the tenor of the thought.

But if a person "burns out" completely, that person's influence and contribution end. Proper health care, rest, and balance will help a leader maintain the ability to persist. A leader must be able to recognize the cost of leadership, both emotionally and physically.

Time to Think

Another price paid by Christian leaders is the time that must be taken for creative thinking and meditation. We do not often think of this as a price to pay, but it is. Most people are too busy to take time to really think.

For the sake of an objective, many leaders want to surge ahead without paying the price of thinking it through to determine the best methodology to meet the goal. It is well said that "the solution is not to work harder, but to work smarter."

Loneliness

A third price the leader has to pay—one we seldom consider—is the willingness to be alone because personal freedom has been lost in the service of others. A true leader promotes others—their interests, values, and goals. At the same time, the effective leader must strive to fulfill personal potential and goals without being absorbed into the group. This leaves him or her living alone, somewhere in between, because he or she has to both identify and be isolated from people.

The leader must be able to welcome friendship, but he has to be mature enough and have enough inner strength to stand alone against opposition.

Identification

Not only must the leader be alone and isolated at times, but paradoxically he or she must also identify with the group. The leader must always remain ahead of the group, but simultaneously walk with the people. This can be a fine line. There must be some distance between leader and followers. It is vital that the leader recognize this principle, yet be able to relate to associates.

This means there must be willingness to be an open, honest human being. Humanness has to come through. The leader cannot be seen as a robot, a cold, mechanical person afraid of letting the true self emerge.

To identify with people, leaders must pay the price of taking time to know their people—to share in their emotions, victories and defeats. Since most goals cannot be reached in isolation, the group must be leaned upon. The leader has to be aware of the group-mind, be willing to make concessions, and lead graciously without losing sight of the long-range objective.

Make Unpleasant Decisions

Many times it becomes the duty of an effective leader to remove someone who is not performing up to the stated standard. Christian organizations often have trouble at this point because leaders are naturally loath to hurt people.

All leaders must be willing to pay this price for the sake of whole. It is not easy, especially when one desires approval from everyone.

In most cases, when a person is relieved because of unsatisfactory performance, we are actually helping him or her; when the person is inadequate on a job, he or she is slowly being destroyed inside by the pressure and strain. Secretly he or she may be praying for deliverance!

Competition

Still another peril of leadership is the effect of competition. There is a price for leaders to pay if they suffer from a "competition anxiety" that takes the form of either the fear of failure or of success.

The fear of failure stifles competition because the leader will be afraid to proceed or become too involved; achievement is curtailed, and a loss of identity is sustained. To overcome this anxiety, the leader must do some serious reality-testing to know what the competitive world really is.

The fear of success can be just as crippling. The leader may appear to be well-adjusted, outgoing, and extroverted, but the price paid by an organization with such people is very high. A leader with this kind of neurosis will develop increasing guilt feelings as he or she and the organization achieve. This kind of person may strive hard, but will usually falter before the actual achievement. He or she will often find some excuse (which to him or her is perfectly logical) to block the realization of the ultimate goal.

Abuse of Power

In the long history of mankind, power has become accepted as a basic characteristic of leadership. In any organization, including a Christian group, when a person is given authority he or she is in a legitimate position to exercise control and influence. For some people this is ego-building and leads to autocracy. It is a peril, and there is a price to pay to keep from falling prey to this insidious temptation.

False Pride and Jealousy

False pride and jealousy are twins. Popularity can affect leader's performance. Feelings of infallibility and indispensability can decrease effectiveness. And it is not uncommon for leaders to go through deep depression.

Every person must have some pride, but pride turns to egotism when we magnify ourselves to the point at which we have no place for the other person. It is false pride when we become so wrapped up in ourselves that other people count for little. This kind of pride or egotism is far different from having a healthy self-esteem.

We all desire to be popular, and there is no great virtue in being unpopular. But there must be balance. A leader should be respected and held in esteem to get the job done better, but popularity can be purchased at too high a price.

When the price of humility is not paid, the temptations of infallibility and indispensability lurk. When people have false pride it is easy to accept the rationalization that they are less liable to make mistakes than others. Unless a person perceives his or her true self-worth and is led by the Holy Spirit, he or she may easily fall into this subtle trap. Despite experience and maturity, leaders often fail to see that all of us are prone to make mistakes. "After all, my judgment has usually proved accurate," is what many reply.

The myth of indispensability is often perpetuated by the best-intentioned people. Frequently organizations face this with their older leaders, who become progressively less able with age to assess their contributions objectively. They may drag their heels and really unconsciously stop—or at least hinder—growth and development.

Utilization of Time

Of all the things we have to work with, the most important is the time God has given to us. There is a price to pay in the use of our time because it seems that we human beings are born congenitally lazy. So we have to alter this process.

In the final analysis, managing our time really means managing ourselves. We have to budget our time just as carefully as we must budget our money.

Rejection

A leader, especially a Christian, must also be ready to pay the price of personal rejection. There is always the strong possibility that somewhere he or she may be maligned for his or her faith or Christian perspective on issues. This was the path Jesus walked: "He came to that which was his own, but his own did not receive him" (John 1:11).

The leader must be able at times to resist praise. He or she must have the courage to stand up against the spirit of the age. The leader must put the praise of God above the praise of men. He or she knows that the "fear of man will prove to be a snare" (Proverbs 29:25). The verdicts or judgments of men do not change one's standard if it is truly God- and people-oriented.

It takes a person with good ego strength to be able to cope with rejection. Normal, well-adjusted people want to be liked; it can become a difficult road to walk if a leader feels the cooling winds of indifference or dislike. Often people who are rejected are not recognized for their strength until they have left or died. Monuments are then built with the stones once thrown at the person in life. This is not easy to accept, but the leader must be prepared emotionally and spiritually to face this possibility.

You may be able to think of other ways in which a true leader must be ready to pay a price if he or she is to retain a responsible position. When all is said and done, when there is a willingness to make the sacrifices necessary for success, the span of service will be marked by high quality and excellence.

Part Two

LEADERSHIP AND THE BIBLE

CHAPTER 4

The Old Testament and Leadership

C hristian leadership represents action, but it is also a set of tools for spiritual men. It is not moral or immoral—it is amoral. Effective leadership methods can be used for ulterior and worldly purposes by people who are not spiritual at all. By the same token, spiritual men can take these tools and use them for the glory of God, whether or not all the tools in the leader's arsenal are spiritual. The issue is the spirituality of the person and how he can better use leadership tools for the glory of God.

But where should the spiritual man look for the tools? Is it enough to borrow from the secular world and its literature?

A legitimate question may be asked, "Is the subject of leadership biblical? Are there valid principles for organization and spiritual leadership? Can we study the Bible and find methods to guide our thinking?" Yes, if we have an open mind to perceive its insights. I believe that every basic, honorable principle in leadership and management has its root and foundation in the Word of God.

God Searched For Leaders

The Bible is filled with examples of God's searching for leaders, and when they were found they were used to the full limit as they met His spiritual requirements, despite their human failings.

Close scrutiny of leaders mentioned in the Bible indicates most experienced failure at one time or another. Many failed at some point in their lives in a marked way, but the key to their success was that they never groveled in the dust. They learned from the hand of failure, repented, and then were used in even mightier ways.

Let us note several Old Testament passages. This is not intended to be exhaustive, but rather to stimulate the thoughtful person to further study and to gain insight into leadership excellence.

First, consider Joseph. Is there in all of history a more magnificent example of leadership skill than his? Remember, he was placed in a high administrative position in Egypt not long after his jealous brothers had sold him to a passing caravan. He was given charge over the monumental harvest in Egypt. Then came the horrible years of famine, the delegation of the work, planning the whole operation, distribution of the materials, the foodstuffs, satisfying the complaints, and handling the grievances. The people he had to work with no doubt helped little (Genesis 41:14–57).

What a magnificent example of organization in Scripture! But God did not simply plant the skills in Joseph's brain so that he did it instinctively without thinking. I believe God does not work that way with men; generally I believe He will guide us to the subjects we need to study and learn if we show and exercise leadership qualities.

In the book I co-authored with my friend, Alec Mackenzie, *Managing Your Time,* I develop a biblical perspective regarding leadership.

Any view of leadership must be based upon one's view of man. The Bible gives us a clear view of man: "We all, like sheep, have gone astray, each of us has turned to his own way" (Isaiah 53:6). Thus, as sheep must be directed to move the entire flock along a single path, so groups of people need direction so that their efforts and energies will be directed toward a common goal.

This direction that people need must come from the top. God has ordained this and Scripture teaches it in many ways. Moses set up lines of authority following Jethro's advice, which we shall examine more closely (Exodus 18:13–27). The Aaronic priesthood was set up with a high priest and orders of priests under him in varying ranks (1 Chronicles 24). The husband is head of the home and a parallel relationship exists in the church (1 Timothy 3:4–5). It is important to recognize that authority flows from the higher levels to the lower in God's plan.

In Christian organizations there appears to be a recurring tendency to forget this. Confusing equality before the Lord with organizational equality, Christian workers may do themselves and their organizations a great disservice by refusing to accept duly constituted authority. We are admonished, "Everyone must submit himself to the governing authorities" (Romans 13:1).

We recall the Roman soldier who asked the Lord to come to his home to heal his servant, saying, "'I myself am a man under authority, with soldiers under me. I tell this one, "Go," and he goes; and that one, "Come," and he comes. I say to my servant, "Do this," and he does it.' When Jesus heard this, he was amazed at him, and turning to the crowd following him, he said, 'I tell you, I have not found such great faith even in Israel'" (Luke 7:8–9).

Place for Responsible Authority

None of this is to imply that all authority, of whatever character, is to be condoned. Authority carries with it great responsibility. Desirable authority is not viewed as being unwillingly imposed, all-powerful, insensitive, and unenlightened. Those entrusted with authority are divinely ordained to use it responsibly for His purposes. His ultimate purposes and those of the organization—hopefully one and the same—must be paramount. Sensitivity to the needs of those who are serving as well as those being served is essential.

The nature of authority may be far more complex than is commonly recognized even by those in management. The probability of this seems clear from the comment of Chester I. Barnard, the noted authority on management:

> A person can and will accept a communication as authoritative only when four conditions simultaneously obtain: (a) he can and does understand the communication; (b) at the time of his decision he believes that it is not inconsistent with the purpose of the organization; (c) at the time of his decision, he believes it to be compatible with his personal interest as a whole; and (d) he is able mentally and physically to comply with it.[3]

Barnard reminds us of not only the complex nature of authority, but also how much it does, in fact, depend upon the attitude with which it is received by those reporting to the person exercising it. Of the forces at work in leadership situations, we must identify those within the leader, those within the followers, and those within the situation. The life of Winston Churchill, who may not be seriously challenged for the title "Man of the Twentieth Century," bears graphic evidence of these three kinds of forces. Recall that after marshaling the morale and the forces of the British Empire in her darkest hour during World War II, he was rejected by his own constituency and replaced as prime minister by Clement

Atlee. He returned as prime minister at the age of 77, but never forgot the bitter lessons learned at the hands of fickle followers and history.

Then There Was Moses

Turning again to *Managing Your Time:*

The Bible has been quoted in numerous instances for its demonstration of management principles. One of the most outstanding examples is the instruction of Moses by Jethro some fifteen hundred years before the birth of Christ (Exodus 18:13–27). Noted below, from the Amplified Version, are these verses along with some of the management ideas and principles they suggest.

18:13 Next day Moses sat to judge the people, and the people stood around Moses from morning till evening. *(Observation and Personal Inspection)*

18:14 When Moses' father-in-law saw all that he was doing for the people, he said, "What is this that you do for the people? Why do you sit alone, and all the people stand around you from morning till evening?" *(Questioning—Discerning Inquiry)*

18:15–16 Moses said to his father-in-law, "Because the people come to me to inquire of God. When they have a dispute they come to me, and I judge between a man and his neighbor, and I make them know the statutes of God and His laws." *(Conflict Resolution—Correction)*

18:17 Moses' father-in-law said to him, "The thing that you are doing is not good." *(Confrontation)*

18:18 "You will surely wear out both yourself and this people with you, for the thing is too heavy for you; you are not able to perform it all by yourself." *(Evaluation—of Effect on Leader and People)*

18:19 "Listen now to me, I will counsel you, and God will be with you. You shall represent the people before God, bringing their cases to Him." *(Coaching—Counseling, Representation, Establishing Procedures)*

18:20 "Teaching them the decrees and laws, showing them the way they must walk, and the work they must do." *(Teaching, Demonstration, Job Specification, Delegation, Selection, Establishing Qualifications,*

Assigning Responsibilities)

18:21 "Moreover you shall choose able men from all the people, God-fearing men of truth, who hate unjust gain, and place them over thousands, hundreds, fifties, and tens, to be their rulers." *(Chain of Command)*

18:22 "And let them judge the people at all times; every great matter they shall bring to you, but every small matter they shall judge. So it will be easier for you, and they will bear the burden with you." *(Span of Control, Judging-Evaluation-Appraisal; Limits of Decision-Making; Management by Exception)*

18:23 "If you will do this, and God so commands you, you will be able to endure the strain, and all these people also will go to their tents in peace." *(Explanation of Benefits)*

18:24 So Moses listened to and heeded the voice of his father-in-law, and did all that he had said. *(Listening, Implementation)*

18:25 Moses chose able men out of all Israel, and made them heads over the people, rulers of thousands, of hundreds, of fifties, and of tens. *(Choosing-Selecting, Assign Responsibility. Span of Control)*

18:26 They judged the people at all times; the hard cases they brought to Moses, but every small matter they decided themselves. *(Judging-Evaluating, Management by Exception)*

18:27 Then Moses let his father-in-law depart, and he went his way into his own land.[4]

Passing the Test

It is clear from this passage that Moses received much direction and encouragement for the great tasks that lay before him. On numerous occasions he demonstrated great qualities of leadership even though his career as a statesman actually did not begin until he was eighty. At the outset, after God had called him, the people did not understand his role in their midst (see Acts 7:23–25). They asked, "Who made you ruler and judge over us?" Note that he never lost sight of his ambition and calling in life, which made it possible for him to emancipate his people from the oppression of Egypt. His steadfast heart and consuming drive to achieve made him an outstanding example for all potential Christian leaders.

Moses' experience at the Red Sea showed how well he had passed the test for would-be leaders when he faced an utterly impossible situation. Who would not have shrunk from the task? Before him lay the Red Sea; behind, the legions of Pharaoh. The people, faced with certain annihilation, were complaining bitterly. But Moses, with a resolute spirit, focused on God's promises and exclaimed to the people, "Do not be afraid." They all had every reason to fear. And because of Moses' faithfulness, God was able to demonstrate His power through one man, and it became a rallying point to assist the Israelites in their march toward the Promised Land. Superb leadership and implicit faith had won the day!

Later in the wilderness Moses had the right attitude, when he knew it was time to train someone else for leadership. He was fearful of being a paternal leader and pleaded with God to give the Israelites a successor. Thus, he did not indulge in self-pity, knowing that he would not lead the people into the land of promise. He was more concerned about the right kind of direction and future leadership.

Well Spoken Of

The New Testament provides a rather comprehensive commentary on the outstanding leadership qualities that Moses possessed, enabling him to succeed (Hebrews 11).

1. Faith (11:24—"By faith Moses, when he had grown up, refused to be known as the son of Pharaoh's daughter.")

2. Integrity (11:25—"He chose to be mistreated along with the people of God rather than to enjoy the pleasures of sin for a short time.")

3. Vision (11:26—"He regarded disgrace for the sake of Christ as of greater value than the treasures of Egypt, because he was looking ahead to his reward.")

4. Decisiveness (11:27—"By faith he left Egypt, not fearing the king's anger; he persevered because he saw him who is invisible.")

5. Obedience (11:28—"By faith he kept the Passover and the sprinkling of blood, so that the destroyer of the firstborn would not touch the firstborn of Israel.")

6. Responsibility (11:29—"By faith the people passed through the Red Sea as on dry land; but when the Egyptians tried to do so, they were drowned.")

It is no wonder that to this day, nearly all Jews—Orthodox, Reformed, and Conservative—consider Moses the greatest of all the prophets and leaders in the long history of Israel.

A Strong Spiritual Leader

David, the second king of Israel, was a striking contrast to Saul, the first king. Whereas David was noble, generous, and admirable, Saul was ignoble and lacked most of the fine qualities one expects in leadership.

David came to the throne about 1000 B.C. and reigned for approximately forty years. He conducted many wars of conquest, laid the foundation of the Solomonic empire, and initiated a period of splendor and power for the Israelite nation that has never been equaled. Behind David's accomplishments was the blessing of God. The reasons for his success are not difficult to find.

When David was approached by the elders of Israel (2 Samuel 5:1–3), they recognized his many sterling qualities and strong traits of leadership.

The nation had been torn by civil war, and the people were weary of strife. The happiness and prosperity of Judah under David motivated the rest of the tribes to desire the administration of David's kingship.

But in addition, the relation of all the tribes to David was an inducement: "We are your own flesh and blood" (2 Samuel 5:1). They would have him know that their feelings toward him were warm and tender. David was no foreigner, unqualified by the Mosaic Law to be king over the Lord's people (Deuteronomy 17:15).

The Israelite tribes through their representatives advanced another good reason for desiring David as their king. They referred to his former valuable service to the nation: "While Saul was king over us, you were the one who led Israel on their military campaigns" (2 Samuel 5:2).

They were telling David that he was the real power in Saul's government. Saul was only a figurehead. It was David who led Israel against their enemies and returned with the spoils of victory. Who then was more qualified to fill the vacant throne?

The strongest reason of all that the Israelite tribes offered for wanting David to rule was that he was God's choice. "The Lord said to [David], 'You will shepherd my people Israel, and you will become their ruler'" (2 Samuel 5:2). Christian leaders serve better when they are convinced they are in the will of God, for then they know they will be equipped for their tasks by God's power.

As a leader, David possessed qualities that attracted others. The elders came to him (2 Samuel 5:3); he did not go to them. He had ruled Judah well for seven years, and there was every reason to believe he would rule all the tribes as well. David took a loyalty oath with the people to protect them as their judge in peace and their captain in war. They in turn obliged themselves to loyalty and obedience to David as their sovereign under God. Such a sacred pact and solemn inauguration inspired much confidence in the people.

Valiant conquest and wise administration were important elements in the glory of David's reign. His very first exploit after he became king over all Israel was to capture Jerusalem from the Jebusites and make it the capital of the twelve tribes. He showed his valor by storming and taking the city. He displayed his political and administrative sagacity as well when he made the city the capital. Jerusalem was not so centrally located as Shechem, but he must have thought through the decision well. Jerusalem was a natural fortress, and it had a high elevation on the central highland ridge in Palestine that made the city a delightfully cool spot through the torrid summer.

Secrets to David's Success

There were several secrets to the glory of David's leadership. First, wise diplomacy distinguished his reign (2 Samuel 5:11). The king's generosity and attractive traits of personality won him many allies. He knew how to placate enemies as well as win friends. He was lovable. He made friends readily, while Saul had the strange ability to alienate people. These traits made David a successful diplomat. Those who did not respond to his generous nature he dealt with by force. But the wise, like Hiram of Tyre, cultivated his friendship and sent representatives to offer him favors.

Hiram I of Tyre (c. 969–936 B.C.) was a contemporary of both David and Solomon. He presided over a commercial kingdom with his capital in Tyre. His people dealt mainly in commerce and were skilled artisans, shipbuilders, and technicians. Hiram had access to the Lebanon forest of cedar in Syria and helped David with skilled labor and building materials for the construction of a palace and, doubtless, other major construction projects.

Thus we see David possessing the ability to reach out and strategically build his own empire. Leaders must have this quality to treat and lead others in such a way that their contributions may be used to good advantage.

Second, David's recognition of the Lord God in all his blessings made his rule outstanding (2 Samuel 5:12). He did not take credit to himself for all his success and prosperity. He was not boastful and self-assuming, as are so many who become power hungry. He humbly attributed his rise to power to the Lord and saw Israel as the Lord's people and himself as the leader under God, responsible to the Lord for leadership. Christian leaders who would lead people in this manner need never worry about success. When they recognize their highest responsibility is to the Lord, it makes all the difference in the world.

Third, David constantly sought the Lord's blessing (2 Samuel 6:12–15). This is the occasion of the ark's being brought to Jerusalem. There had been an earlier attempt to get the ark, but a Levite named Uzzah put out his hand to support the ark in defiance to a command of the law (Numbers 4:15).

The ark was left in the care of Obed-edom the Gittite. Those who watched the ark saw that the entire household of Obed-edom was blessed because of its presence in his house. They told David the news. When David heard it he proceeded to bring the ark into the city.

He knew the absolute necessity of having God's blessing upon his work and administration. The Christian leader today needs no less desire for his life and work.

Fourth, as a leader David was not ashamed to be involved in spiritual exercises. He was able to acknowledge the need for sacrifice for sin (2 Samuel 6:13). This time every precaution was taken to insure the proper conduct of the ark to the city. He rectified the former mistake. He did not place the ark in a cart now, but ordered those whose business it was to carry it on their shoulders to do so.

At the outset, when the Levites "had taken six steps," David offered sacrifices of "a bull and a fattened calf" as atonement for former errors (2 Samuel 6:13). When the Levites finished their task in safety, a thank offering of seven bullocks and seven rams was brought (1 Chronicles 15:26).

David was also unashamed to praise and thank the Lord: "He danced before the Lord with all his might" (2 Samuel 6:14). He leaped for joy because his heart was so filled with gladness, and he was so taken up with the Lord's glory that he became almost oblivious of the fact that he was, after all, a dignified king. This more than anything else gives us insight into the heart of a man who loved the Lord so much that he did not concern himself about what people thought.

Lastly David, as a strong leader, led his people in praising the Lord (2 Samuel 6:15). The great king thought it no disparagement to his dignity to lay aside his royal purple and put on the simple garb (a linen ephod) in order to minister better to his people. Such a garb was used in religious exercises by those who were not priests, as in the case of Samuel (1 Samuel 2:18).

The result was that the people brought the ark to Jerusalem with loud acclamations; they were demonstrative and joyful. They brought the ark to the city of David and put it in the place that the king had provided (compare 1 Chronicles 15:1; 16:1). In the presence of the ark, God was in the midst of His people.

David illustrated clearly that the Christian leader, too, must be willing to exercise spiritual means to mold, stimulate, and continually challenge his colleagues and subordinates. In spiritual work we rather expect it; in the secular world many shy away from it. However, the principles abide: God will always bless those who highly regard Him, no matter what the endeavor.

A Leader of Leaders

A striking example of strong leadership is Nehemiah, who along with Ezra and Zerubbabel was instrumental in rebuilding Jerusalem's temple and wall. Talk about organization! He possessed many qualities prerequisite for leadership excellence. His character was beyond reproach; he was a praying man; he displayed great courage in the face of much opposition; he had a deep concern for his people exhibited by his insight, tact, impartiality, and decisiveness. Furthermore, he did not shirk responsibility given to him.

Nehemiah had a tremendous ability to encourage his countrymen and then express appreciation when it was in order. He quickly dealt with problems before they became too severe. Thus he was a strong leader who was able to inspire his people to great heights.

His organizational ability, disclosed by his skillful strategy and detailed plans, is a challenge to every would-be leader. Read the entire book of Nehemiah, looking for every leadership and management principle.

The books of Ezra and Nehemiah tell of the returning exiles from Babylon and how they were absorbed into the Jewish community at the time. The accounts are a grand illustration of the importance of planning. Ezra stated that in all, 42,360 exiles returned with 7,337 slaves and 200 singing men and women. The priests numbered 4,289, there were 74 Levites, 128 singers of the children of Asaph, 139 porters, and 392 Nethinim and children of Solomon's servants.

Complete Reorganization

At this time some of the social and religious traditions were changed, especially in music. During the days of reconstruction there were more singing guilds, and the temple ministry was reorganized. The musical staff was enlarged (1 Chronicles 6:33–37). Details are preserved of the organization of the Levites as well as the porters who were distributed among the different gates. The Levites were divided into various areas of responsibility such as work in the chambers and the treasuries (compare 1 Chronicles 9:26–32; 23:24–32). These accounts were no doubt referring to the period of Nehemiah.

Three Facts Stand On

In summarizing this great leader, we can say that Nehemiah is known in Bible history as the great builder. In Nehemiah 3:1–6:16 three facts stand out. We see how great he was as an administrator. He knew what he wanted to do, how it had to be done, and who was to do it. The what, how, and who are tremendously important. They spell the difference between success and failure. Nehemiah had a clear objective or goal, a sound technique, and a good enlistment program. His function as an administrator included the ability to *analyze.*

He also succeeded in a program of total mobilization after he determined the plan. Everyone in and about Jerusalem was involved, from the high priest and his fellow priests to the goldsmith and the merchants (Nehemiah 3:1–31). The two rulers of Jerusalem as well as the common citizens were involved. At first some nobles did not feel it was proper for them to do such work, but apparently they changed their minds (compare Nehemiah 3:5; 4:14). Thus Nehemiah mobilized the entire population, revealing his ability to *deputize* and *delegate.*

Finally we see how Nehemiah achieved perfect coordination. In Nehemiah 3 it is almost tedious to read the phrase "'next to him (or them)." It appears over a dozen times, and "beside him" or similar another dozen or more times. Every man had his work and his place. Such perfect coordination enabled the wall to be finished in record time. We clearly see Nehemiah's ability to *supervise.*

Indeed, Nehemiah stands forever as a model for all would-be leaders who aspire to the heights of success, because he organized the whole nation and fulfilled his role as leader.

God Ordains People to Lead

The ancient Wisdom Literature of the Israelites, such as Psalms and proverbs, addresses itself a great deal to leadership principles. One of the Proverbs says that the hand of the diligent shall rule. The *Living Bible* reads, "Work hard and become a leader" (Proverbs 12:24). A true leader will use his imagination to improve his work and anticipate the next task.

That God ordains men to serve is clear from Psalm 75:6–7: "No one from the east or the west or from the desert can exalt a man. But it is God who judges: He brings one down, he exalts another."

The Bible constantly discloses the fact that God searches for people whom He can count on as leaders. Note the following examples:

1. 1 Samuel 13: 14: "The LORD has sought out a man after his own heart and appointed him leader of his people."

2. Jeremiah 4:25: "I looked, and there were no people."

3. Jeremiah 5:1: "Go up and down the streets of Jerusalem, look around and consider, search through her squares. If you can find but one person who deals honestly and seeks the truth, I will forgive this city."

God's plea for stable and effective leadership is probably best epitomized by the prophet Ezekiel, who said. "I looked for a man among them who would build up the wall and stand before me in the gap on . . ." (Ezekiel 22:30).

CHAPTER 5

Christ and Leadership in the Gospels

Any study of Christian leadership is incomplete unless the life of Christ is studied. It is essential to recognize at the outset that He epitomized the concept of leadership by His own statement: "For even the Son of Man did not come to be served, but to serve; . . . I am among you as one who serves" (Mark 10:45; Luke 22:27).

If Christ spent so much time with the disciples, it is certain that He wished to impress them with the example of His life. He came to serve, and so should they. This was His method of leadership. He unselfishly gave of His life, which culminated in His death on the Cross. The Old Testament predicted the Messiah would be a "suffering servant." His service did not degenerate into servility; He was humble, but retained dignity.

His kind of service set an example. He was willing to wash His disciples' feet. His perfect, sinless, human life ended in self-sacrifice at Calvary. Thus He showed His followers how to serve, and He demanded no less of those who would carry on His work on earth. Jesus teaches all leaders for all time that greatness is not found in rank or position but in *service*. He makes it clear that true leadership is grounded in love, which must issue in service.

When we take a closer look at His earthly service, we discover that His ministry was mainly teaching. He spoke with authority. At times, the greatest learned men of the synagogue were startled by His teaching. He knew that the only way to perpetuate truth was to pass it on, so He set out to train His disciples.

Furthermore His leadership demanded that others be obedient. He did not want His disciples to use their position for selfish purposes. So His leadership was largely carried out through teaching and training as well as through keen interest in individuals and their problems.

Another major consideration is that Christ's service was redemptive. He came to provide freedom for mankind: "The truth will set you free" (John 8:32). This idea must dominate the relationship between any true leader and the group. There must be a dynamic, living relationship—that is what is meant by *redemptive.* Men who had faith in Christ not only found eternal life, but were changed in the here and now. The Christian leader, following the pattern of Christ, will not use the group to achieve his own ends without regard for people who constitute the group. He will want to allow people to be themselves and thus be liberated. It is not a slavish conformity to the group that he seeks, but to help people serve a cause with joy, commitment, and a motivation that is prompted by Christ Himself.

Christ and Ambition

All Christians live under the mandate to develop their lives to their utmost. The apostle Peter urged us to "grow in the grace and knowledge of our Lord and Savior Jesus Christ" (2 Peter 3:18). This calls for sanctified ambition, with a strong drive to forge ahead and achieve. For centuries Christian mystics and others have written and spoken disparagingly of ambition, in the ordinary sense of the word, thinking it to be sinful.

However, ambition when used to the glory of God is praiseworthy. The word comes from the Latin meaning "canvassing for promotion." It is true that men can have much selfish ambition to control others, enjoy power for power's sake, and be unscrupulous in money-making and the control of other people. But Jesus gave to the disciples a different standard of ambition and greatness. "Jesus called them together and said, 'You know that those who are regarded as rulers of the Gentiles lord it over them, and their high officials exercise authority over them. Not so with you. Instead, whoever wants to become great among you must be your servant, and whoever wants to be first must be slave of all'" (Mark 10:42–44).

This passage reveals the true nature of ambition for a Christian leader. It is not to be according to worldly standards where men seek gain. Ambition is to be clothed with humility. It is not the number of one's servants that matter, but the number whom one serves. Greatness of exaltation is in proportion to greatness of service humbly rendered. True greatness, true leadership is achieved in selfless service to others. This is the clear teaching of our Lord. History and the contemporary scene are replete with those who have exemplified this selfless service:

Florence Nightingale, Mother Teresa of Calcutta, Sadhu Sundar Singh, Watchman Nee, Martin Luther King, Ken Taylor—a contemporary who has contributed all profits from the printing of the *Living Bible* and the *New Living Translation* into a charitable foundation—and so many, many more.

My good friend, Kenneth O. Gangel, who has stimulated my thinking about leadership, has made a vital contribution to the understanding of this biblical concept in his outstanding work, *Competent to Lead.* He has already done the major research in aptly setting forth both the positive and negative aspects of New Testament leadership. The remainder of this chapter and part of the next are adapted from his book as we consider this important theme (see *Competent to Lead,* 11–16).

What Leadership Is Not

Biblical leadership in terms of Christ's life is also clearly seen when we consider the negative side of the question.

A marvelous passage in Luke 22 holds some valuable principles for helping us analyze our Lord's view of leadership. The passage itself is contained in verses 24 through 27, but the context is of great importance also. The Lord had just ministered to the disciples in the final supper together in the upper room. They had finished sharing the bread and the cup and had experienced among themselves a worship relationship of the highest order, with the incarnate God in their midst and with the Father in heaven. It is almost unbelievable that the scene recorded in these verses could have followed that experience.

1. *New Testament leadership is not political power-play.* Immediately after sharing the symbolical representation of Christ's flesh and blood, the Scriptures record that the disciples fell into a dispute. The word is *philoneikia* literally means "rivalry." What is even more interesting is that this word does not describe an accidental falling into argument on occasion, but rather the possession of a habitual contentious spirit. To put it another way, because of their fondness for strife, the disciples verbally attacked one another in an attempt to gain political prominence in what they expected would be an immediately forthcoming earthly kingdom. Martin Buber once said that persons' inability to "carry on authentic dialog with one another is the most acute symptom of the pathology of our time."

Political power-play in the church is even more reprehensible than it is in the world. Yet it is striking that even before the first church was organized at Jerusalem; before a pastor ever candidated for appointment to a congregation;

before an official board ever met to design a building program, the church knew how to be contentious! Toward the end of the first century, John bemoaned that in at least one church there was a man named Diotrephes who liked "to have the preeminence among them," and the Diotrephesian tribe has multiplied in nineteen hundred years of history.

2. *New Testament leadership is not authoritarian attitude.* Luke 22:25 records our Lord's reaction to the arguments of His disciples. He offered first a comparison and then a contrast. The comparison is that their behavior at that moment was like the behavior of the Hellenistic monarchs who ruled in Egypt and Syria. Their leadership style is described as "exercising lordship"—using the word *kurieuo*—which appears frequently in the pages of the New Testament. At times it is used to describe the authority of God (Romans 14:9). Paul used the word often to refer to a negative control, such as death's attempt to hold dominion over Christ (Romans 6:9); the power of sin in the life of the believer (Romans 6:14); and the hold of the law on men freed by the gospel (Romans 7:1).

A similar word *(katakurieuo)* is used to describe Gentile rulers; the control of demons over men (Acts 19:16); and as a negative example in describing the behavior of elders with saints in the church (1 Peter 5:3). The verb form is never used positively of Christian leadership. To put it simply, *Christian leadership is not authoritarian control over the minds and behavior of other people.* Peter remembered the lesson of this night, for in writing his epistle he warned the elders not to "lord it over those entrusted to you."

The first part of Luke 22:26 has a grammatical construction of strong contrast: "but you are not to be like that." The kings of the Gentiles wished to be called "benefactor" for any little deed of kindness they might show to their subjects; it was expected they would practice autocracy and demagoguery. Whether that is right or wrong is not the issue; the point is that *Christian* leadership is *not* that kind of authoritarian control. Indeed, in defiance of that culture, our Lord added that one who is greatest in the church is actually *as* the younger, and the "boss" (leader) is *as* the worker.

3. *New Testament leadership is not cultic control.* One of the beautiful words in the work of the church is *diakanos*. It means "service" and is precisely what Christ did for His disciples in that upper room. The questions of verse 27 seem to be rhetorical: who is more important, the waiter or the dinner guest? Obvious answer: the dinner guest of course! But who is the guest and who is the waiter at this Last Supper? Answer: "I am among you as one who serves."

Conclusion: *New Testament leadership is not flashy public relations and platform personality, but humble service to the group. The work of God is to be carried on by spiritual power, not personal* magnetism, as Paul clearly pointed out in 1 Corinthians 1:26–31. Some leaders may *serve* the Word, and some leaders may *serve* tables, but all leaders *serve* (Acts 6).

The positive pattern of Christ in developing leadership in His disciples is clearly enunciated in A.B. Bruce's helpful book, *The Training of the Twelve*.[5] He suggested that the total report of the Gospels covers only thirty-three or thirty-four days of our Lord's three-and-one-half year ministry, and John records only eighteen days. What did Christ do the rest of the time? The clear implication of the Scriptures is that He was training leaders. What kind of leaders? How did He deal with them? What were the important principles of His leadership development program? Although it is not the purpose of this book to deal with the total subject of leadership development, certain principles may be helpful in making a transition to a positive declaration of what New Testament leadership is.

The Positive Side

Dr. Gangel suggests four positive declarations of what the leadership of Christ was like:

1. The leadership of our Lord focused on individuals. His personal conversation with Peter, recorded in John 21, is a good example of the way He gave Himself to His men in an attempt to build His life and ministry into them.

2. The leadership of our Lord focused on the Scriptures. His treatment of God's absolute truth was not diluted by relativistic philosophy. It held the Old Testament in highest esteem. The rabbis had distorted God's revelation, and the Leader of leaders now came to say, "You have heard that it was said, . . . but I tell you . . ." (Matthew 5:21–48).

3. The leadership of our Lord focused on Himself. Remember, in John 14:9, how He found it necessary to say to one of the disciples, "Philip, have you been so long with Me and you still have not known the Father? Take a good look at Me because if you understand Me you understand the Father" (author's paraphrase).

4. The leadership of our Lord focused on purpose. Christ had clear-cut goals for His earthly ministry, and a limited time in which to achieve them. If you knew you had to leave your present ministry within three-

and-one-half years and turn it over completely to subordinates you would be allowed to develop during that period of time, how would you go about doing it? You could do no better than to follow the example of Jesus, and the result would probably be a great deal like the leadership that characterized the New Testament church.[6]

CHAPTER 6

The Epistles and Leadership

There is a temptation, when dealing with the issue of New Testament leadership, to turn to the book of Acts because of its vivid description of early church life. It does provide a pattern for church government that is normative for church organization even though it is highly undeveloped. Among the vital lessons to be learned and taught, the book discloses the necessity of Christians to work together.

It is interesting to note that Christ did not reveal a complete church order, ready-made, when He gave the keys of the kingdom to Peter and the other apostles. The structure of the New Testament church unfolded as the church applied itself to its task through the leadership of committed people. There were the formation of missionary teams, the gathering together of workers in various groupings, the utilization of house-churches as well as the development of city churches, and the diversification of forms of Christian service. Sound leadership was required.

We are told in Acts that the Christians of that era turned the world upside down for Christ. This was not done by random and haphazard preaching of the gospel by a few vigorous men. It took much planning and strategy to effectively reach that generation.

But for a biblical study of leadership the book of Acts is insufficient by itself, because it is primarily a historical narrative, not a developed ecclesiology. We will be better helped by looking at the epistles of Paul and Peter, who apparently were commissioned by the Spirit of God to organize local churches and to speak God's plan and pattern for the functioning of those churches. A passage in 1 Thessalonians 2 will serve as a model.

New Testament Leadership Is Nurture

Nurture is a botanical term that describes the care and feeding of a young plant so that it grows properly to maturity. In 1 Thessalonians 2:7–8 Paul used some distinctive words to describe what nurture really is in the eyeball-to-eyeball relationships that mark leadership responsibility. He speaks of being "gentle"— the word *epioi,* used often of a teacher who is patient in the nurturing process of seemingly incorrigible students. In 2 Timothy 2:24 Paul used the word to describe "the servant of the Lord." As if that emphasis weren't enough, he referred to the gentleness of a caring mother, not a hired baby-sitter (1 Thessalonians 2:7). The word is used in the Old Testament to describe Jehovah's care of Israel.

But there is more to this emphasis on nurture. A gentle mother "caring for her little children." The word is *thalpe,* which literality means "to soften by heat" or "to keep warm." Deuteronomy 22:6 in the Septuagint uses the word to describe a bird caring for its young by spreading its feathers over them in the nest. Such a mother is "affectionately desirous" of the growing children, a term that seems cumbersome but appears in the Thessalonians passage in the King James Version, American Standard Version, and Revised Standard Version texts. The implication is a "yearning after" for the good of the group, which ultimately, as 1 Thessalonians 2:8 indicates, results in a sacrifice on the part of the leader.

Where is the manliness in all this? Where is the image of the sharp voice barking orders and "running a tight ship"? Where do we see the legendary Marine sergeant? Again a pagan culture distorts our understanding of spiritual reality. We identify masculinity with toughness and ruggedness, but God identifies it with tenderness. We think of leadership as "handling" adults, but God thinks of it as nurturing children. Joyce Landorf's book addressed to husbands is so appropriately entitled *Tough and Tender.*[7]

New Testament Leadership Is Example

The hard work of Paul's leadership spills out in 1 Thessalonians 2:9. During both day and night with great effort he worked among the believers. His life and his colleagues' lives were examples of holiness, justice, and blamelessness before God. Note that this was behavior *before the believers,* not an attempt at evangelism. In 2:5–6 Paul assured the Thessalonians that their leaders were "men," not some kind of superhuman ecclesiastical giants who wanted to run the organization by sheer executive skill and personal power.

New Testament Church Leadership Is Fatherhood

What does a father do? According to Ephesians 6:4 he is responsible for the nurture of children. Consequently the model of the family is used to describe not only regeneration in terms of infant birth, but also leadership functions as the teaching role of a father in the home. The words rendered "exhorted and encouraged" in 1 Thessalonians 2:11 are the words *parakalountes* and *paramuthoumenoi*. These are commonly used together in Paul's writing. The former is often used of divine ministry, but the latter is always a human word. *It is never used directly for God's comfort, but rather is descriptive of the way He uses people to minister to other people in the community of faith.*

A father also "charges" his children. The word has the idea of admonishing or witnessing truth so that they walk in patterns acceptable to God. I can think of many who have ministered to me so effectively and personally in the "father" role—men like Paul Rees, Carlton Booth, the late Jacob Stam, Herbert J. Taylor, and others. How we should thank God for those who have modeled this role in our lives!

Earlier we noted the positive pattern of Christ in leadership training. Now we mention the example of the apostle Paul. The development of the New Testament church is the multiplication of the lives of the few people described in Acts 1. Many early church leaders were personally trained by Paul; he was, in effect, the "pilot project." Timothy, Silas, Titus, Epaphroditus, the Ephesian elders, and many others grew out of his life and ministry.

There are local churches today that look much like the worldly leadership condemned by our Lord in Luke 22. If we are to serve our own generation with power and effectiveness, we must stop pretending that being a Christian leader is like being a king of the Gentiles.[8]

Paul's Words to Timothy

A key passage stating the qualifications of leaders is 1 Timothy 3:1–7. This is a crucial passage on church government. It deals with a man who was a bishop, an overseer. Two terms are used for church leaders in this text: *elder* and *presbyter.* These terms are applicable to the same person, as borne out by such passages as Acts 20:17 and 28 (see also Titus 1:5–9).

Two legitimate questions may be asked. First, if they were one and the same person, why were different terms used? Most modern scholarship concludes that there is little difference in the terms. It could be pointed out that *presbyteros,* the elder, describes the leaders as they personally were; they were the older, more respectable men. *Episkopos,* the bishop, the overseer, describes the function and task; a bishop was to superintend the church.

Second, if the elder and bishop were the same, how did the bishop become what he did become? The answer is that as the early church grew, it became essential for a leader to emerge from the elders. The elder who arose became known as the overseer.

Several factors produce this kind of thinking. For example, in Titus 1:5 we are told that the ministers were to appoint elders everywhere; this was clearly done in the church wherever they went. In Acts 14:23 we are told that after the first missionary journey, Paul and Barnabas appointed elders wherever there was a church.

Then we find that the qualifications of the two are really for all purposes identical. Titus 1:5 says, "For this reason I left you in Crete, that you might set right what was defective and finish what was left undone, and that you might appoint elders and set them over the churches in every city as I directed you" *(Amplified).* Paul when speaking of elders in the middle of the passage changed the term and called them bishops or overseers (1:7). The qualifications of 1 Timothy 3 and Titus 1 thus appear to be identical.

Again, after his third missionary journey, Paul called upon the elders of Ephesus to meet him at Miletus (Acts 20:17), and in verse 28 he referred to them as overseers. So the same title may be applied to both elder and bishop.

Then the question may be asked, "How did the term *bishop* come to be used?" It is a truism that wherever you have a body of people together, some will emerge as leaders. They will evolve naturally. So from these elders emerged some leaders, and they became known as bishops. They were then ordained or set apart, to be ministers or leaders of local flocks.

A Long History

The institution of elder had a long history even preceding the constituted church. We get the word *Presbyterian* from the Greek word; today a church by that name is built around a court of elders. In Numbers 11:16 we read of the appointment of seventy elders to help Moses in the administration of the people: "The Lord said to Moses: 'Bring me seventy of Israel's elders who are known to you as leaders and officials among the people. Have them come to the Tent of Meeting, that they may stand there with you.'"

Now, there were elders even before they were appointed. They were the officers to guide the Israelites. The Holy Spirit was not revealed at that time to all believers, but He came upon individuals one at a time for a unique ministry. To this day every orthodox synagogue has its elders who are recognized as the spiritual leaders in the community. In the formation of a synagogue, ten men, called a *minyan,* were required to initiate a formal congregation. They were usually strong community leaders. What a help it would be if we Protestants had more community leaders to serve also as leaders in the local congregation.

These elders or *presbyteroi* were respected, fatherly figures used by the Lord to give direction to the church.

The second term in 1 Timothy 3, *episkopos,* gives us the English word "Episcopalian." It is translated "overseer" or "superintendent." This concept also has a long and honorable history. In the Septuagint this word is found several times. In 2 Chronicles 34:17 there is a description of the men who were overseers of the public works projects. The Greek translation from the Hebrew used the word of those who were sent out to establish new colonies. It is a picture of an individual who has the oversight of something. In the New Testament it would be a person who has the oversight of a church or a group of churches.

Set Apart

Before we briefly study their major qualifications, it is to be noted that New Testament leaders were formally set apart for their office. They were ordained (Titus 1:5). The elders were given honor and duly recognized. They had to undergo a time of testing to prove themselves (1 Timothy 3:10). They were paid for their work (1 Timothy 5:18). They were liable to censure (1 Timothy 5:19–22). The tenor of these passages discloses that they were not novices.

Paul saw their duty as being not only to the church, but in other areas also. If they failed there, Paul said, chances were strong that they would also fail in the church. The first was the elder's duty in his home: a man who could not properly instruct his own household, Paul reasoned, would not be able to train a church. The second concern was the bishop's responsibility in the world: he must have "a good reputation with outsiders" (1 Timothy 3:7). He must be respected in the day-to-day living beyond the four walls of the church. That is the real test. Few things have hurt the church more through the centuries than leaders who have failed in their societal obligations.

Paul developed other key qualifications in 1 Timothy 3. First, he said, the Christian leader must be a man "above reproach" *(anepileptos)*. This word is used of a position that is not open to attack. It is an extremely high standard, for this person must be free not only from definite civil charges, but must also be beyond criticism. In this life, of course, no man can fully attain such a position, but it is an ideal that we must expect to be more nearly met in true leadership.

Second, the leader must be "the husband of but one wife." Several interpretations grow out of this text. But in the context we may be quite certain that it means he is a loyal husband, preserving his marriage vows and the sanctity of the Christian home. He must be able to manage his household well. As is obvious from the rest of the New Testament, this does not mean how well he can dictate and control his family, but rather how well he has developed the relationships within his family that are Christ-honoring and people-honoring.

Next, the Christian leader must be "temperate" *(nephalios),* and a few verses later he is told not to overindulge in wine. The word *paroinos* means to be addicted to wine. *Nephalios* also means "watchful" and "vigilant"; *paroinos* also means "quarrelsome" and "violent." So the burden of the passage is that the leader must not allow himself any indulgence that would stain his Christian witness.

Then Paul used two words to describe two more essential qualities for the Christian leader: *sophron,* translated "prudent"; and *kosmios,* translated "well-behaved."

The word *prudent* is translatable a number of ways, including possessing a sound mind, discreet, chaste, and having control over sensual desires. In biblical times a person having this quality was considered self-controlled. Spiritually, in this kind of a person Christ reigns supreme.

The well-behaved leader is so because he is *sophron* in his inner life. *Kosmios* means externally orderly and honest. So a leader's passion must be in control, and outwardly he must have recognized beauty.

A leader must also be hospitable. Much stress is found in the New Testament on this theme. The word *philoxenos* contains the idea of one who keeps an open heart and an open house; he does so without grudge. In the early church there were wandering teachers and preachers who needed homes to stay in. The true leader is sensitive to those in need.

Next, the Christian leader must have an aptitude to teach *(didaktikos),* says Paul. Instruction is a vital part of any meaningful and successful enterprise.

The Christian leader must not be a striker *(plektos)*. The individual is not to assault others when they err, but tries to be reconciled with those with whom he disagrees.

Gentleness is another important characteristic. The word is *epieikes,* and it is difficult to translate literally. In classical Greek it connotes the quality of correcting the law when the law appears to be unjust. A true leader, then, is one who knows when to retreat from the rigid, unjust letter of the law and can apply it with the right spirit. It could also include the notion that a leader should remember good rather than evil.

Two final thoughts remain in this passage. First, the Christian leader must be peaceable *(amachos)*. He knows how to achieve ends through tranquil means rather than by bullying people. He also must be free from the love of money *(aphilarguros);* he measures achievement of both himself and his subordinates without continually attaching a dollar bill or self-enhancement. His perception is more in terms of the intrinsic value of people and labor.

These qualities outlined by Paul were recognized even in the pagan world. William Barclay quotes an ancient writer who once described an ideal commander: "He must be prudent, self-controlled, sober, frugal, enduring in toil, intelligent, without love of money, neither young nor old, if possible the father of a family, able to speak competently, and of good reputation."[9] How much more does God expect of His children who are leaders!

Peter Speaks Up

The apostle Peter speaks to the issue of Christian leadership in his first epistle (1 Peter 5:1–7). When he wrote this letter he was a prominent figure in the early church. Besides being very close to Jesus, he became honored and respected because of his vital role in the formation of the first church at Jerusalem. It was he who preached a mighty sermon the very day the Holy Spirit was revealed to believers at Pentecost (Acts 2).

Thus it is important to hear his advice. Few passages show the significance of Christian leadership more clearly than 1 Peter 5. The writer began by addressing his words to his fellow elders; he set down the perils and privileges of leadership. First, Peter said, leaders are to care for the flock. They are to be properly motivated—not by coercion, but out of willingness. He will accept his responsibility, not merely out of duty, but with real compassion for others.

Second, Peter pointed out the high calling of leadership. A man must be interested in more than making a shameful profit, so that he will not be affected in his task or decisions by any personal gain that is unbecoming his office. Next, a leader is not to be dictatorial, a petty tyrant; his major consideration is to be a worthy example for his flock. He is not driven by the love of power or authority.

Humility, said Peter, should be shown in his relations with others, but he must also be challenged to react humbly to the testings that God allows in his life: "clothe yourselves with humility" (5:5).

Finally, the true Christian leader will not resist or rebel against the experiences of life, but will accept God's hand upon his life. He will be aware that God is molding him more like His Son through trial. Through suffering God can settle a man as well as restore one who has been trusting in his own flesh.

These qualities are essential if a leader is to serve effectively.

CHAPTER 7

"The Pattern We Gave You"

Aside from the passages in Timothy and Titus, which talk about the qualifica-tions of an elder or an overseer, it seems to us that the Bible has little to say about special qualities of Christian leaders.

But . . . the Bible does seem to indicate that the life of a Christian leader is to be such that it can be used as a model for those who follow. Consider Paul's comments to the Philippians, "But join with others in following my example, brothers, and take note of those who live according to *the pattern we gave you*" (Philippians 3:15).

There is a way of living that is first noticeable, and second, reproducible. The style and the ethos of organizations are the result of the pattern of leadership. It is certainly a pattern of management and leadership. But more importantly, it is a pattern of life.

What kind of a pattern are we giving the members of our organization? We can become so results-oriented, so production-oriented, so program-oriented that we forget we are in the business of developing people. Unlike the warrior chief who led his band into battle, most of our training is given before the battle, in the quiet times of reflection and discussion.

"Rejoice in the Lord always. I will say it again: Rejoice!" Easy to say. Difficult to do.

But we are not asked to rejoice in the environment that surrounds us. Rather, we are asked to rejoice *in the Lord.* What a privilege we have. First, to be in the Lord: One of Paul's favorite expressions is "in Christ." We too need to see our-selves as being in Christ, in the Lord. From a human perspective we fail continu-ally. We make wrong decisions, bad decisions. We are discouraged by the failure of our actions to produce a desired result. We are disheartened by staff members who fail to live up to our expectations for them. We are buffeted and tossed about by problems that are not of our own making. But we are in the Lord! From this perspective, the world takes on an entirely different hue.

And we can rejoice in the Lord because He is Lord. He is Lord of all. He is the One who said I will never leave you nor forsake you. He is the One who knows the end from the beginning. He is the One who works all things together for good. It is His kingdom that reigns over all.

This is the pattern that our followers need to see in us. There may not be much in the everyday reports we are receiving in which to rejoice. But in the Lord and for the Lord there is always the potential for rejoicing. We Christians have a straight-line view of history. We believe in a blessed hope. We believe that there will be a triumphant culmination of all things.

This is not to say that we should have a false enthusiasm or an "anything goes" attitude about others. Rather, it should encourage us to have a quiet confidence that though we walk through the valley of the shadow of death, He is with us. His correcting rod and His steadying staff comfort us.

There are times when we have to give direct orders. There are times when we must call people to account for what they have done. There are times when we must command the attention of our followers with vigor and determination. But in all, Paul asks us to "let your gentleness be evident to all" (Philippians 4:5).

Enthusiasm, but gentleness.

Sternness, but gentleness.

Activism, but gentleness.

A demand for excellence, but gentleness.

Why gentleness? "The Lord is near" (Philippians 4:5).

The Lord is near. "He walks with us and He talks with us." His coming again is nearer today than it was yesterday. The Lord never slumbers nor sleeps. His gentleness is what He asks of us.

"Live according to the pattern we gave you." Have a reputation for gentleness.

Will we meet our budget this month? Will the volunteers we need step forward?

Can I find someone who really understands how lonely it is to be in this position of leadership?

Can I keep up with this latest advance in technology?

Can we afford to send our son to college on my salary?

These are days of great anxiety. The very uncertainty of the world gives us adequate reason to be anxious. What is the antidote: "By prayer and petition, with thanksgiving, present your requests to God" (Philippians 4:6).

We are not suggesting a veneer of superficial piety. It is a truism of life that the familiar quickly becomes unrecognizable. We need a pattern. And yet we need a way of bringing to that pattern a freshness, a uniqueness that is the result of a freshness within us.

For the activists among us (probably the majority of Western Christian leaders) there is a need for us to turn our activism toward active prayer and petition. If prayer and petition are not a normal part of our everyday business, then perhaps we need to schedule them as part of that everyday business. What about leaving the last ten minutes of every meeting to ask one another what requests need to be made to God as a result of the meeting?

The world longs for leaders who have a quiet confidence that things are under control. When our private worlds are falling apart, we want desperately to know that there is someone to whom we can turn who will hold us up in the middle of our distress. When the organization is going through the storms that so often break over us, we need to turn to the person at the helm and find reassurance in calmness and control.

Rejoicing. Gentleness. No anxiety. Three pieces of the pattern. There is a fourth—contentment.

"I know what it is to be in need, and I know what it is to have plenty. I have learned the secret of being content in any and every situation, whether well-fed or hungry, whether living in plenty or in want" (Philippians 4:12).

Not a contentment with the status quo. Not a contentment that you are all right, and I don't have to be concerned for your welfare. Rather, it is a contentment that this situation right now is all right for us.

Perhaps it is easier for some of us to be content when in want. When we are in need, we tend to draw close to God and depend upon Him more. It seems much more difficult to have a feeling of dependence when budgets are being met and forecasts are being realized. Perhaps more than any other time we need to learn to be content in the midst of plenty. For it is He who gives the increase.

Rejoicing. Gentleness. No anxiety. Contentment.

Nothing about effective communication or good cost control or dynamic planning. Those are all skills, along with a host of other management skills, which we can learn. Rather a quality of day-to-day living that so permeates our lives that it leaves the sweet perfume of Christ wherever we go.

"Finally, brothers, whatever is true, whatever is noble, whatever is right, whatever is pure, whatever is lovely, whatever is admirable—if anything is excellent or praiseworthy—think about such things. Whatever you have learned or received or heard from me, or seen in me—put in practice. And the God of peace will be with you" (Philippians 4:8–9).

CHAPTER 8

Building on Biblical Priorities

What is a priority? Some will respond in terms of putting one thing before something else. Others may think in terms of ranking items. Priorities have both a "when" and an "if."

There are many priority questions. For the Christian organization there is the question of which purpose—of all the possible ministries with which we could become involved—is the one that God wants for *our* organization? Once we become involved in a ministry, we face the question of a choice between goals. Thus, of all the things that we could do to carry out the ministry, which seem most important to us now? Which should be postponed? Which should be abandoned? We can also think of priorities in terms of allegiance. What claims the highest priority in our lives?

Levels of Christian Priority

Christian organizations are comprised of the people of God in relationship. Although other organizations may claim to represent relationships, the Christian organization represents a special association, since each of its members is part of a larger family, the body of Christ.

In addition, the organization itself claims to be part of this larger body of believers—the church—that is both mystical and physical. The Bible indicates that the work of Christ is to be done by people in relationship, not by individuals. In Ephesians we are told that individuals are built up and gifted so that they in turn can strengthen a body which is to do the work (see 4:16).

The Bible does not tell us much about organizational structures. Through the ages, the leaders of the church have often disagreed on ecclesiastical structures or organizational relationships. But the Bible does have a good deal to say about the quality of relationships within its organizations. In fact, it goes so far as to assume that the key to organizational success lies in the *quality* of those relationships. Jesus told His disciples that men would know that they were His disciples by the quality of love they had for one another (see John 13:35). In His high priestly prayer, He even goes so far as to say that the basis of the world's belief in Him will derive from this oneness. Jesus said:

> "My prayer is not for them alone. I pray also for those who will believe in me through their message, that all of them may be one, Father, just as you are in me and I am in you. May they also be in us so that the world may believe that you have sent me" (John 17:20–21).

And although the Bible has its ringing command for service, it seems much more concerned with how this service will be carried out (and how the people who carry it out will live with one another) than it is with how the work will be accomplished. Evidently, the work of Christ is to be done by the church, caring for its members with the same concern that it has for the task it has been commissioned to do. And the Bible gives no simple answer as to when it is acceptable to sacrifice the good of the individual for the work of the local fellowship—or when aims of the fellowship are to be put aside for the good of the individual.

But we do have some models of people who are set aside for ministry. Certainly the commissioning of Paul and Barnabas in Acts 13:2 is an example. One can infer from this example that, from time to time, "healthy" people are to be sent out from the local fellowship and somehow given a different set of responsibilities. What does this have to say about Christian priorities as they apply to the individual and to the organization? We see three levels of Christian priority:

1. *Commitment to God and Christ.* This is of the highest priority. Everything begins here. It is a commitment so radical that Jesus demands that all other relationships be forfeited for it.

2. *Commitment to the body of Christ (the church).* This is a commitment as Christians one to another.

3. *Commitment to the work of Christ.* This is commitment to all the things we are called upon to do in His name.

Christian organizations and individuals ignore these priorities to their peril. After these commitments come all the rest of life.

Priorities in Christian Organizations

From what the Bible tells us, there are no permanent answers to the dilemma of "building up the body" and sending off the same people to carry out the work of Christ in the world. But it does appear that the Christian organization (as distinguished from the local church) has to put more weight in the direction of its goals.

Unlike the local church, the Christian organization begins from a different base. It is founded for a specific purpose. Unless it is primarily fellowship, this purpose is to carry out the *work,* although the dimension of fellowship will still be there. There are obvious expectations that one will experience Christian love and compassion. There is no question as to what comes first in the Christian organization: the *purpose* to which the organization is committed. The organization therefore accepts only "healthy" people. It recruits volunteers or paid staff on the basis of what they can contribute to the purpose (work) of the organization.

Thus, the Christian organization must ultimately put the good of the organization over that of the individual. If an individual is unable to perform the task which the organization calls for him to do, the organization must replace that person with someone who is able. It is true, of course, that there are times in the everyday life of an organization when the business of the organization should be temporarily halted to care for the individual. But what we are speaking of here is the long-range and ultimate decision that must be made.

The local church does not have such a clear point of decision, since it has two seemingly irreconcilable goals: (1) caring for the individual in relationship to the body of Christ; (2) doing the work of Christ. The local church cannot say to the individual, "We're sorry, friend, but you are no longer able to perform, and therefore you can no longer be a member of our organization."

There is a paradox to all of this. On the one hand, the individual is called upon to put the health of the church and its individual members before the work of Christ. (The assumption here is that if the church is healthy, the work of Christ will get done.) On the other hand, the group of individuals, the organization, must from time to time put what appears to be the immediate good of the individual aside for the good of the organization.

Recognizing the Priorities

But having stated the paradox, what do we do? First, we must recognize the tension and our human limitations. There will be individuals in the organization who will come out on different sides of the question. People who are by nature task oriented will tend to put the task before relationships. On the other hand, people who are more concerned with relationships in life will tend to see these as the major emphases. There needs to be a continual reminder that there are no easy answers. This is part of our struggle to be Christians in a sinful world.

Second, we must hold up our highest priority—the Person of the Lord Jesus. We can become so busy with "doing" that we can forget the reason for it. The question should always be: "Will this bring glory to God?"

Functional Priorities

Having made this rather cursory venture into the general spiritual priorities of the organization, let us look at priorities among goals. Which goals have the highest priority? How do we keep on the right track?

- We can't minister to everyone. To whom do we want to minister?

- We can't do everything. What must we do first?

- We can't be everything. What is most important to be at this time?

Because both needs and situations change, these questions must be asked again and again. The cycle continues. We will face new problems and receive new information about the world in which we are working. Thus, we need to review our priorities continually.

Posteriorities

Organizations have a great deal of natural inertia. Once individuals have been assigned to a task, and suborganizations such as boards or committees or departments have been formed, the groups tend to generate lives of their own. It is easy to stop asking, "What is the goal of the Christian Education Committee this year?"—and start wondering, "What should we do this year?

What we need are *posteriorities,* statements of things that we are *not* going to do this year. Picture an organization as an alligator—it has a great tendency to grow a very large tail. Periodically someone needs to chop off the tail, so the alligator can keep moving! Perhaps we need a committee to decide each year which 10 percent of all the things we did last year we are *not* going to do this year.

Part Three

CHRISTIAN LEADERSHIP

CHAPTER 9

Christian Leadership—What Is It?

Leadership can be looked at from many different angles. Leadership is a *position.* Companies have leaders. Organizations have leaders. Groups have leaders.

Leadership is a *relationship.* Leaders are persons who have followers—by definition. People may follow because of inspiration, self-interest, or because of organizational structures, but followers there must be.

Leadership is *actions.* Leaders are known by the leadership acts they perform. A person may have a long list of the attributes or traits of a leader, but if he never takes leadership action, he is not (yet) a leader.

Christian leadership differs from other forms of leadership basically in its motivation, the "why?" of its actions.

How to Define a Leader?

For years there has been a running argument about how to define a leader. Is he a leader because of the qualities or attributes he brings to the role? Is he a leader as a result of his relationship to a group? Is he a leader because of the things that he does?

There has been a general confusion between the person or role of the leader and that of the manager (or administrator or executive or director or general or ruler or whatever name the position carries). This confusion is quite natural. Persons who turn out to be good leaders find themselves in positions of leadership. Since they are seldom identified as leaders until the time they assume the leadership role, it is difficult to distinguish between the man and the role.

"Leadership is of utmost importance. Indeed, there is no substitute for it. But leadership cannot be created or promoted. It cannot be taught or learned." So wrote the dean of management experts, Peter Drucker, in *The Practice of Management* (Harper & Row, 1954, 158). Drucker believes that the task of the organization is to create the conditions under which potential leadership qualities become effective.

To put it another way, leadership qualities are part of the basic makeup of the individual. They will not necessarily become evident until that individual is found in a leadership situation. Most, if not all, the men and women who are found in leadership positions have been put there because their leadership ability has been recognized. If you or your associates do not have the basic makeup of a leader, you will not become one. But it does not follow that men and women who are potential leaders will automatically find leadership roles.

Are There Basic Qualities?

Are there, then, basic qualities that all leaders will have to some measure? Observers of leaders, and men who have been leaders themselves, seem to point to a handful of attributes that seem to be universal. Some of these attributes are either genetic or are closely wrapped up in the social environment. Others are acquired.

Selfless dedication is how General Eisenhower describes the first one ("What Is Leadership," *Reader's Digest,* June, 1965, 50). There is about a leader a belief in what he is doing, the goal he is trying to reach, the cause he espouses, that transcends himself. He is willing to sacrifice even himself to accomplish the task.

This takes *courage.* To hold on in spite of the apparent obstacles, to make a decision with inadequate information, to risk reputation and material well being, require a courage based on conviction.

A major portion of this courage will demonstrate itself in *decisiveness.* Decisions must be made. Other men vacillate. The leader makes a decision and moves ahead.

Leadership requires *persuasiveness.* If men and women are to follow, they must be convinced that the goals and aspirations of the leader are worthy of their dedication and be motivated to attempt them.

Interestingly, there is almost universal agreement that the most outstanding leaders have had a *humility* which has resulted in their accepting responsibility for failure as well as success.

Up to this point we have been describing qualities that might be held by almost anyone in any walk of life. But for the vast majority of leadership situations there must be *competence,* the individual must have skills in the area in which he is working. Without competence few wars will be won, no ocean liner will dock, no organization (Christian or other) will long survive. Competence, of course, assumes intelligence and creativity to whatever degree required.

Many people think of leaders as having a great deal of personality. Both personal observation and a small amount of research will quickly show you that "personality" is *not* one of the basic qualities. There are leaders who are personally warm and affable. There are others who are cold and aloof.

Nor can leaders be typed by the way in which they go about their task. There are many different styles of leadership—dictatorial, autocratic, benevolent, democratic. Some men lead by example. Others lead by sensing the direction of the crowd. Some are problem solvers who work well in groups. Others may pride themselves on their decision-making ability and rejoice in the personal quick decision. In the complex societies in which most of us work, men who hold positions of leadership in dynamic organizations have learned to adopt their style to the situation.

How to Find Good Leaders

But if Drucker is right, if leadership "cannot be taught or learned," what can we do to find, equip, and select the best leaders? The answer lies in building organizations that encourage and promote these basic qualities. Leadership *is* situational. It is a combination of the right leader leading the right group in the right set of circumstances. (The most competent leader is the one who can continue to exercise leadership in the broadest number of situations.) Do you want to attract and nurture good leaders? Build into your organization goals and objectives that require dedication and courage. Set high standards of conduct, responsibility, and performance. Demonstrate respect for the individual and his work. Create a climate where good leaders will be recognized and nurtured.

Once such a climate exists, good leaders will begin to identify themselves. It is at this point that training can begin. As we said earlier, a leader must have adequate competence in his field. If a man or woman is to assume broader responsibilities, he must have the specific training needed. This can be obtained formally by more academic work or on-the-job. If on-the-job, then care should be taken that both he and his supervisor understand the (measurable) objectives of his training.

It does not follow that because a man is technically outstanding that he is necessarily a leader. Putting a technically competent person in a leadership position when he is not a leader may only serve to prove the Peter Principle. ("All men eventually rise to the level of their incompetency.")

Are There Leadership Capability Tests?

Yes, there are. Enough has been learned by now to predict with reasonable accuracy whether an adult is a potential leader. Your local university, state employment service, or private testing agency may all be able to help.

What Is Christian Leadership?

So far we have said very little about *Christian* leadership other than to note that it differs basically in its motivation. However, it has been of continuing interest to us that those organizations that place a high priority on the worth of the individual, on high standards of personal conduct, on good communication, both up and down, organizations that have righteous convictions, out-perform the others. It has also been our observation that too often Christian organizations have had lower standards of individual and corporate performances than secular ones.

What is *Christian* leadership? It is leadership motivated by love and given over to service. It is leadership that has been subjected to the control of Christ and his example. The best Christian leaders exemplify to the utmost all those attributes of selfless dedication, courage, decisiveness, compassion, and persuasiveness that mark the great leader.

The truly Christian leader has discovered that leadership begins with the towel and the basin—in the role of a servant.

Selfless dedication is possible because the Christian knows that God has a grand strategy of which he is a part.

Courage is magnified by the power that comes through the indwelling Spirit.

Decisiveness comes from knowing that ultimate responsibility does not lie with him.

Persuasiveness is based on allegiance to a cause that transcends all causes.

Compassion is the human expression of Christ's concern for the individual.

Humility results from knowing that it is God who does the work.

Are You a Leader?

Are you a Christian leader? Lead! The *purpose* of leadership is to lead.

CHAPTER 10

A Christian Philosophy of Management

I recently had a letter asking my views on a Christian philosophy of management. I really worked this one over. What was it about my being a Christian that impacted on my management philosophy? As a student of management, an active manager in a large Christian service agency, and a teacher and resource person in management seminars, I obviously should have an answer. And I find I do. But the trouble is most people will think it is the wrong answer. For I don't think there *is* a Christian philosophy of management any more than I think there is a Christian philosophy of bus driving! To me the question reflects an attempt to divide the secular and the sacred. They refuse to be divided.

David Secunda, former vice president of the American Management Association and a thoughtful Christian, sums it up this way in a recent letter:

> Management, as I see it, contains nothing that is incompatible with Christian principle or belief. It is a means to an end—not an end unto itself and does not presume an agreement on ends. At its core is the effort to enhance the human potential and without this, it becomes a box of tools and techniques, useful but also subject to good intelligent misuse. Likewise there is no excuse to justify the bad or ill-managed Christian organization. Believers have no more license to be ineffective when dealing with human resources than does a surgeon. Lives are at stake in both cases.
>
> But, management as a process can benefit from change or an additional dimension. One such is a sounder being that would emerge from a blending of management and Christian fundamentals. We

have not done this but there is no reason why you shouldn't try. However, it can't be done from books and computers, even though they have a place. The understanding of each alone takes much of a man—to do both demands unusual commitment, but the prize may be worth the try.

Our Failure Is Practice, Not Philosophy

Now, there no doubt are men in management positions (both secular and Christian) who are operating in very unchristian ways. They are using their position to manipulate for their personal gain; they are conducting their business in ways that violate accepted ethics or perhaps even the laws of the land. They may be dealing with other human beings in very unloving ways. But as I read most current management theory, it seems very Christian indeed! There is increasing awareness that helping an individual grow as a person within the context of the organization's goal is good for the organization and good for the individual. Like good bus driving, the rules of a well-played game are reasonably obvious. The failure is not in the philosophy, or lack thereof, but in the practice. Again we are reminded that it is not things that are sinful, but men!

Christian Organizations Are Not Black and White

I have had the opportunity to be involved with a good number of Christian organizations from local churches to denominational headquarters, from overseas mission staffs to mission organizations within the United States. The black-and-white picture that I hoped would emerge as I compare the "secular" to the "Christian" world has just not come into focus. In fact, if anything, I would have to say that the situation is even a mushier gray than it was before.

Why Is This So?

Why is this so? Why should my experience be that I have found many Christian organizations that act in a much less Christian manner than some of their secular counterparts? I have thought about this a great deal, and I would offer the following suggestions.

Many Christian organizations do not have the luxury of clear-cut measures of performance. The profit-making company must make a profit in order to stay in business. It may have other more altruistic goals than just making a profit. But without that profit it cannot exist. Most Christian organizations, on the other hand, find it very difficult to set up standards of measurement against which they can audit their own performance.

Christian organizations usually assume a common allegiance to a higher purpose. Because this is so they have few checks and balances in asking their employees to put out more work, whether it be in the form of overtime, extra responsibility, or sacrificing family for the organization. It would be my belief here that they are operating in a very unbiblical manner, because of my strong conviction that the Bible puts our commitment to one another above the work to which we are called. The other side of this coin is the fact that many of the employees, who are usually working for a wage considerably less than the standard outside, feel that they are part owners of the organization and as such have a right to question anything that goes on or instructions that they receive.

"This is the Lord's work . . ." is used in a number of other ways. I am sure that most of what is done is quite unconscious, but too often we excuse poor working conditions, low pay, poor quality, or generally substandard personnel relations on the basis that we are conserving the Lord's money.

"We are all Christians here . . ." is used as an excuse for not having thought out procedures, particularly personnel procedures. Too often the assumption is made that being a Christian automatically gives one a common ethical base on which to work. As a result we can easily slip into business practices that are less than ethical.

What Can We Do to Improve?

If, as has been my personal observation, Christian organizations come out second-best when measured against secular organizations, what is the answer? As a Christian, what should be my philosophy of management? Just good management.

Excellence

It would always begin with excellence. If it is "the Lord's work," and it is worth doing, then it is worth doing with *excellence*. Every standard we set should be set as high as we can possibly set it.

Purpose

Christians then need a clearly defined purpose that is undergirded by a set of equally clear goals, goals that are both measurable and accomplishable. These purposes and goals should be used as the basis of the people we hire, the procedures we write, the facilities we acquire, the programs we carry out.

Communicated Goals

Christians should communicate. If we are the body of Christ, let's have the nervous system working. Goals should be clearly communicated to all those who are responsible for them. Here we enter the whole area of management by objective, the common building and sharing of goals. There is a need for goals to flow up from the bottom and to come down from the top. There is a need to identify and creatively resolve conflicts between management and subordinate goals, not necessarily to the mutual satisfaction of all concerned, but certainly with the mutual understanding of all concerned.

Goals center our thinking on the task and keep us from becoming functionally obsolete. There is nothing worse than an organization that has become so wrapped up in its function that it has lost sight of its purpose. Goals are like a suspension bridge that at one end rests on purpose, and on the other rests on function. They make certain that there is an open road between the two. The moment we discover that our Christian organization has become more interested in self-perpetuation than accomplishing a purpose, that's the time to push the self-destruct button. (And that takes courage!)

The Needs of People

Finally, I would continually struggle with the needs of people. In every organization that attempts to concern itself with its own people, there will always be a tension between caring for the individual and reaching the goals of the organization. It is in this area that we probably have more biblical guidelines than in any other area of management. A Christian view of management must include a constant review of the needs of the individuals involved. There will be many times where the desires, or even the personal welfare, of the individual may have to be subordinated to the good of the group or the achievement of the task. But let's make certain we spend enough time to recognize the particular conflict and the implications of its resolution.

A Christian philosophy of management? Perhaps. More appropriately, let's have a Christian view of *life*.

CHAPTER 11

Manager or Minister?

Minister or manager? Unfortunately, too many Christian organizations are led by men or women who have a gift for ministry and little training (or perhaps even an inclination) for management. Witness the large number of leaders of Christian organizations who are ordained. Of course, ordination does not exclude a person from having management gifts and skills, but it does give an indication of the leader's basic training and probable bias. The emphasis is on ministry.

But assuming that we have selected the best managers that we can find to lead the organization, do we not still have a responsibility to minister to each other? Of course.

Even a hardened army sergeant knows that people are the ultimate key to a successful organization. A great deal of thought and study has been given to make people more productive. Giving them more satisfying work, providing adequate remuneration, placing them in an environment that is conducive to their well-being, and helping them to feel good about themselves, the organization and their task, are among the most successful means. Most of the management literature indicates that all of this is done for the good of the organization, or for the good of the product. This is probably only a half-truth. Most men and women, be they Christian or non-Christian, enjoy helping others and seeing others operate effectively. And as a society, we seem to be learning about the innate responsibility of organizations to society.

But what about the Christian manager? If he or she is leading an organization made up of members of the same mystical body of which he or she is a part, is there not some special relationship implied?

What guidelines can we give?

If the organization is to survive, ultimately the organization must have first priority. There will be times when the organization will permit itself to be diverted from its task for the good of the individual. However, if the leadership of the organization believes that the organization exists as a part of God's purpose, eventually the tragic choice between the good of the organization and the good of one individual must be settled in favor of the organization. (We are assuming that every Christian organization has a fundamental responsibility for people.)

It does not follow that the manager never puts aside purposes for people. Most situations that will face the Christian manager will not be a clear-cut question of the choice between the organization and the individual. Usually they will be situations in which he or she can respond to the need of an individual without jeopardizing the organization. But nevertheless, the purpose is what the organization exists for.

How do we minimize the tension between caring for people and accomplishing our goals?

Start with the selection of staff. There are three common reasons why individuals seek to join a Christian organization. First, they may have a strong belief in the organization's purposes. Second, they may be attracted by the idea of working with other Christians in an environment that is usually less competitive and where, by definition, people are more likely to be concerned for the individual as a person. Third, there will be those who come to work in the Christian organization because for one reason or another they could not succeed in a secular organization. Too often, the Christian organization's lower salary structure is such that it tends to attract people in this last category.

Go for excellence! Look for the best people whom you can find. Concentrate on those who have a high sense of Christian calling balanced by the necessary skills and experience. One is not a replacement for the other. Both are needed.

Demonstrate in your own lifestyle what you expect of others. Model the desired characteristics of how the business of the organization ought to be carried out. The marks of a Christian organization are intangible. Simply because a gospel text is on the wall doesn't make the organization effectively Christian. Rather it is a spirit that is evident among the people, a spirit that is constantly engendered, prayed for, and modeled by those who are to set the pace.

Encourage members of the organization to minister to each other. Help them learn to respond to felt needs, moving into situations carefully and cautiously, guided by the Holy Spirit.

Recognize that you are an authority figure. We need to remember that although we are Christian brothers and sisters, the manager or leader is a very significant person in the life of the staff members. We are responsible for the person's well-being to the extent of his salary and working situation. There is an authoritative role that is forced upon each manager. Some of your staff will feel more "ministered to" if they see you as acting in the role of a peer. Others will need a father (or mother!) figure. The latter have a need to know that someone is in charge and that their personal welfare is in good hands.

Don't use "Christian" manipulation. Because many staff members are highly motivated to be workers in God's kingdom, we may be tempted to use this motivation inappropriately. Because they are doing the "Lord's work" does not give us license to take advantage of the individual's personal time. We must be careful not to expect our staff to work consistent unpaid overtime, nor accept all our pronouncements as divinely inspired.

Finally, be a lover. "Love God and do as you please." This suggestion made by St. Augustine assumes that if we loved the Lord with all our mind and heart and strength, what pleases us would please Him. How do we know we love God? By how we treat each other. "A new command I give you: Love one another. As I have loved you, so you must love one another. By this all men will know that you are my disciples, if you love one another" (John 13:34–35). Jesus said that. We can't improve on it.

CHAPTER 12

When Is It Time to Pray?

It is appropriate that we end this section on Christian leadership with a call to prayer. We live in an increasingly complex world. More and more we have a sense of impotency both as individuals and organizations. Too often we quietly ask ourselves, "What difference do we make anyway?"

But in such a world-gone-out-of-control the Christian organization has a special advantage. Because we believe in a God who stands outside the creation, because we believe *his* purpose will ultimately be accomplished, we can rest in the confidence that we *do* make a difference. We are part of a much greater "plan." Just because we cannot clearly comprehend how all we do will ultimately work together for good does not dissuade us from believing that we are plugged into the Source of all life.

Thus we can believe in prayer, we can call one another to prayer. We can make prayer an integral part of our daily lives. For we believe that prayer is the medium through which we carry on conversations about the business in which we are involved.

Christian Organizations Are Different

There is, or there should be, something different about Christian organizations. It is not enough that an organization have Christian purposes. There is a basic assumption that the leadership of this organization owes its first allegiance to God in Christ. Therefore, though we realize that most "Christian organizations" are those who are about some specifically defined Christian task, our primary qualification for Christian organizations is the relationship of its staff to Jesus Christ as Lord.

Suppose one had the opportunity to continuously observe the *behavior* of the individuals within the Christian organization? What would one discover? Should not one come to the conclusion that these indeed are Christians? Is not the tree most easily identified by the fruit it bears?

What Behaviors Should We Expect?

On a horizontal level, on the level of our relationships with all people, the Bible calls us to love. The measure of one's commitment to Jesus Christ is the gauge of this relationship. "By this all men will know that you are my disciples, if you love one another" (John 13:35). So in a Christian organization one should expect to observe acts of love, acts that demonstrate such a relationship.

In the vertical dimension one would expect to find acts of prayer, times of praise, petition, thanksgiving, and intercession that demonstrate that the individuals within its organization see themselves as part of a dimension much greater than themselves.

The Mystery of Prayer

It is not our purpose here to attempt to define prayer, or even to justify it in the life of the Christian. We are *called* to pray (Jeremiah 33:3); we are *commanded* to pray (Colossians 3:17).

At the same time, we need to understand the mystery of prayer. On the one hand, although we are asked to pray about everything, this does not excuse us from being responsible nor from attempting to be effective managers. On the other hand, the fact that we are doing an excellent job of leadership and management does not reduce the need or the demand for prayer.

The mystery is much like that of the sovereignty of God and the freedom and responsibility of man. The Bible states categorically that God is completely sovereign and will give his glory to no one. It states just as categorically that men have freedom and responsibility to act. Any attempt to bridge these two concepts intellectually is bound to fail. But as any mature Christian can testify, if one lives as though both were equally true, the results demonstrate that they are.

For reasons known only to the mind of God, prayer is always God's *modus operandi*, not only in our personal lives but in our organizations as well.

What Happens in the Organization?

Unfortunately, many of us can also testify to the fact that within our organizational life prayer has become a sterile thing at best. Too often it is almost formalized into a certain cultural role within an organization. Meetings may be opened or closed with prayer. There are set times when people are called upon to pray. To many, prayer is viewed as a duty imposed by the organization, rather than the natural response of the individual within the organization.

Perhaps even worse is the secret feeling of embarrassment we may have as executives and leaders in Christian organizations that others will think our desire to pray is just something we feel forced to do as part of our position.

When Is It Time to Pray?

The obvious answer is that it is always time to pray. Every successful leader in the Bible was an individual who recognized the importance and value of prayer.

We need to petition God for guidance and wisdom as well as blessings upon decisions that we have made. Praise should be continual.

Prayer is probably the single most important factor of uniting hearts together in a ministry.

Prayer is a statement of belief, a statement of faith. It acknowledges that our times are not in our own hands. It is not a substitute for decisions, nor the substitute for planning. Note that James does not condemn the planning of those who say, "Today or tomorrow we will go to this or that city, spend a year there, carry on business and make money." Rather, he wants people to acknowledge that the future is in the Lord's hands: "Instead, you ought to say, 'If it is the Lord's will, we will live and do this or that'" (James 4:13–15).

Where to Begin?

It is the responsibility of Christian leadership to model a life of prayer. This is true both in the personal life of the executive and the way staff associates are called to prayer with regularity and frequency.

We *need* to begin with formal times of prayer together. There *should* be a specified time at least once each week when the entire staff of a Christian organization within a given locality comes together to acknowledge themselves as Christians, to worship the Lord and to pray together.

But there needs to be something beyond this. In the paragraphs that follow, we describe some of the approaches with which we have had experience.

A Weekly Time Together

There is nothing sacred about coming together weekly, but it does seem that coming together as an organization within the context of a week of Christian life gives a spiritual rhythm and heartbeat to an organization. We are not suggesting that such a once-a-week gathering should be always devoted exclusively to prayer. Prayer should certainly be a part of such a time and there will be some times when we will want to spend the whole time praying together, perhaps corporately, perhaps by breaking up into smaller groups.

Certainly this is the time to share the needs of the organization or church and to demonstrate that we believe "prayer changes things," and particularly matters pertaining to our organization.

A Daily Group Devotional

By having staff gather in small groups of four to fifteen it is possible to give opportunity for a wide range of worship and prayer experiences. There is always the danger that such a regular meeting can become mere routine. Consequently, it is necessary to use your creative imagination in designing the program. One of the best ways of doing this is to have members of the staff involved in planning the kind of experiences they would like to have. This responsibility can be rotated within the group. Perhaps planning a month ahead is useful.

Prayer Partners Are Helpful

By pairing up individuals as prayer partners within the organization for a week or a month you give opportunity for more in-depth praying and sharing. Experience shows that this, too, can become no more than a formal nod toward prayer involvement. This tendency can be overcome by encouraging people to share prayer requests, get together for lunch, or have a coffee break together.

If you do establish such a system, it is also important that someone be made responsible for it.

Circulate Prayer Requests

These can come not only from within the staff, but also from outside the immediate staff. Whether you are a local church or a Christian service agency, there will always be those whom you know who need to be brought before the throne of grace. By specifically asking people to pray, you sharpen their own awareness of their own need.

Special Time of Extended Prayer

It would seem almost self-evident that the organization attempting to be sensitive to its role as part of the kingdom of God should discover times when the most appropriate response is to put aside all normal business and have an extended time of petition and praise!

Can we say a word here about asking people to volunteer their time? We know that most members of a Christian organization will have a strong desire to undergird that organization in prayer at all times. However, if times of corporate prayer are relegated to "after-hours," the message we transmit is: "The work is more important than prayer. Consequently, we haven't time to stop working to pray. We'll have to do that after we're through working." You get the point. At World Vision we call together over four hundred of our staff members each week to invest an hour of our time in prayer.

Prayer Retreats

We have also made it a practice at World Vision to encourage each working unit, whether it be a division or a department, to spend at least one day a year away from the office. Many times this can be used for praying about specific needs of the work unit. Again, the message given is that people are important as individuals and their spiritual contribution is a vital part of the organization.

Spontaneity in Prayer

This is where your individual leadership is really needed. Others are not going to feel comfortable with breaking into a discussion or a meeting with a suggestion that this might be an appropriate time for prayer unless you take the lead in doing it.

How easy it is to be driven by the urgency of the matter, the schedule of the next meeting, or the pressure of the next appointment to believe that we probably don't have time to pray.

A Ministry of Prayer

People who are given a special ministry of prayer need to be encouraged and undergirded. The local church needs a band of individuals with whom to share special prayer requests.

For the Christian organization, this may mean building up a group of people who will commit themselves to support that organization in prayer. For example, World Vision International has a ministry called International Intercessors. Over ten thousand individuals have agreed to receive monthly information about how they can offer their prayers of petition or praise in support of our work.

"May the God of Peace . . .

. . . who through the blood of the eternal covenant brought back from the dead our Lord Jesus, that great Shepherd of the sheep, equip you with everything good for doing his will, and may he work in us what is pleasing to him, through Jesus Christ, to whom be glory for ever and ever. Amen" (Hebrews 13:20–21).

Part Four

EXCELLENCE IN LEADERSHIP

CHAPTER 13

Give Up Your Small Ambitions

An American Indian tells about a brave who found an eagle's egg and put it into the nest of a prairie chicken. The eaglet hatched with the brood of chicks and grew up with them.

All his life, the changeling eagle, thinking he was a prairie chicken, did what the prairie chickens did. He scratched in the dirt for seeds and insects to eat. He clucked and cackled. And he flew in a brief thrashing of wings and flurry of feathers no more than a few feet off the ground. After all, that's how prairie chickens were supposed to fly.

Years passed. And the changeling eagle grew very old. One day, he saw a magnificent bird far above him in the cloudless sky. Hanging with graceful majesty on the powerful wind currents, it soared with scarcely a beat of its strong golden wings.

"What a beautiful bird!" said the changeling eagle to his neighbor. "What is it?"

"That's an eagle—the chief of the birds," the neighbor clucked. "But don't give it a second thought. You could never be like him."

So the changeling eagle never gave it another thought. And it died thinking it was a prairie chicken.[10]

What a tragedy. Built to soar into the heavens, but conditioned to stay earthbound, he pecked at stray seeds and chased insects. Though designed to be among the most awesome of all the birds, instead, he believed his neighbor's counsel: "Hey, you're only a prairie chicken . . . Come on, let's go find us some insects."

Right now, you may find yourself in a situation much like that changeling eagle. You know you are designed to perform tasks far greater than you've performed to date. You know you have the ability to move well beyond your present self-imposed limitations. But for some reason, you do not choose the path of excellence. You're an eight-cylinder automobile straining on four.

You say, "After all, it's so much easier to scavenge for insects than to soar among the heavens. It's so much easier to accept the status quo than to venture out." Of course it is. It's also easier to enjoy long, nonproductive lunches and attend seminar after seminar on "how to do it" than to sit down and get the job done.

But that which is easy and undemanding is seldom truly fulfilling. And it is 180 degrees away from the path toward personal excellence.

As we work out a strategy for pursuing excellence in these chapters, I think you'll realize that today is the day to start giving up your small ambitions. Right now, you can begin living your life with a vigor, enthusiasm, and intensity you never before imagined. Starting today, you can begin to draw from your own deep inner resources and cut a swath through mediocrity that will give your life a whole new significance. The results of your efforts may so surprise you that you'll wonder why you waited so long. You'll also find that your mind, stretched to a new idea or new action, will never retreat to its original dimension.

But a word of caution: Every truly worthwhile achievement of excellence has a price tag. The question you must answer for yourself is, How much am I willing to pay in hard work, patience, sacrifice, and endurance to be a person of excellence? Your answer is important, because the cost *is* great. But if you are willing to be the person you were meant to be, I think you will discover that *for you* the sky is the limit, because each one of us is called by God to become personally involved in an act of creation. Excellence is not restricted to sex, age, race, or occupation. This means a life of excellence is for *you*.

You may be a pastor, a student in seminary, a carpenter, an executive, a teacher. You may be a mother who every day tries to relate to two- and three-year-olds. You may be a parent of teenagers (a special prayer is said here for you). You may be young, or you may be in retirement. Whoever you are, today *is* the first day of the rest of your life—a day of new resolve and new beginnings. What will you make of these precious hours? Are you going to live the half-life of a prairie chicken, scratching for seeds and insects? Or will you choose to soar, to build a personal reputation for excellence . . . to live your life as God intended, knowing that He loves you dearly and that He wants the very best for your life? I hope you'll accept the challenge to make this day a truly new day.

J.B. Phillips paraphrases Philippians 1:10 as follows: "I want you to be able always to recognize the highest and the best, and to live sincere and blameless lives until the day of Christ." In the New International Version the apostle's prayer is that we "may be able to discern what is best."

The highest and the best—this should be the goal of every man and woman of God.

Be the best person you know how to be, in your personal life and on the job.

If you're not stretching yourself and your talents, ask yourself why not? And then do something about it.

Give up your small ambitions. Believe a big God; remember that "God is greater"!

Get angry with your own mediocrity, and then do something constructive to get yourself out of the same old rut.

Don't wait for the seventh wave of success to carry you on to the comfort of the shore. That's the thinking of the irresponsible and the lazy. With God as your strength, take responsibility for your own actions and begin living life with a fresh point of view.

An exciting life of excellence awaits you—and it can begin today.

The admonition of the apostle Paul in Colossians 3:17 is to the point: "And whatever you do, in word or deed, do everything in the name of the Lord Jesus, giving thanks to God the Father through him." No greater standard for excellence can be found anywhere!

Again the apostle says in Philippians 4:8, "If anything is excellent . . . think about such things."

But among many Christians, there are some serious tensions in the pursuit—or nonpursuit—of excellence. There are conflicts over what is highest and best. Some people feel the church should be a nickel and dime operation. Others choose to mortgage their grandchildren's future on the building of lavish cathedrals. Often, there's a curious mix.

I once visited a beautiful chapel on a new church college campus. In contrast to three obviously expensive chandeliers was a hand-drawn Sunday school attendance chart taped on the foyer wall. Twenty-five hundred dollars for chandeliers, but the best they could do to communicate what was happening to people was a crude graph.

A few years ago, we at World Vision were strongly criticized for purchasing first quality plumbing for a new building (a long-term investment that has paid good dividends). But at the time, to some, it seemed "too good." There's also been occasional criticism for our having carpeting in many of our offices, instead of less expensive tile. "It looks too posh," one said. "It doesn't look Christian," said another. (I've never quite figured out what a Christian carpet might look like!) Someone else offered, "It won't be a good witness. It looks too nice." Well, I couldn't disagree more. Somewhere in my files I have the actual yearly cost breakdown of how much World Vision has saved in floor wax alone. But that carpet also reduces noise and distraction, and thus helps our staff get the work done in considerably less time. As far as the Christian witness is concerned, we believe that appearance *is* important. We make no apologies for first-class appearance, because we as Christ's people are called to excellence. Further, we believe we are to *set the standards* of excellence for ourselves and others.

But "clothes don't necessarily make the person," and there is always the issue of confusing style with substance. Carpet on the floor will not hide shoddy work at the desk. That is why the quality of excellence must pervade our entire lives. It's so much more than just appearance. Scripture reminds us, "Let *all things* be done decently and in order."

In his book *Making It Happen*, Charles Paul Conn writes:

> Whatever It Is
> However impossible it seems
> Whatever the obstacle that lies between you and it
> If it is noble
> If it is consistent with God's kingdom, you must hunger after it and
> stretch yourself to reach it.

Have you ever watched a dramatic movie about mountain climbing, where the camera follows the climbers close up as they inch their way into the heavens, grasping and reaching for every little crevice of rock that in turn gives them a new footing to move up still a few more inches? And haven't you felt, Wow, I could never do that? You've got to be born a mountain goat to make that kind of a climb. But some of you *have* tried it, haven't you? And you've actually lived to discuss the experience. Sure, it was tough, exhausting, and frightening. But you did it. You moved beyond yourself. You gave up the comfort of the common plateau and headed toward greater heights. And you made it!

But mountains aren't the only challenges. What about your everyday life? How exciting are your sixteen waking hours each day? Are you constantly challenging yourself, straining your muscles? Or are you settling for less than the best?

If so, is it because you feel uneasy with the idea of having the best, being the best, or doing something that is truly outstanding? Do you find it easier to handle "excellence" if you can shift the responsibility for it onto someone else—or *onto the Lord*: "The Lord has really blessed his ministry," or, "The Lord really gave her great gifts"? Do you even feel somehow less spiritual if there is direct praise for a job done with *excellence*?

"To God be the glory" is more than the poetry of a song. It's the truth. God is the source of all our strength and to Him all glory and honor is due. But God has always chosen to use people like you and me. Frail? Yes. Prone to mistakes? Of course. Perfect? Never. But with all the things we can list that are wrong with us, there is still one overriding cry from the heavens: "I love you, and you are my child." When it comes to people, God has never made junk.

Striving for excellence in our work, whatever it is, is not only our Christian duty, but a basic form of Christian witness. And our nonverbal communication speaks so loudly that people often cannot hear a single word we say.

Dr. David McClellan, professor of psychology at Harvard, says, "Most people in this world can be divided into *two* broad groups. There is that *minority* which is challenged by opportunity and is willing to work hard to achieve something, and the *majority*, which really does not care all that much."

Which camp are you in? Are you willing to work at being good at something? Really good? Are you willing to spend your life building a reputation? Or will you settle for the life of a prairie chicken and never even come close to fulfilling your potential?

Dr. Melvin Lorentzen reminds us that "we must stress excellence over against mediocrity done in the name of Christ. We must determine to put our *best* into the arts, so that when we sing a hymn about Jesus and His love, when we erect a building for the worship of God, when we stage a play about the soul's pilgrimage, we will not repel people but attract them to God."

Perhaps part of our problem is just some defective theology. Many of us have difficulty living with the biblical truth that a sovereign God is doing it all—and the parallel truth that man has not only been given complete responsibility for his actions but is commanded to *take action*! This is part of the tension between theology and living, a tension that will never be—nor should it be—resolved. The following story may illustrate what I mean.

A pastor once made an investment in a large piece of ranch real estate he hoped to enjoy during his years of retirement. While he was still an active pastor, he would take one day off each week to go out to his land and work. But what a job! What he had bought, he soon realized, was several acres of weeds, gopher holes, and rundown buildings. It was anything but attractive, but the pastor knew it had potential and he stuck with it.

Every week he'd go to his ranch, crank up his small tractor, and plow through the weeds with a vengeance. Then he'd spend time doing repairs on the buildings. He'd mix cement, cut lumber, replace broken windows, and work on the plumbing. It was hard work, but after several months the place began to take shape. And every time the pastor put his hand to some task, he would swell with pride. He knew his labor was finally paying off.

When the project was completed, the pastor received a neighborly visit from a farmer who lived a few miles down the road. Farmer Brown took a long look at the preacher and cast a longer eye over the revitalized property. Then he nodded his approval and said. "Well, preacher, it looks like you and God really did some work here."

The pastor, wiping the sweat from his face, answered, "It's interesting you should say that, Mr. Brown. But I've got to tell you—you should have seen this place when God had it all to Himself!"

It takes action to achieve excellence—deliberate, careful, relentless action. There are no shortcuts to quality.

In his fine book, *Excellence*, John Gardner says, "Some people have greatness thrust upon them. Very few have excellence thrust upon them . . . They achieve it. They do not achieve it unwittingly by 'doing what comes naturally' and they don't stumble into it in the course of amusing themselves. All excellence involves discipline and tenacity of purpose."

Simple? No. Costly? Yes. Worth it? You bet. But before you take action, and before you move beyond your small ambitions, you need to make some basic decisions. You must know where you are going.

CHAPTER 14

Don't Just Stand There, Do Something!

D o what? you ask.

There are so many things to do. How can I possibly decide what is really important for me and my life? How can I be sure that what I *choose* to do is what I really *ought* to do?

Perhaps the simplest advice to you who face this dilemma is *Do something.* Choose a goal and work toward it. Later you may modify it, expand it, or even eventually abandon it for a better one. But first, make a decision. Decide to decide. Or, plan to plan. But don't be like the overenergetic cowboy who raced into the corral, saddled up his bronco, and rode off in all directions.

It may be difficult to choose a specific goal, but unless you do, you may find yourself forever frustrated, nonproductive, and eventually emotionally distraught.

Psychiatrist Ari Kiev of Cornell University, in his fine little book, *Strategy for Daily Living,* writes about the importance of *setting a goal* for a person's mental health.

> In my practice as a psychiatrist, I have found that helping people to develop personal goals has proved to be the most effective way to help them to cope with problems. Observing the lives of people who have mastered adversity, I have noted that they have *established goals* and sought with all their effort to achieve them. From the moment they decided to concentrate all their energies on a specific objective, they began to surmount the most difficult odds . . . The establishment of a goal is the key to successful living.

And we can add that the people who truly excel in their endeavors are invariably the ones who early on (1) determine clear-cut goals, and (2) habitually direct all their energies toward fulfilling them. The *decision* to go after a goal is the key to success. The *determination* to stay with it is what brings out the quality of excellence.

Let's take *you* as an example.

Let's say you are a pastor. What are some of your goals?

A Sunday school of five hundred?

A counseling program for all ages in your church?

Your own summer camp?

Two books published in the next three years?

Preparation of four really strong sermons that will stand the test of time?

Obviously you cannot do all these things at once, but what would happen if you took them one at a time? Let's take the goal of writing four truly effective and unforgettable sermons.

Let's say you invested one hour each day, five days a week, toward your goal of producing four great messages. That would be five hours a week, twenty hours a month, two hundred forty hours a year. That's a lot of working hours toward your goal—two hundred forty hours of productive, uninterrupted time. I think you'll agree that with that kind of time spent you could produce some sermons that would become classics.

But what would happen if you were to approach your decision in *this* manner?

> Well, I'd really like to write a few great sermons within the next few years. But I'm still pretty young, and I have lots of time. I think that next summer at the lake would be the perfect time to get moving on the research. Or if that doesn't work out, then maybe I could get started during a couple weekends away next fall.

Good intentions, but will you ever prepare those sermons? Without a conscious decision to start—and finish—will you achieve the quality you want? Will they be truly great? Probably not, because the pursuit of excellence is precisely that—a pursuit! A hot pursuit, if you like, for something you want very much. Dr. Kiev says, "Always have the next goal in the back of your mind, since the most satisfaction comes from *pursuing* a goal, not simply from achieving it."

You may recall the marvelous swimmer, John Naber, who won five gold medals at the Olympic Games in Montreal in 1976. John is a Christian, and it was he who led the victorious American contingent around the Olympic track following the games, triumphantly waving a small American flag.

On his return home to Southern California, he spent an evening in my home church and told of the events of the Montreal Olympics; then he said something that rather startled all of us.

John indicated that following the euphoria of the victories and the adulation he received upon returning home, and after all of the press interviews, he went into deep depression. He knew this wasn't what he ought to feel and sense as a Christian, and he could not figure out what had happened after he had achieved the goals toward which he had worked so hard and so long. He then realized, he reported, that he did not have at that time any other goals beyond winning the Olympic events. As a Christian, he realized that there were better and higher things toward which he needed to strive, and he needed to reset his goals in serving Christ. Recognizing this and facing the situation, he established new goals and testified to the way the Lord met him at this particular point of need.

In contrast, you may recall young speed skater, Eric Heiden, who, with his sister, was a favorite of the 1980 Olympic Winter Games in Lake Placid, New York. Eric also won his share of gold medals but did not share the problem John Naber faced. Throughout his training and participation, the Olympic wins were simply a step along the way to the achievement of a greater goal—to be a successful surgeon like his father.

Remember, the most satisfaction comes from pursuing the goal, not simply from achieving it!

Remember how Elijah, in the Old Testament, following the stunning victory which God granted to him over the priests of Baal at Mount Carmel, sat under the juniper tree and pouted? He was completely defeated, even though God had given him great victory. Why? At that moment he did not have further direction for his life. But the Lord met him at his point of need, and Elijah went on to further victories in God's name.

As you pursue excellence, you will find that the world around you will have an almost uncanny way of stepping aside when you say, "This is my goal. I am going to reach it." Og Mandino, in his classic *The Greatest Secret in the World,* indicates the importance of sticking with your goal, step by step:

> The prizes of life are at the end of each journey, not near the beginning: and it is not given to me to know how many steps are necessary in order to reach my goal. Failure I may still encounter at the thousandth step, yet success hides behind the next bend in the road.

Never will I know how close it lies unless I turn the corner . . . I will be likened to the rain drop which washes away the mountain; the ant who devours a tiger; the star which brightens the earth; the slave who builds a pyramid. I will build my castle one brick at a time, for I know that small attempts repeated will complete any undertaking.[11]

Small attempts repeated
One hour a day
Twenty hours a month
Two hundred forty hours a year!

Are you willing to make that kind of commitment toward fulfilling one of your goals? Which of your goals would *not* give up in submission to this kind of relentless discipline?

Many years ago I set a goal, and I set it high. I determined to be the best and most effective manager I could possibly be—not necessarily better than anyone else but better than the Ted Engstrom I saw in the shaving mirror the morning before. What an exciting adventure it has been! I'm sure it is quite obvious to my associates that I haven't always managed well, but I've always *strived* to manage well. My journey is far from over, and I still read everything I can on the subject of management. I read articles, books, specialized magazines, and news clippings. I attend management seminars (and also lecture on the subject several dozen times every year); I spend time with the best management consultants, picking their brains. Every day of my life is another twenty-four hours when I try to manage better than I did the day before. And I'm still learning and seeking to sharpen what I feel is my God-given gift of administration.

An ego trip? I hope not.

A power play to keep others in subjection? No.

I have simply decided to excel in this one area. And it's a decision for which I thank God daily.

Early in his ministry, the great Bible teacher Martin Lloyd-Jones vowed he would master the book of Romans. He did. During the years he pastored in the great Westminster Chapel in London he preached through this epistle several times, taking as much as three years at a time to do so, verse by verse, sentence by sentence, word by word, thought by thought. He excelled in his understanding and exposition of this great doctrinal book of the New Testament. Certainly Dr.

Jones took to heart Paul's admonition in 1 Corinthians 14:12: "Excel in gifts that build up the church"!

History is replete with examples of men and women who changed their world because they dared to accept the challenge of a dream—a goal—of a Mt. Everest . . . a four-minute mile . . . a symphony . . . a *Pilgrim's Progress* . . . a walk on the moon . . . a city reached for God . . . a slum beautified. Augustine, Savonarola, Martin Luther, John Calvin, John Wesley, D. L. Moody, George Washington Carver, Martin Luther King—they all had a dream, a goal. Large ambitions, high goals, great dreams are free to all of us.

And being careful not to exclude the personal, what about goals involving relationships? Your wife, husband, children, employees, co-workers, neighbors?

Dorothy and I have been married for over forty years, and we often remind each other of goal commitments we made even before our marriage, often renewed in the early months, that we would never end a day without the assurance that the lines of communication were open between us and that, as best we knew how, we would "not let the sun go down while we were still angry." Obviously, there have been tensions, healthy arguments, disagreements. I am a scrapper; she's a conciliator. I am feisty, much of the time in a hurry, a perfectionist; she is cool, collected, even-tempered. We're a good match. Our goal has always been to be not only lovers, but best friends, and we have achieved it.

As the children came along and grew into adulthood, we agreed to seek to model this relationship for them. We haven't said, "Here's our goal," but we have been aware of it and trusted osmosis—and the Lord—to reveal it and hopefully transmit it.

What am I saying? A strategy for excellence in our relationships calls for goals which can be measured and accomplished, to which we can refer as benchmarks or guideposts along life's path.

I think we can all take comfort in knowing that none of us will be judged on the *perfection index*. In the final analysis, the questions to each of us will be: Did you make the most of your talents? Did you work toward developing your potential? Did you choose excellence, or did you coast? Did you rise above the commonplace, or did you survive on mediocrity?

The wisest of all men, Solomon, said: "Whatever your hand finds to do, do it with all your might" (Ecclesiastes 9:10). That's ancient wisdom that is desperately needed in today's society, so addicted to the status quo.

Someone has said that the difference between an amateur and professional is about *five minutes more*.

Just five minutes more of reading toward your goal.

Just five minutes more of working out a communication problem with your spouse.

Just five minutes more with a son or daughter who may be having difficulties in school.

Just five minutes more of asking God to give you the special guidance you so desperately need.

Are you an amateur, or are you a professional? Are you willing to give it that extra five minutes? Are you determined to strain your muscles until they cry out for relief, to keep on trying when you want to quit?

Og Mandino writes:

> I will never consider defeat and will remove from my vocabulary such words and phrases as *quit, cannot, unable, impossible, out of the question, improbable, failure, unworkable, hopeless* and *retreat*: for they are the words of fools. I will avoid despair, but if this dis-ease of the mind should infect me, then I will work on in despair. I will toil and I will endure. I will ignore the obstacles at my feet and keep mine eyes on the goals above my head, for I know that where dry desert ends, green grass grows . . . I will forget the happenings of the day that is gone, whether they were good or bad, and greet the new sun with confidence that this will be the best day of my life.[12]

If you didn't accomplish all you wanted to today, if you're discouraged and you feel let down by others, just run through the lines of the old song, "Just pick yourself up, dust yourself off, and start all over again."

In the pursuit of excellence, don't just stand there, do something!

CHAPTER 15

"Mistakes" Are Important

O ne of the greatest obstacles we face in attempting to reach our potential is the fear of making a mistake, the very human fear of failure. And yet *excellence* is based on failure, usually one failure after another.

The genius inventor Thomas Edison was one day faced by two dejected assistants, who told him, "We've just completed our seven hundredth experiment and we still don't have an answer. We have failed."

"No, my friends," said Edison, "you haven't failed. It's just that we know more about this subject than anyone else alive. And we're closer to finding the answer, because now we know seven hundred things not to do." Edison went on to tell his colleagues, "Don't call it a mistake. Call it an education."

What a marvelous perspective. I don't know how many additional tries it took before Edison achieved success, but we all know that eventually he and his colleagues *did* see the light. Literally.

Whether you are an inventor, a housewife, a student, a pastor, or a business executive, you must adopt the same principle that guided Edison in his laboratory work: Learn from your mistakes and keep going. In fact, don't call them mistakes at all; call them *learning experiences.*

I cringe when I recall some of the horrendous mistakes I have made during my lifetime. I have made gross errors in judgment and have been insensitive toward people I really loved. I have unintentionally bruised colleagues and employees. But I've tried to evaluate those mistakes down through the years so that I could learn from them. I hope I have.

I am not alone, however. I am in the company of millions. Because who among us has gone through a single day without committing some error, some mistake?

I'd like you to consider doing this little exercise. Take a few minutes today or tomorrow to carefully observe yourself and people around you. For the sake of this exercise, watch them carefully and see if they make any mistakes. Here's what you may find:

The cashier at the supermarket rings up the wrong amount for your head of lettuce and has to correct the error.

The mechanic forgets to tighten that last nut on your car and you leave the repair shop with an annoying rattle in your car.

Your young daughter is learning how to walk and makes mistake after mistake as she forever tumbles to the carpet.

Your spouse is harsh with you over breakfast and in the evening tells you that he or she couldn't wait to put things right.

You inadvertently run a red light and immediately start praying that the police are patrolling in another part of town.

Mistakes. Errors in judgment. Some simple, some critical. As we look around us, we notice that no one is immune. And yet when we look at ourselves, we tend to be mercilessly critical. We speak of ourselves as failures, instead of as having failed in that one task. We're like the proverbial cat who, having sat on one hot stove, swore never to sit on any stove again.

Someone has quipped, "If Thomas Edison had given up that easily, you and I would be watching television in the dark." But he didn't give up, not even after seven hundred "learning experiences." All great discoveries have come about through trial and error. So will yours—whether it's a cure for cancer, a new technique for communicating with teenagers, or a better mousetrap.

I've always been encouraged by the words of Charles Kettering: "You will never stub your toe standing still. The faster you go, the more chance there is of stubbing your toe, but the more chance you have of getting somewhere." And, like the turtle, you really will go nowhere at all unless you stick your neck out. So it's back to our basic decision to *act*. To *do something*. I've heard psychologists say that action—any kind of action—is also a tremendous cure for depression, even if it's no more than a walk around the block.

Today is a good day to start believing that you don't need to live a life of quiet desperation, fearful of any new challenge. Starting today, you can begin to enjoy using and developing your gifts. For a start, you may want to risk something small—like a toe rather than a neck.

For example, if you've always wanted to write, then write something, a short article, a poem, an account of your vacation. Write it as if it were going to be published; then submit it somewhere. If you're a photographer, gather your best pictures together and submit them as entries in a contest. If you think you're a fair tennis player or golfer, enter some tournaments and see how you do. You may not win the top prize, but, think how much you'll learn and experience just by trying.

Or perhaps you've always felt weak in math, or foreign language, or book-keeping. Enroll today in a basic, nonthreatening course at a local college or a community program. The fact that you may have received a poor grade in the subject at 16 has little bearing on how you'll handle the subject matter at age 25, 30, 50, or 65.

Have you wanted to learn to play the piano? You can! Line up an instructor, set up a schedule for lessons, and set aside forty-five minutes a day for practice. In a year you'll be amazed at how well you will do.

Gourmet cooking appeals to you? Get some new recipe books; experiment with one meal each week. So what if the soufflé is scorched the first time? The second one will be better. Before you know it, your culinary delights will be lauded and in demand—at least by your family.

Franklin D. Roosevelt once said, "It is common sense to take a method and try it. If it fails, admit it frankly. But above all, *try something*." It's the only way you'll ever begin to realize your God-given potential. And it can be the glorious beginning in your pursuit of a life of excellence.

Don't be afraid of failure. It's by failure that we learn and profit. Ted Williams, one of the greatest baseball batters of all time, failed six times out of ten in his best year when he batted .400! Learn from your failures and mistakes, and move on.

Let me give you two personal examples of how I failed miserably, but how, through sticking with it, made something good of those mistakes.

One Sunday morning, many years ago, I was scheduled to preach in a siz-able Indiana church. It was Mother's Day, although I had paid scant attention to that. Upon arriving at the church, the pastor reminded me that it was Mother's Day and said that he hoped I would address the congregation with this particular day in mind. Most unwisely, I agreed that I would. While the congregation sang the hymns, while the choir sang the anthem, and while the ushers received the offering, I prepared a new sermon using the acrostic M-O-T-H-E-R. Rarely has a poorer sermon been preached! I blush to this day as I recall that Sunday morn-ing. But I learned! I learned always to seek the mind of the Lord in preparing a message and, having done this, stick with it. (And never on the spur of the moment.)

On another occasion, I was scheduled to address a large youth rally in Portland, Oregon. I arrived at the meeting utterly fatigued, after traveling and speaking for a number of days and suffering from a severe cold and a splitting headache. Within minutes after beginning to speak, my voice faltered. I began to sound like a croaking frog and finally had no voice at all. I had to sit down in utter defeat, the address barely begun! What did I learn? Get some rest before a message; always have a lozenge available; and make certain that a glass of water is near the pulpit! Thank goodness that experience has not been repeated.

Don't simply commence to get ready to begin to live. Start now. Today. Don't prepare indefinitely to take that course, or teach that Bible class, or ask for that promotion. Do it now. If you're scared to death, admit it. You'll find that the admission alone will quiet your heart and unwrinkle your brow.

Paul Tournier, the well-known Swiss psychiatrist, has said, "God's plan is fulfilled not just through the obedience of inspired men, but also through their errors, yes, their sins."

The Bible is replete with examples of how God turned people's failures—and forgiven sins—into great triumphs. That's His business.

Look, for example, at King David. David failed to discipline his sons, and as a result a whole chain of sorry events occurred. David failed to discipline Amnon after his immoral relationship with his sister, Tamar. This led David's other son, Absalom, to avenge his sister by killing Amnon. Finally, the entire kingdom was totally disrupted when Absalom led a rebellion against his father.

Great warrior that he was, perhaps David lacked what many today are calling "tough love." He had an obvious strong emotional attachment to his children, as when he wept for Absalom after he was killed leading a rebellion, but somehow he could not bring himself to discipline his children as was needed.

We also recognize that David failed to control his physical passions. When David added to his sin with Bathsheba the sin of murder of her husband Uriah, a faithful warrior in his army, he demonstrated a basic character flaw in not being willing to own up to sinful behavior soon enough to avoid adding another sinful act as a cover-up.

Yet, despite his great failures, David stands as one of the truly great men of God and of all time. He was a man after God's own heart in his devotion to Him and in his eagerness to honor Him and seek His glory. He did not shake his fist at God after a failure but repented and earnestly prayed that God's Spirit would never be taken from him.

Now look at Sarah. In her day, being childless in marriage was often construed as being a failure. A wife's purpose and role were very closely related to rearing children and maintaining the family name and heritage. Sarah had to bear this sense of failure until she was ninety years old. An example of how deeply affected and hurt she was by this sense of failure can be seen in her harsh treatment of Hagar when she was able to bear the child Ishmael. Hagar fled to the wilderness in her despair at Sarah's treatment of her. At the age of ninety, Sarah was undoubtedly a frustrated, disappointed, and bitter woman. It is understandable how she could laugh, though she denied it, when she overheard God telling her husband, Abraham, that she would bear a child. Yet Sarah is listed in the "Hall of Fame of Faith" in Hebrews 11. Her faith grew, and she drew strength from her deep faith in God. The apostle Peter uses her as a key example in his teaching of how wives are to relate to their husbands in honor and obedience (1 Peter 3:6).

Samson is another example: His failures are most evident in his relationships with women. Against the advice of his parents, he chose to marry a woman who evidently did not worship the Lord. This led to much bloodshed between his people and the Philistines and eventually to the death of his wife and her father.

Samson later entered into an immoral relationship with a harlot in the city of Gaza, and the people of that city sought to take his life. And, of course, what follows is the familiar story of the Philistines persuading the beautiful Delilah to entice Samson into telling her where he received his great and unusual strength. He made a game out of the whole situation, leading her along into many false assumptions about the source of his strength. But, finally, persistent Delilah persuaded him to tell her the truth. This led to Samson's capture and imprisonment and eventually to the gouging out of his eyes. Yet, Samson was used greatly by the Lord in helping to rescue Israel from the tyranny of the Philistines. And despite his failures, he was God's man, presiding over and judging the nation of Israel for twenty years.

Then there is Jonah. The reluctance of Jonah to do what God had asked him to do stands out as a glaring example of great stubbornness and rebellion, and perhaps fear. His was no passive resistance, but rather an active effort to get as far away from the place and purpose of God as possible. He was told to go to the great city of Nineveh and proclaim God's great displeasure with the wicked and godless ways of the people there. When Jonah finally got turned around, in a most unusual manner, and did what he was told to do, he displayed a selfish anger with God and the people of Nineveh. Rather than rejoicing that they had repented and were responding favorably to God, he displayed a great deal of contempt and selfish anger toward both God and the Ninevites. Then Jonah went outside the city gates, and in his despair—and perhaps exhaustion—asked that his life might be taken.

Still, Jonah remains one of the great examples of a man delivered and used by God, almost in spite of himself. It is recorded that a whole city of people, favorably affected by Jonah's preaching, turned away from their sins. And Jonah's prayer for deliverance, one of the great prayers of the Bible, was even quoted by the Lord Jesus Christ in His earthly ministry.

Turning to the New Testament, we find the apostle Peter, who drew stern rebukes and was told of the shameful denial that he would make of his Lord. At one point, when Jesus was talking about the death that He would die, He perceived that the very thoughts of Satan were coming out of Peter's mouth. And, of course, the three denials of Peter in the course of one evening, disowning any allegiance or association with Jesus, are familiar to all. Though he was irresistibly attracted to being with Jesus, for he knew that He held the very words of life, Peter could not readily accept the ways of Jesus. Even after Jesus had ascended to heaven, Peter had great difficulty in accepting many of the things he had been taught by Jesus.

The apostle Paul found it necessary to rebuke Peter and tell him face to face that he was showing prejudice and false standards in dealing with Jews and Gentiles. Yet, who could deny the greatness of Peter, the man who gave pivotal leadership to the early Christian church and was at the forefront of the earliest recorded people movements to Christ. His two New Testament epistles, which relate to bearing up under suffering, have provided great comfort and endurance for Christians throughout the centuries. His loyalty and devotion to Jesus Christ in his latter years have been an inspiration to all believers for two millennia.

God does not expect perfection; He expects obedience. And through obedience He can turn failures into triumphs.

Each of these Bible characters was unique. So are you. Develop your own style. No one has had the life experiences you have had; no one has the contributions to make that *you* can make. So it's not a question of being better than someone else. Excellence demands that you be better than yourself.

Some people are outgoing, while others are introspective. Some are thinkers rather than doers. Some are leaders; some are followers. Some are ahead of their times; many are behind. Some are musical geniuses; most are not. Some are great preachers; many are not. But whatever category you are in, right now you can make that single, deliberate move toward a life of excellence.

We are all aware of true and challenging illustrations of hosts of people who have triumphantly overcome seemingly impossible handicaps and disabilities. Let me illustrate with just two familiar and moving examples. The first is my friend Joni Eareckson.

At the age of eighteen, Joni became paralyzed from the neck down after a diving accident in shallow water at Chesapeake Bay. She had total quadriplegia, the result of a diagonal fracture between the fourth and fifth cervical levels.

Joni survived the critical first few weeks but soon came to the point of total despair and frequently wanted to commit suicide. Her reasons were understandable. Her appearance was grotesque—at least to her. Her weight had dropped from 125 to 80 pounds, her skin was jaundiced, her head had to be shaved to help hold her in a brace, and her teeth had become black from medication. Added to that was her sense of extreme limitations and her fear of the future. However, she let Christ turn that tragedy into triumph, those limitations into unlimited opportunities, and her fear into fortitude.

She has since done some utterly remarkable things. For example, she learned to draw and paint by holding a pen or brush in her teeth, and her work is truly remarkable. She refused to remain cloistered, and began accepting numerous speaking engagements, including appearances on television programs such as the *Today* show and *Larry King Live*. As a result she has spoken to millions of people, telling her story and encouraging them to find the hope and purpose which a life in Jesus Christ makes possible. And she has developed a ministry called Joni and Friends, which seeks to encourage others who are handicapped and to increase the understanding of those not handicapped.

The second person I want to remind you of is Helen Keller. At the age of nineteen months, because of illness, Helen became totally blind and deaf and speechless. Needless to say, it would have seemed that she had no future.

But Helen was a highly spirited girl and was tremendously encouraged by the loving care of her mother. When Helen was seven, the "beloved teacher," as Helen called her, came into her life. Anne Mansfield Sullivan was greatly responsible for unleashing in Helen Keller the great desire to express herself.

Through Anne's help, Helen went on to graduate cum laude from Radcliffe College. Helen had been determined to attend college years earlier, and it was due to her own insistence that she was finally enrolled. Devoting her life to helping others deprived of sight and sound, she traveled all over the world on their behalf, giving lectures. She wrote several articles and books, including an autobiography.

Her contribution was such that Mark Twain said that the two most interesting characters of the nineteenth century were Napoleon and Helen Keller.

What about you? Whether *your* handicap is physical or emotional, today can be the day you begin to chip away at that granite mountain of self-defeat. You can read books about how to do it. You can attend seminars on assertiveness training. You can discuss your plans for change with your friends and pray about it until the cows come home. But ultimately it's up to you to take action. And to take action that is productive you must know who you are . . . and what you are. It is my hope that today you will recognize that God made you in a special way for His special purpose. He wants you to be all He meant you to be. And He wants you to perform with class.

It was said of Jesus, "He has done everything well" (Mark 7:37). A Jesus of mediocrity, a Jesus of the average, is not the Jesus of the Bible. And if we want a model of one who took risks and lived a life of excellence, we can find none better than the life of our Lord.

He confronted the religious leaders of His day, mincing no words. (Very risky.)

He claimed to be the Son of God. (This ultimately cost Him His life.)

He took a whole series of shopworn religious legal statements and suggested that they could best be summed up as: Love your God, and love your neighbor as yourself. (Tampering with sacred tradition.)

He spent huge amounts of time with so-called second-class citizens: tax collectors, prostitutes, lepers, disabled, Samaritans. (Misguided indeed.)

He was furious when His Father's house was turned into a noisy marketplace. (Tampering with temple economics.)

He had the audacity to reach out and heal the sick on the Sabbath. (Couldn't He lay off for just one day?)

He encouraged the little children to come to His side so He could tell them He loved them, too. (Judea was hardly a child-centered society.)

And during His last days on earth, He chose to love those who persecuted Him, mocked Him, and exposed Him to every human indignity imaginable.

During the later part of His earthly ministry Jesus also said that His followers— you and I—would do greater things than He had done. Have you ever wondered if He really meant that? If He did, then we need His discipline and His courage. We need His anger at injustice and His untiring concern for those who suffer. We need His capacity for taking risks. And we need to know more of His great love.

CHAPTER 16

How High Is Your Attitude Quotient (AQ)?

One day a man who took great pride in his lawn found himself with a large healthy crop of dandelions. He tried every conceivable method he knew to get rid of them, but they still plagued him and his lawn. Finally, he wrote to the Department of Agriculture, enumerating all the things he had tried, and closed his letter with the question, "What shall I do now?" In due course came the reply, "We suggest you learn to love them."[13]

Each of us faces people and situations every day that exasperate us. And often, despite our Herculean efforts, the exasperation simply won't go away. It's then we realize that perhaps the biggest risk of all is *changing our attitude.*

Jim Rohn of Adventure in Achievement shared these observations on what he called the "diseases of attitude":

Indifference: The mild approach to life. Don't let this rob you of the good life.

Indecision: The greatest thief of opportunity. A life of adventure is a life filled with many decisions—good ones and bad ones.

Doubt: One of the worst is self-doubt. Turn the coin over. *Belief* is a better gamble than doubt.

Worry: The real killer. Worry in its final stages can reduce you to begging. It causes health problems and financial problems.

Overcaution: Some people will never have much. They're just too cautious. Let the record book show you won, or let it show you lost, but don't let it show you failed to play the game.

A recurrent theme in Rohn's lecture is this: *The major key to your better future is you.* Not your boss, not your salary, not your "situation," but *you.*

I guess at times we all wish things were easier. We wish interest rates would come down so we could buy our dream home. We wish our children would start to appreciate all we've done for them. We wish we could just coast once in a while on our way to a life of excellence. And sometimes we just have a large umbrella wish that life would be a bit fairer to us.

Well, we can wish all we want. We can dream pipe dreams of a utopia where the other guy does all the work and where we get all the money and all the credit. But that's all it will ever be—a dream, because there's an ancient law that is still powerfully in effect. It's as old as the farmer who put that first seed into the earth thousands of years ago. *You reap what you sow.*

If you don't like the crops that are coming up all around your feet, you may want to check and see what you're planting these days: Cabbage still gives cabbage, and apples still produce apples. A smile breeds a smile. Negative thoughts stimulate the growth of more negative thoughts.

This law is as old as the hills, and as far as I know, the cleverest attorney has yet to find a loophole. So it's probably best not to try to beat the system. Instead, if you don't like what you see, check your bag of seeds—the seeds of attitudes—and determine what you've been growing in your emotional garden.

Let me illustrate this "sowing and reaping" law from the Scriptures:

Haman was a high official of the court of King Ahasuerus (Xerxes of Persia) who became furious when a Jew named Mordecai refused to bow down to him, as the king had commanded. Thus, Haman set out to destroy Mordecai and all the other Jews in Persia. He even prepared an unusually tall (seventy-five feet) gallows for Mordecai.

As it turned out, the queen, Esther, was also a Jew and was the cousin of Mordecai. At a special dinner that she prepared for the king and Haman, she revealed Haman's evil plot to the king. The king became furious and ordered that Haman and his sons be hanged on the very same gallows that Haman had prepared for Mordecai and that the Jews would take up arms to defend themselves against any who were seeking to harm them under Haman's previous plans. Here we see one of the most ironic biblical examples of the principle of sowing and reaping.

We can also see in the life and reign of King Solomon the results and rewards of a kingdom founded on the righteous reign of his father, King David. In David's forty years as ruler of Israel, he sought to build his kingdom on the foundation of God's statutes, commandments, and ordinances.

Solomon, gifted by God as the wisest man ever to live, ruled over all the kingdoms from the Euphrates to the land of the Philistines and to the border of Egypt. To Solomon was given the great privilege of building the house and temple of the Lord in all its magnificence. Solomon sought to be diligent in following the Lord, as did his father David. We see this in his benediction prayer for the newly completed temple, in which he says: "May the Lord maintain the cause of his servant, and the cause of his people Israel . . . that all the peoples of the earth may know that the Lord is God; there is no other."

The life of Solomon is an example of reaping positive results from the very positive sowing done earlier by his father David and by himself.

Joseph is another positive example of the sowing and reaping principle. Abandoned to a desert well to die, sold into slavery by his brothers, falsely accused of adultery by his master's wife, and finally cast into prison, Joseph remained faithful to God. He continued to give God credit for his abilities and special insight. God rewarded Joseph's faithfulness, and Joseph became a ruler under Pharaoh and was instrumental in helping the entire nation of Egypt to survive a famine of seven years, as well as in assisting his family through those famine years.

Finally, think of the story of Ananias and Sapphira in the book of Acts. To lie to another human being is a sinful deed, but to lie to God Himself has awesome consequences; and it cost this couple their very lives.

They said that all the proceeds from the piece of property which they had sold were going into the Lord's work among the early apostles, when in fact they were keeping some of the money for their own use. Each was questioned separately about the land sale and whether or not their claim about giving all of it was true. They each chose to lie about money which they were withholding for themselves, and both, as they finished their statement of falsehood, were immediately struck dead. This is one of the most dramatic examples in the Scriptures of instant consequences resulting from a sin. They immediately reaped the results of the lie they had sown. While we do not often see this sowing and reaping principle so readily apparent, it continues to operate!

Let me ask you a question. Do you know any grumps? I mean real bonafide grumps—the kind who frown, mumble incessantly, belittle others, and walk about with a little gray cloud forever hanging over their drooping heads? Not much fun to be with, are they? They are afflicted with a disease of attitude. By six o'clock each morning they already *know* it's going to be a lousy day!

And then there are our friends who always seem to be "up," pleasant, interesting, and interested. They are, in contrast, a joy to be around. Their warmth and good humor are contagious. They have the capacity to share their gift of encouragement with everyone they meet. Their attitudes are healthy.

One of the ingredients for a life of excellence is just that—healthy attitudes. One smile is still worth a hundred frowns in any market.

A smile

- costs nothing but creates much.

- enriches those who receive without diminishing the wealth of those who give.

- happens in a flash, but the memory of it can last a lifetime. None are so rich that they can get along without it and none so poor but are richer for it.

- creates happiness in the home, fosters good will in a business, and is the countersign of friends.

- is rest to the weary, daylight to the discouraged, and nature's best antidote for trouble.

- cannot be bought, begged, or stolen, for it is of no earthly good to anybody until it is given away.

- And if any person should be too tired to give you a smile, why not give one of your own?

- For nobody needs a smile so much as one who has none to give.[14]

Charles Schwab, the man to whom Andrew Carnegie paid a million dollars a year because of his ability to motivate people, once said, "A man can succeed at almost anything for which he has unlimited enthusiasm." Show me a person who has that approach to life, and I'll show you a man or woman who has attitudes that are positive and constructive.

One of my heroes, Theodore Roosevelt, said this about attitudes:

It is not the critic who counts: not the man who points out how the strong man stumbled or where the doer of deeds could have done them better. The credit belongs to the man who is actually in the arena; whose face is marred by dust and sweat and blood; who strives valiantly; who errs, and comes short again and again, because there is no effort without error and shortcoming; who does actually try to do the deed; who knows the great enthusiasm, the great devotion, and spends himself in a worthy cause; who, at the worst, if he fails, at least fails while daring greatly.

Far better it is to dare mighty things, to win glorious triumphs even though checkered by failure, than to rank with those poor spirits who neither enjoy nor suffer much because they live in the gray twilight that knows neither victory nor defeat.

That "gray twilight" zone of mediocrity is no place for a person committed to a life of excellence—and certainly no place for a child of God.

Following a serious World War II accident that involved a shattered hip, I was told I would have limited leg mobility and a noticeable limp and undoubtedly would have played my last game of golf, which was my favorite recreation and sport. It was a devastating announcement. But I determined that bad hip or no, I was once again going to enjoy golf.

Three surgeries later, with a rehabilitated and rebuilt hip and a lift on my right spiked golf shoe. I play eighteen holes with regularity (almost as often as I wish I could!).

It's the "attitude quotient" that counts!

We began this chapter by talking about what Rohn called "diseases of attitude." But what are the cures for those ailments of the spirit? How can we bring our attitudes back to a state of healthy well-being? Let's take them one at a time.

Indifference: The most effective cure for this "mild approach to life" is to get excited about something. Point yourself in one direction and move toward it. It could be anything from being the best gardener on the block to running an effective organization. But you will *never* know the thrill of the hunt until you get yourself worked up about something. Today, start putting everything you've got into everything you do. It's the perfect cure for this killer disease.

Indecision: The antidote for indecision is simple. In fact, we've already talked about it in chapter 14: *Don't just stand there, do something!* Get off the dime and get a move on. You don't have to discover the cure for some rare disease. Your decision may simply be to read a book on how to further your career, or it may be patching up a relationship that is significant to you.

Doubt: This is the greatest killer of all. Especially self-doubt. The Scriptures tell us not to think overly impressive thoughts of ourselves. But they also encourage us to think realistically about our strengths, abilities, gifts, and talents. The cure for self-doubt is belief—not a blind allegiance toward doing the improbable, but a healthy belief in ourselves and in the gifts God has so generously given to each of us. That includes *you*. Everyone has God-given gifts. What are yours?

Worry: The Word of God is such a comfort if we will but choose to believe what it tells us. First Peter 5:7 reads, "Cast all your anxiety on him because he cares for you." I can think of no greater assault on the problem of worry than to quietly take our pain and frustration and place them at the feet of the Savior. Among the most visible benefits may even be a reduction in your lower back pain or fewer attacks of peptic ulcers.

Overcaution: This is the "what if" syndrome. You've been there. *What if* I speak up and declare my own point of view on this issue? I might lose some friends in the process. *What if* I decide to do something nice for myself, like buy a car or take a long trip? "They" might think I'm selfish. *What if* I buy a new home, get saddled with high payments, and then lose my job? I can't prove it statistically, but I would be willing to wager that 95 percent of our worries *never ever* come to pass.

The opposite side of timidity and overcaution is adventure—taking risks and accepting challenges that are beyond your immediate ability to deliver. This is what a life of excellence is all about.

But these diseases of attitude are always lurking, always ready to infest and infect the garden of your mind. So be on guard. Keep sowing attitudes that are constructive, that will bring you a step closer each day to the goals you have set for yourself. It's part of the pursuit of excellence. And it will help keep you from being afflicted with that most dread of all diseases—the status quo (which someone has said is Latin for "the mess we're in"!).

CHAPTER 17

You Don't Have to Be Average

I wonder how many of you would have bought this book if the title had been *How to Be Below Average,* or *How I Achieved Mediocrity,* or *How I Got to Be Less Than the Best!* Oh, you may have leafed through a few pages just to see what kind of a crackpot had put the volume together, but I seriously doubt if many would have chosen to make the investment. After all, who among us needs any encouragement to be average? For millions that's already the problem. The majority of people in our country live every day beneath their God-given potential. Instead of responding to life's challenges with personal growth and a commitment to specific goals, they are addicted to a dead-end status quo.

Beginning today, you can move beyond that dismal gray existence of mediocrity and start exploring new heights. But this new adventure will begin only with your personal commitment to becoming better than you have known or seen yourself to be.

When Britain's late, great Prime Minister, Sir Winston Churchill, was a young teenager, he attended a public school called Harrow. Young Winston was not a good student; as a matter of fact, he was quite a rascal. Had he not been the son of the famed Lord Randolph Churchill, he probably would have been expelled from the school. However, he completed his work at Harrow, went on to the university, and then embarked on a brilliant and illustrious career in the British military, serving in both Africa and India.

At age sixty-seven, he was elected prime minister of the British Empire. It was he who brought great courage to the nation through his speeches and leadership during the dark days Britain faced in World War II.

Toward the very end of his leadership as prime minister, the old statesman was invited to address the young boys at his alma mater, Harrow. In announcing the coming of their great leader, the headmaster said, "Young gentlemen, the greatest orator of our time—perhaps of all time—our prime minister, will be here in a few days to address you; and it will behoove you to listen carefully to whatever sound advice he may bring to you at that time."

The great day arrived, and the prime minister appeared at Harrow. Following a glowing and lengthy introduction by the headmaster, Sir Winston stood up—all five feet, five inches and 235 pounds of him! After he had acknowledged the effusive introduction, he gave this brief but moving speech: "Young men, never give up. Never give up! Never give up! Never, never, never, never!"

Start "not giving up" right now. Today. And one of the best ways to get started is to begin observing those who seem to be better than average.

When Dr. Elton Trueblood was a student at Harvard, his mentor, Dean Sperry, said to him, "You must have some great models." That's when Trueblood realized that the real enemy is mediocrity and that he should seek excellence. And he realized that the way to seek excellence was to soak his life with characters who had achieved excellence.

These may be community leaders, pastors, housewives, teachers, parents, or co-workers. Watch them carefully. Talk with them. Find out what they read. Explore their interests. Talk to people who work with those who are excelling in their occupations and in their personal lives. Give careful attention to their style. If a person is making $80,000 a year, perhaps he or she has an $80,000 smile. Perhaps that person has learned how to listen better than anyone else around.

Success leaves clues. And as you carry out this private research, I think you'll also discover that achievers are not born. They are made. The same can be said for underachievers—for the average man or woman.

As you observe those who excel, be on the lookout for specific qualities that set them apart, qualities you would like to implement in your own life. Qualities such as the following:

Personal discipline: Those who excel are people who, first of all, take charge of themselves. They plan their work and then they work their plan. They are neither burning out nor coasting along; they have achieved a balance in their lives. They know they have physical, emotional, intellectual, and spiritual needs; and they see to it that those needs are met.

Vision: Above-average people have developed the foresight to see how things will work out as a result of their policies and methods. They are always looking ahead, so they also have the insight to make good decisions.

Optimism: People who excel are not "downers." Of course they have their moments of discouragement, but for the most part they respond to life with a cheerful spirit and an attitude that "this problem can be solved." An optimist laughs to forget; a pessimist forgets to laugh! The pessimist sees a difficulty in every opportunity and the optimist sees an opportunity in every difficulty.

A sense of adventure: Above-average people create their own adventures and engineer a large measure of their own happiness. These people take risks, push themselves to the limit, and stretch their minds and bodies in pursuit of their goals.

Courage: Above-average people know that it is always too soon to quit. That excellence demands courage in the face of defeat. Many games have been won in the bottom of the ninth because of *one* pitch-hit single. The highest degree of courage is seen in the people who are most fearful but refuse to let fear defeat them. However fearful they may have been, God's leaders in every generation have been commanded to be of good courage. Remember God's word to Joshua, "Be strong and courageous . . . for the LORD your God will be with you wherever you go."

Humility: People of excellence do not talk excessively about themselves or their many accomplishments. They are content to let their track records do the talking. More than likely, you will have to pry stories of great achievements out of them. The apostle Paul said in 1 Corinthians 15, "I am the least of the apostles and do not even deserve to be called an apostle."

Humor: Above-average people know that "a cheerful heart is good medicine." Humor can relax the most difficult of situations and create an atmosphere of good will. Perhaps one of the most outstanding qualities of above-average people is their ability to laugh at themselves. A good laugh at oneself is better than a tonic. It saves many difficult situations.

Confidence: People of excellence know that if they don't believe in themselves, no one else will believe in them either. Self-confidence is not unspiritual. Quite the contrary, it is an honest belief in the gifts and talents given to you by God.

Anger: Above-average people are healthy enough to get angry, but angry at the right things—like injustice, incompetence (especially in themselves), and poor use of time and money. This quality of anger was present in our Lord when

He swept the moneychangers from the temple and when He spoke so harshly of the ancient laws that had such little regard for people. The apostle Paul said, "In your anger do not sin."

Patience: Above-average people are patient. They are careful listeners. Only after all the facts are in do they make a decision.

Integrity: A life of excellence is one which has trustworthiness as its base. Above-average people can be trusted. Their word means something. They can be counted on to deliver. They have a deep sense of personal responsibility. They will not cheat on themselves, their family, or their work.

Finally, being above average is not dependent upon race, age, or sex.

Babe Ruth had hit 714 home runs during his baseball career and was playing one of his last full major league games. It was the Boston Braves versus the Reds in Cincinnati. But the great Ruth was no longer as agile as he had once been. He fumbled the ball and threw badly, and in one inning alone his errors were responsible for most of the five runs scored by Cincinnati.

As the Babe walked off the field after the third out and headed toward the dugout, a crescendo of yelling and booing reached his ears. Just then a boy jumped over the railing onto the playing field. With tears streaming down his face, he threw his arms around the legs of his hero.

Ruth didn't hesitate for one second. He picked up the boy, hugged him, and set him down on his feet, patting his head gently. The noise from the stands came to an abrupt halt. Suddenly there was no more booing. In fact, hush fell over the entire park. In those brief moments, the fans saw two heroes: Ruth, who in spite of his dismal day on the field could still care about a little boy; and the young boy, who cared about the feelings of another human being. Both had melted the hearts of the crowd.[15]

That's being above average!

CHAPTER 18

A Creative Attitude

You and I walk the halls of the great Smithsonian Institution in Washington, D.C., and we overhear ourselves say, "My, we are obviously seeing the handiwork of some of the inventive geniuses of our age."

We travel to Europe and move past row upon row of paintings and sculptures in the Louvre in Paris, and we know we are viewing the work of the world's true creative giants—Rembrandt, Van Gogh, da Vinci, Michelangelo and many others.

But whether it's a time-honored museum that houses the world's great art treasures or an afternoon of sidewalk art in Santa Monica, Phoenix, or Chicago, we are never far from the artistic talent of men and women we have labeled "creative." On canvas, on the printed page, in the concert hall, on the movie screen, their work is everywhere.

But I would like to suggest that we give the word *creative* a somewhat wider berth, one that will include not only the renowned artistic geniuses of our time, but also you and me. I'm referring to expanding the idea of *creative* into the larger concept of a *creative attitude,* an attitude that says, "I am willing to be 'fully born,' to abandon the secure certainties of life, and to part company with my many illusions. I will live a life of faith and courage, even if it means aloneness and 'being different.'"

The Bible is full of examples of courage to challenge us. Think, for example, of Abraham. Abraham displayed courage by doing what God had told him to do, even though the outcome was unclear and uncertain. Abraham was told to leave his home in Haran and go in the general direction of Canaan, not certain exactly of where he was going. And this at the age of 75! All that he had was the promise from God that He would lead him and that He would make of him a great nation. Not only was Abraham at an age when tearing up familiar roots of family and friends would be particularly difficult, but also he did not yet have any children of his own from which a nation could emerge. It should be noted also that Abraham was a very rich man, and so he was not motivated by economic necessity to move on to "greener pastures" in order to survive and make a better living. It was simply a matter of believing God and having the courage to translate that belief into the action necessary to see a promise of God fulfilled.

Young Daniel's courage had to do with the very essence of what it means to worship the Lord God and none other. He had the courage of his convictions, choosing to stay true to his devotion to the Lord rather than to continue living and compromise his commitment to almighty God. The issue was whether or not Daniel would take thirty days off from any outward display of prayer to God, so that the only prayers offered would be to King Darius. After all, some would say, he could still pray secretly in his heart and not show any physical sign of praying to God and thereby feign obedience to the edict from the king. But this was not for Daniel. He knew the intention of the edict, and he would have nothing to do with it. Though it could cost him his life, he would not give dual devotion and worship to God and the king. His courage was rewarded with deliverance from a den of lions, but he was well prepared to pay with his life for his convictions.

Or think of Moses. There is a brief account in the book of Exodus that displays the physical courage of Moses. (Of the two, physical and moral courage, most say that moral courage is the most difficult; but examples of physical courage are much-needed in our day when soft and comfortable living may ill prepare us for displaying it.)

One day Moses was sitting by a well where seven daughters were attempting to water their father's sheep. Some shepherds came and drove them away, evidently not willing to wait their turn and knowing that the women were not capable of opposing them. "Moses got up and came to their rescue (the women) and watered their flock" (Exodus 2:17). Though outnumbered, Moses opposed those men, standing up for the oppressed women.

The man named Saul had been breathing threats and murder against the early disciples of Jesus Christ. He would literally drag men and women from their houses and commit them to prison because of their Christian faith.

This same Saul had a dramatic conversion to Christianity, became Paul, and began to proclaim to others this new life in Christ. He wanted to fellowship with the Christians in Jerusalem, but the Christians there were afraid and distrustful of him. They just could not believe that their enemy was really a Christian now. However, there was one man who was willing to stick his neck out and proclaim that Paul's conversion was genuine. This man was Barnabas. "Barnabas took him (Paul) and brought him to the apostles" (Acts 9:27).

It takes courage to get involved in a controversial issue and take up the defense of someone whom most or all of your friends and close associates oppose. Barnabas did and was instrumental in helping to launch Paul's career as a missionary statesman throughout Europe and Asia Minor. This one act of courage was important in gaining the support of the Jerusalem believers, which Paul needed as he began his new role as an apostle of Jesus Christ.

These obviously were creatively courageous people. To be truly creative means much more than painting a picture, or writing a play, or inventing a machine. Creativity has been built into every one of us; it's part of our design. Each of us lives less of the life God intended for us when we choose not to live out the creative powers we possess.

John Gardner, in his modern classic *Self Renewal,* says:

> Exploration of the full range of his own potentialities is not something that the self-renewing man leaves to the chances of life. It is something he pursues systematically, or at least avidly, to the end of his days. He looks forward to an endless and unpredictable dialog between his potentialities and claims of life—not only the claims he encounters but the claims he invents. And by potentialities I mean not just the skills but also the full range of his capacities for sensing, wondering, learning, understanding, loving, and aspiring.[16]

Gardner is right. But you may have fallen into the trap of believing that creativity is only for the other person. Not so. A life of richness awaits you, whether you ultimately hang a painting in the Smithsonian, or whether you become the best mother or father it's possible for you to become.

In *The Self in Pilgrimage*, Earl A. Loomis, Jr., asks an important question: "Why are we afraid to embrace our virtues? Why do we mask them behind inaccurate estimates and unreasonable fears?" He then suggests this answer: "Basically we resist recognition of our assets because once recognized they must be *used.*"

What is more tormenting than recognizing a potential and then refusing to put it to work? It's like possessing a miracle drug capable of saving the lives of thousands but keeping it in a locked vault.

What is more personally tragic than love unused? Generosity kept to oneself? Friendship unshared? The world's literature is filled with tales of men and women who knew their own potential, recognized their own talents but refused to use those gifts. Consequently, they are the truly tragic figures of history. It would be far better not to know of a gift than to be aware of it and refuse to use it.

I was cleaning out a little desk drawer once when I found a flashlight I'd not used for over a year. I turned it on but was not surprised when it gave no light. I unscrewed it and shook it to get the batteries out, but they wouldn't budge. Finally, after some effort, they came loose. What a mess! Battery acid had corroded the entire inside of the flashlight. The batteries were new when I put them in a year before, and I certainly had stored the flashlight in a safe, warm place. But there was one problem. Those batteries were not built to be safe and warm. They were designed to be turned on—to be used. That was their only reason for existing.

It's the same with us. You and I were made to be "turned on"—to put our love to work, to apply our patience in difficult, trying situations. We are called upon to take the energies God has given us and compel them to do productive labor for ourselves and others. *This* is what it means to be creative. This is what is means to be *fully born.*

Right now, is there an attitude, a skill, or a talent in your life that is wasting away? Are you letting it disintegrate, atrophy?

It's easy to coast. But except for cream, I know nothing else of quality that floats to the top. A life of excellence takes work, perseverance, and discipline; but it's worth every ounce of sweat and determination. If you choose to let your talents slide, be ready to accept the harsh verdict of that ancient law: What you refuse to use, you will surely lose.

And if you fail at one pursuit, don't become a recluse. Life has not come to an end. It's not what happens that's critical. *It's what you do about what happens* that's important.

The apostle Paul spent months in prison, in Philippi, Rome, and elsewhere. His prison epistles have inspired millions for over two millennia. In the darkest night, in the most desperate of circumstances, his bright, cheerful outlook encouraged the early church, and these letters continue to encourage the church today.

Mother Teresa, who became a legendary humanitarian figure in our time, was born of impoverished Albanian parents in Yugoslavia. Albania, where there had been no public worship of any kind for decades, was once the most hard-core Communist nation in Eastern Europe. Yugoslavia was likewise a part of the atheistic Communistic society. From such an unlikely background came this beautiful person who ministered grace, lovingkindness, and mercy to the destitute and dying in Calcutta, the filthiest city in Asia. She was loved by the mighty and the lowly alike. Visit her Home of Mercy next to the wretched Kali Temple in the heart of the slums of this slum city, as I have, and you will encounter a slice of heaven on earth. Here, because of Mother Teresa's concern and care, the beggars, the indigent, and the homeless died with dignity—and the word whispered in their ears is that God loves them!

My friend, Tom Skinner, a black Harlem gang leader, tough and ready to battle with the lifting of a knife, met the Savior through the loving witness of a friend and today ministers the gospel to thousands of university students, conducts large and effective community-wide crusades, and heads up one of the most effective evangelism efforts in our nation today.

The apostle Paul, Mother Teresa, Tom Skinner—and thousands of others with the most unpretentious of backgrounds or unlikely circumstances have made a difference in their world. They pursue excellence, for Christ's sake. So can you and I.

Background, education, circumstances . . . none of these can hold back a creative spirit.

Think, for example, of Abraham Lincoln, who was elected president of the United States in 1860. He grew up on an isolated farm and had only one year of formal education. In those early years, he was exposed to barely half a dozen books. In 1832 he lost his job and was defeated in the race for the Illinois legislature. In 1833 he failed in business. In 1834 he was elected to the state legislature, but in 1835 his sweetheart died, and in 1836 he had a nervous breakdown. In 1838 he was defeated for Speaker of the House, and in 1843 he was defeated for nomination for Congress. In 1846 he was elected to Congress but in 1848 lost the renomination. In 1849 he was rejected for a federal land officer appointment, and in 1854 he was defeated for the Senate. In 1856 he was defeated for the nomination of vice president, and in 1858 he was again defeated for the Senate.

Many people, both at home and abroad, consider Lincoln to be the greatest president of all time. Yet it should be remembered how many failures and defeats marked his life and how humble and unpromising his early beginnings were.

Martin Luther was born into the peasant class, his father a poor mine worker. The peasants were considered to be the most religiously conservative element of the general population. Roland Bainton said that there was "nothing whatever to set Luther off from his contemporaries, let alone to explain why later on he should have revolted against so much of medieval religion." Luther was a common man, and he entered the monastic life in order to make his peace with God and with a more than ordinary devotion to follow the way prescribed by the church. Yet Luther began a protest for reform which shook the very foundations of Western civilization, and some point to the days of Luther as the beginning of modern times. Even within the Catholic Church today, there are leaders who are grateful to Luther for the reforms that he helped stir within the church itself.

Shirley Chisholm, the strong, black congresswoman from the Bedford-Stuyvesant section of Brooklyn, came from a family that was very poor. Both of her parents worked when they could, her mother as a seamstress and her father as an unskilled laborer in a burlap bag factory.

Shirley was a bright child and did well in school. She graduated from Brooklyn College and intended to be a teacher, but she became increasingly angry at the injustices she saw around her and decided she would have to fight the system, "even if I had to stand alone." She eventually entered politics as a congresswoman, thereby becoming the first black woman to serve in Congress.

Shirley knew that Congress was badly in need of reform and that their priorities must be changed. She was convinced that a great number of the leaders in Congress were out of touch, out of tune, with the country. Her first assignment as a congresswoman from an urban constituency was a seat on the Agricultural Committee! She challenged the House leadership before the Democratic caucus and won. They changed their minds and asked her to serve on the Veterans Committee, which was at least relevant to many of her districts.

Shirley Chisholm credits her grandmother for much of her philosophy today:

> She always used to say, "You must have courage and conviction, and remember that when you take a stand on things in this world, quite often you are going to find yourself alone . . ." She imprinted on my mind the necessity to fight for that in which you believe, even though you may not always have supporters.

Shirley Chisholm credits the church with having a terrific influence in giving her stamina and strength.

> When I am disillusioned, all I have to do is get on my knees and pray, and in ten minutes I seem to have gotten a new lease on life. I get a kind of inner strength from God. I don't seem to need anybody to stand with me in what I do. The only thing I want and need is to look to my conscience—and God.

Much of her standing alone has been in her fight against injustice toward black people in her district. And her word to those who are black and poor in her district is to make education the number one priority and to "realize that the world has no room for weaklings, and that it is only weaklings who give up in the face of obstacles."

Do you feel that if only your circumstances would change, then you could work on your creativity? Nonsense. The "perfect" environment hasn't been invented yet—and probably never will be.

Once again, look around you at the people whom you admire for their lives of excellence. What do you see? More than likely, you will see many of the following traits.

1. Drive—a high degree of motivation

2. Courage—tenacity and persistence

3. Goals—a sense of direction

4. Knowledge—and a thirst for it

5. Good health

6. Honesty—especially intellectual

7. Optimism

8. Discernment

9. Enthusiasm

10. Chance-taking—the willingness to risk failure

11. Dynamism—health and energy

12. Enterprise—willing to tackle tough jobs

13. Persuasion—ability to sell

14. Outgoingness—friendly

15. Communication—articulate

16. Receptive—alert

17. Patient yet impatient—patient with others yet impatient with the status quo

18. Adaptability—capable of change

19. Perfectionism—seeking to achieve excellence

20. Humor—ability to laugh at self and others

21. Versatility—broad interests and skills

22. Curiosity—interested in people and things

23. Individualism—self-esteem and self-sufficiency

24. Realism-idealism—occupied by reality but guided by ideals.

25. Imagination—seeking new ideas, combinations, and relationships.[17]

None of the above comes easy, not even for the geniuses of our world.

J.C. Penney once observed, "Geniuses themselves don't talk about the gift of genius. They just talk about hard work and long hours."

Edison believed that genius was 1 percent inspiration and 99 percent perspiration.

Paderewski, when called a genius, said, "Perhaps, but before I was a genius I was a drudge."

So if at first you don't succeed, try and try again. Remember, it took Thomas Edison over seven hundred attempts before he saw the light.

Start today! Develop an attitude of creativity. Be determined to make *your* mark. It's an important part of your pursuit of excellence.

We Can Overcome

Some of the world's greatest men and women have been saddled with disabilities and adversities but have managed to overcome them.

Cripple him, and you have a Sir Walter Scott.

Lock him in a prison cell, and you have a John Bunyan.

Bury him in the snows of Valley Forge, and you have a George Washington.

Raise him in abject poverty, and you have an Abraham Lincoln.

Subject him to bitter religious prejudice, and you have a Disraeli.

Strike him down with infantile paralysis, and he becomes a Franklin D. Roosevelt.

Burn him so severely in a schoolhouse fire that the doctors say he will never walk again, and you have a Glenn Cunningham, who set the world's record in 1934 for running a mile in 4 minutes and 6.7 seconds.

Deafen a genius composer, and you have a Ludwig van Beethoven.

Have him or her born black in a society filled with racial discrimination, and you have a Booker T. Washington, a Harriet Tubman, a Marian Anderson, a George Washington Carver, or a Martin Luther King, Jr.

Make him the first child to survive in a poor Italian family of eighteen children, and you have an Enrico Caruso.

Have him born of parents who survived a Nazi concentration camp, paralyze him from the waist down when he is four, and you have an incomparable concert violinist, Itzhak Perlman.

Call him a slow learner, "retarded," and write him off as uneducable, and you have an Albert Einstein.[18]

CHAPTER 19

Believing in the Process

Several years ago I was browsing through the shelves of a large Christian bookstore in Los Angeles when a young man came up to me and asked if he could be of assistance. For a moment I didn't even hear his question because my eyes were fixed on the large red button he wore on his shirt collar. There was no slogan, no political message—only these letters: PBPGINFWMY.

Since I've never been accused of being overly shy, I asked him what on earth those letters meant. And with a smile that told me he was glad I'd asked, he said, "It means. 'Please be patient. God is not finished with me yet.'"

What a marvelous reminder for all of us—to be patient with ourselves and with others as we all move through this long, often tedious process called life.

Some of us learn the ropes quickly, while many of us invariably cross the stream at the widest point. But *no one at any time* has it made. No one has yet learned the answers to all the questions.

In his *Letters to His Son,* Lord Chesterfield writes, "There is hardly anybody good at everything, and there is scarcely anybody who is absolutely good for nothing."

So if your progress seems slow while it appears those around you are engaged in remarkable successes, just remember: Patience! God is not finished with you yet!

The apostle Paul recognized the importance of the Christian life as a day-by-day process when he wrote: "I do not consider myself yet to have taken hold of it. But one thing I do: Forgetting what is behind and straining toward what is ahead, I press on toward the goal to win the prize for which God has called me heavenward in Christ Jesus" (Philippians 3:13–14).

Paul was a man of particular brilliance, trained at the feet of the great Gamaliel in the traditions of ancient Israel. Through study and experience, he learned to be comfortable in both the world of the Greek and the Jew. He was an orator of no small merit and a man who would compose some of the most poignant letters—from some of the most surprising places—ever recorded in the history of humanity. This man of such great academic and spiritual accomplishment could have rested on his laurels. He could have lived as if he had arrived, but he didn't. He put aside the past, lived in the present, and pressed on toward the goal of conforming himself to the image of his Lord.

That's what it means to believe in the process. And it's an important ingredient in the pursuit of excellence.

We Americans are probably more prone to the I-want-it-now syndrome than any other people on earth. The tremendous post-World War II growth of our economy and our subsequent demand for and acquisition of endless creature comforts have somehow tricked us into believing we can have anything we want, *when we want it!*

We go on crash diets so we can lose three pounds in a day, rather than learning to eat sensibly. Our how-to-do-it books, while often helpful, too often present us with false hopes for instant riches, instant success, and instant acceptance. We often sow our wild oats and then pray for crop failure, rather than seed quality into our lives and work for a mature harvest.

All of this only demonstrates that we don't understand how things work. Lasting success, true excellence seldom comes overnight. And it always has a price.

One night after he had given one of the greatest concerts of his brilliant career, Paderewski was greeted by an overeager fan who said, "Oh, I'd give my life to be able to play like you do." Paderewski replied quietly, "I did."

If you want to be a truly effective pastor, you must work on being effective. Establish a standard for your ministry. Business people, do the same in your business. Build a reputation for excellence, and recognize that it will take time and that it will not come easily. It takes decades to grow an oak to maturity. Nature knows that it takes time to produce something that will endure.

I recall one day a dozen years ago when a young, unprepossessing seminary student came to my office to share his dream of reaching Japanese students for Christ by teaching them English in centers nearby major Japanese cities. Ken Wendling had never been to Asia, but he had the burden. I recall thinking, "Young man, it's a worthwhile idea, but what makes you think you can pull it off, with no backing, no experience, no funding?"

Today, there is possibly no ministry more significant among Japanese students than the Language Institute for Evangelism (LIFE). Ken's dream has become a reality because of his dogged determination, his never-give-up spirit. It has been a long-term process with him. Now every year teams of young people are formed for short-term service in Japan; English language centers have been established throughout the country; evangelism concerts regularly attract thousands; the Protestant church in Japan has been meaningfully supported and has evidenced growth because of the ministry of LIFE, Ken Wendling's dream and his lifetime work.

Earlier in the twentieth century, an almost-illiterate major league baseball player, an alcoholic, came to the end of himself and one day wandered into Chicago's Pacific Garden Mission. There he met Jesus Christ and received him as Savior and Lord. Bill Sunday's life was magnificently transformed. He immediately began to share his newly found faith with his ballplayer buddies and ultimately became the best-known evangelist in America. But—it took time. Sunday's significant ministry evolved gradually, over many years. Again, a process. Sunday overcame lack of education, the scorn of fellow preachers, suspicion of his unusual preaching style, and jealousy of peers to become a legend in his time. He became obsessed with pointing men and women and boys and girls to Christ in great evangelism crusades across America. Tens of thousands are in heaven today because of the fearless preaching and the burden of this evangelist—including my father-in-law, who met Christ in a Billy Sunday crusade. To this intrepid gospel crusader, nothing was more important than preaching Christ. He exemplified excellence in his calling to serve God through his public evangelism.

It has been well said, "Those who attain to any excellence commonly spend life in some simple pursuit, for excellence is not often gained upon easier terms." Choose your top priority and stay with it.

Perhaps you're blessedly afflicted with many gifts. You're a Jack or Jane of many trades, but you really excel in none of them. Perhaps it's time to put down your shotgun and turn to your rifle. Instead of blasting recklessly into the sky of blue, hoping you'll hit something, pick your target, take careful aim, and go for the *one thing* you want most.

It's too easy to be like the Texan who waltzed up to the ticket agent at the Dallas-Fort Worth Airport and said, "Ma'am, I'd like you to sell me a first class ticket." The agent asked, "But where to, sir?" The Texan replied, "It don't really matter, ma'am. I got business everywhere."

There's nothing wrong with having business everywhere, but it's to your advantage to take care of your tasks one at a time and to recognize that each of your goals will take effort, determination, and time.

The organization I represent, World Vision, began as a dream of a young missionary-evangelist and Christian humanitarian. However, Bob Pierce never dreamed when he promised to pay for the care of one needy Chinese child, White Jade, that one day the organization he founded would care for 600,000 needy children! The ministry grew a step at a time—10 children, 100, 1,000, 10,000, 100,000. One village of hungry fed, then two, then scores. One man and a secretary, no support, but a driving passion to help the needy. Fifty years later World Vision has become the largest evangelical relief and evangelism ministry in the world. This is a result of the dream of one man, of careful attention given to details, of the diligence and determination of a team of committed people, of sacrifice of time and energy—and of the blessing of God.

Excellence is a process that should occupy all our days, whether it is tied to a specific piece of work done or not. Just as you must work at life, so you must work at the spirit of excellence. It will become a part of you only through a singleness of purpose and a determination to see your goals through to the end.

Remember, "It's always too soon to quit." You and I will make mistakes today. We'll make errors in personal judgment and mistakes in administration. But we do ourselves no favors if we judge ourselves on the performance of the last several hours. Instead, we need to ask, What is our track record? What kind of progress have we made during the past six months—the past year? Are we closer to our goal? Have we gained new insights into ourselves as a result of our work?

Courage is the ability to "hang in there" five minutes longer.

We've written considerably in these chapters about attitudes, goal-setting, priorities, motivation, and believing in the long process that excellence demands. But there's another quality that's equally important: the ability to relax and enjoy.

Some time ago I came across this homily by an aging monk, Brother Jeremiah, who was reflecting on his many years of Christian service. He'd worked hard, sometimes too hard. He'd taken life seriously, often too seriously. And as he approached the end of his active service to others, he sat down and wrote these words:

> If I had my life to live over again, I'd try to make more mistakes next time. I would relax. I would limber up. I would be sillier than I have been this trip. I know of very few things I would take seriously.

I would take more trips. I would climb more mountains, swim more rivers, and watch more sunsets. I would do more walking and looking. I would eat more ice cream and less beans. I would have more actual troubles and fewer imaginary ones.

You see, I am one of those people who live prophylactically and sensibly and sanely, hour after hour, day after day. Oh, I've had my moments, and if I had it to do over again, I'd have more of them. In fact, I'd try to have nothing else. Just moments, one after another, instead of living so many years ahead each day. I have been one of those people who never go anywhere without a thermometer, a hot water bottle, a gargle, a raincoat, aspirin, and a parachute. If I had it to do over again, I would go places, do things, and travel lighter than I have.

If I had my life to live over, I would start barefooted earlier in the spring and stay that way later in the fall. I would play more. I would ride on more merry-go-rounds. I'd pick more daisies.

In my book, *The Making of a Christian Leader,* I address the importance of such balance in our living.

A person can become a workaholic by overcommitting himself financially, by making unrealistic plans, or simply by failing to recognize a personality defect. Often he may use work as an escape mechanism. Thus he has to drive himself to the exclusion of what should be his priorities.

It is most unfortunate that we deplore drug and alcohol addicts but somehow promote and admire the work addict. We give him status and accept his estimate of himself. And all the while his family may be getting so little of his time and energy that they hardly know him.

Overwork is not the disease itself. It is a symptom of a deeper problem—of tension, of inadequacy, of a need to achieve—that may have neurotic implications. Unfortunately for the workaholic, he has no home; his house is only a branch office. He won't take a vacation, can't relax, dislikes weekends, can't wait for Monday, and continues to make his own load heavier by bringing more work onto himself. Such a person also is usually defending against having to get close to people.[19]

Obsessive, compulsive striving for our goals is *not* the way to pursue a life of excellence.

When the apostle John wrote his three brief but beautiful and intimate epistles, he was a very old man, possibly in his nineties. As he reflected on his life and the human needs that continued to surround him, all he chose to say, basically, was, "Little children . . . love one another."

Life has its rhythm, and the process takes many convoluted turns. The ambitions of youth are seldom the desires of the old. So much happens in the interval, and it's all part of the process.

What is happening in your interval? What are you doing to ensure that your life is holding all the splendor and promise God has intended for you? Are you devoting your energies toward a pursuit of excellence in every area of your life?

You can, and you can start today.

Now is the time to develop new habits, new goals, and new perspectives that will give your life a quality that will bring honor to the God who loved you so much that He gave His life for you.

Don't just think about it. Do it!

The poet James Russell Lowell has said it so well:

> Life is a leaf of paper white
> Whereon each one of us may write
> His word or two,
> And then comes night.

> Greatly begin, though thou have time
> But for a line,
> Be that sublime,
> *Not failure, but low aim, is crime.*

CHAPTER 20

Christian Excellence

In 1961 John Gardner, who was then head of the Carnegie Corporation, and was subsequently to move on to prominent roles of leadership in HEW and Common Cause, wrote a book with the simple title, *Excellence* (Harper and Row).

The book was subtitled, "Can We Be Equal and Excellent Too?" In this book, Gardner was attacking the idea that it is almost undemocratic to excel at something over your fellow man.

Gardner was on the right track. We need to excel. And yet, Christians also fall into this same trap of believing that no one should be better than someone else. We become uneasy with the idea of having the best, being the best, or doing that which is outstanding. In our thinking too often we don't mind "excellence" if we can shift responsibility for it onto the Lord. "The Lord has really blessed his ministry," or "The Lord really gave him great gifts." But we may become suspicious if someone is praised directly for doing an excellent job.

There are some real tensions here, and they work themselves out in strange ways:

- We once visited a beautiful chapel on a new church campus. In contrast to three obviously expensive chandeliers was a hand-drawn Sunday school attendance chart taped on the foyer wall. The chandeliers cost $1500, but the best they could do to communicate what was happening to people was a crude graph.

- Another time, World Vision was criticized for purchasing first quality plumbing for a new building, a long-term investment that has paid good dividends, but at the time seemed "too good" to some.

- In contrast is the pride we exhibit when a Christian makes the "big time" in athletics or politics. For some reason it's all right to praise a man for other *non-Christian* things!

A Problem of Theology

Part of our problem is just defective theology. Most of us cannot live with the biblical (paradoxical) truth that God is doing it all—he is in all and through all, and the parallel, and just as completely incomprehensible, truth—man is the one who has not only been given complete responsibility for his actions, but is commanded to act. All of this is part of our tension in theology and life. We constantly struggle with the concept of operating a business and a ministry. They do not conflict; both are vital.

But we are called to excellence. And we are called to set standards of excellence for ourselves and all men. In Philippians 1:10 Paul prays that we may have the ability to approve those things that are excellent.

"Be perfect as your heavenly Father is perfect" is the standard. But where to begin? Does a call to excellence mean a call to excellence in everything?

Colossians 3:17 admonishes us, "Whatever you do, in word or deed, do everything in the name of the Lord Jesus, giving thanks to God the Father through him." No higher standard could be found.

And yet most of us must admit that there are large segments of our life where this is not our experience. What's the answer? How do we as Christian leaders apply these criteria?

Let's start with some definitions.

Excellence Is a Measure

First: Excellence is a measure. It demands definition. One of the trite replies of our day when asked how we like something or how well something is going, is "Compared to what?"

But excellence is like that. It assumes a standard.

And conversely excellence assumes inferiority. It assumes there's a way of doing or being something that is

- less than the best.
- less than what it could be.
- less than worthwhile.

Excellence Assumes a Goal

Second: Excellence assumes a goal, an objective. Excellence demands that we think beyond dreams, think beyond concepts; that we think into reality—in terms of what can be, what should be.

Excellence Assumes Priorities

Third: Excellence assumes priorities. It not only has to do with doing one thing well, but is concerned with a choice between goals. There are some goals that are less worthy, less honoring to God, goals that fall short of all that God intends us to be. It is not that there is one right way for all men, but rather that a potential for excellence in some area lies in all men. We are called to live a life in which we need to do many things to live our life, but within which we are called to do some things with excellence. Certainly to excel in prayer. Perhaps to excel in one book of the Bible or to exercise one gift to its fullest potential. (Some of us have great gifts, but we are too lazy to unwrap them.)

Excellence Is a Process

Fourth: Excellence is more of a process than an achievement. Similarly, life is a process; management is a process. There are times in history when we can look at an individual or event and pronounce it excellent, but it is continually pressing on that marks the man dedicated to excellence.

> I do not consider myself yet to have taken hold of it. But one thing
> I do: Forgetting what is behind and straining toward what is ahead,
> I press on toward the goal to win the prize for which God has called
> me heavenward in Christ Jesus (Philippians 3:13–14).

Excellence Should Be a Style of Life

Fifth: Excellence has to do with a style of life. Know yourself. What is your style? What can it be? People are tremendously different. They have different gifts. They have different callings. There are: outgoing and introspective people, thinkers and doers, leaders and followers, logical and intuitive persons, teachers and learners.

Some people are ahead of their time, some are behind. A few are musical geniuses, most are not. Some are great preachers, some are not. Some are conceivers of grand ideas, others are people of small detail.

But for each of us, excellence demands that we be true to the best that God has placed within us. My style of life should be one of excellence. The Christian can adopt nothing less as his goal.

Excellence Has to Do with Motivation

Sixth: Excellence has to do with motivation. Excellence is not achieved easily. The first 80 percent of an excellent solution comes easily. The next 15 percent is difficult. Only the highly motivated person reaches 100 percent.

There is a joy in such achievement that is an all-too-rare experience for most of us. One of the mysteries of living is that the goal which is achieved easily brings little inner satisfaction or reward. Old victories will serve for old age, but before that I must forget what lies behind and press on to the high calling that lies ahead.

Think big! Believe a big God! Remember that "God is greater . . . !"

Excellence Assumes Accountability

Seventh: Excellence assumes accountability, either to our own inner standard or the standard of the group. Oh, how we Christians have so often missed that!

- Excellence is a measurement, and that assumes a standard of accountability. Yes or no. Make it or not.

- Excellence demands a goal, and that's sticking your neck out to others.

- Excellence demands priorities, and that's telling people what comes first in your life.

- Excellence is a process, and that means continually checking progress.

- Excellence has to do with style and that means deciding what gifts God has given me and how I should be responsible for those gifts.

- Excellence has to do with motivation, and that's what it's all about!

How Do We Respond to the Goal of Excellence?

1. Sort out your goals. You can't do everything. You can't be everything. And that's all right.

2.   Of those goals you believe you must push toward, decide which have top priority. Do these with excellence.

3.   Decide who you are and what you are, or, paradoxically, decide how God made you and what he wants you to be. Do that with excellence. It was said of Jesus, "He has done everything well." Can we do less?

4.   As we seek Christian excellence, keep it in perspective. Some things are more excellent than others. Before that verse in Philippians 1:10, Paul tells us how we will be able to judge that which is excellent.

> And this is my prayer: that your love may abound more and more in knowledge and depth of insight, so that you may be able to discern what is best and may be pure and blameless until the day of Christ, filled with the fruit of righteousness that comes through Jesus Christ—to the glory and praise of God (Philippians 1:9–11).

The *purpose* is glory and praise of God. The *goal* is excellence.

Note that the steps to the goal are knowledge and discernment thoroughly mixed together with abounding love.

The *measurement* is the fruits of righteousness.

The *power* comes through Jesus Christ.

All glory to Him!

Part Five

INTEGRITY IN LEADERSHIP

CHAPTER 21

Semper Infidelis

Semper Fidelis, "always faithful"—the official, etched-in-stone motto of the U.S. Marine Corps. But in the light of the sex-for-spying scandal in Moscow, the leathernecks have had to answer to "Semper INfidelis." For 200 years, and from the halls of Montezuma to the shores of Tripoli, the Marines have stood for loyalty, discipline, and faithfulness. We still hear it: "The Marines are looking for a few good men." Now, it seems, they're looking for more than just a few!

In early 1987 two Marine guards at the U.S. embassy in Moscow allegedly escorted Soviet agents into the most sensitive chambers of the consulate—including the "secure" communications center. The damage? Incalculable. Entire lists of secret agents, threatened. Transmission codes, compromised. Plans, immobilized.

And what force overpowered the men who had supposedly received the finest military training in the free world? Was it firearms? Torture? Nuclear blackmail? No, it was *sex*. Lust of the flesh held sway over the strength of armor.

But surely this incident was merely some bizarre exception. Who wants to believe our armed forces could be neutralized by the arms of women? I, for one, still have a great deal of confidence in our young soldiers. Maybe that's because I once wore the Army green as a young man myself. What concerns me most is not that something like this can happen in the U.S. Marines, but that it seems to be happening all over the world in so many other institutions. If a small, highly trained group of elite soldiers cannot take the hill, what of the civilians who follow behind?

What about our lawmakers? Do they obey their own laws? Have our preachers heard their own sermons on repentance? Is the business world sold on ethics?

Are "lovers" truly loving one another? Are parents producing character in their children or just raising characters?

This morning, I threw down my copy of the *Los Angeles Times* in disgust. It was more of the same . . . filled with further explicit allegations of the sexual misconduct of a prominent TV evangelist, along with new stories about his wife's spending habits that are beginning to make Imelda Marcos seem conservative. As a fellow Christian, I believe in grace and forgiveness. But what makes this TV evangelist's sexual impropriety particularly damaging is that his tryst took place *seven years ago.* Allegedly, too, it involved drugged wine and unnatural acts against the woman's will. Not only that, he arranged payment of more than $265,000 in hush money. And he "confessed" only after the incident received national attention.

Like loose threads on a sweater, one revelation led to another. Next he announced the transfer of his entire nationwide broadcast organization to a rival preacher. Later he claimed that same preacher had seized control through a hostile takeover.

Several other well-known television ministers exchanged heated charges and countercharges with this "gospelebrity." Did he and his wife pocket undisclosed millions in bonuses and cash while claiming only a modest salary? Were there other sexual encounters? Are there any political figures involved?

The stakes behind this one prodigal personality are enormous: Thirteen million viewers, $172 million in assets, a 2,300–acre religious theme park (second only to Disneyland and Disney World in attendance). For lack of integrity, this evangelist lost it all.

Unfortunately, there are other prominent preachers calling the integrity of God's servants into question. Another evangelist retired to his prayer tower until supporters could raise eight million dollars to bail him out of acute financial difficulties relating to his medical school. If he didn't get the money, God was going to "call him home." Fortunately, the dollars arrived and he survived. Unfortunately, Christian integrity had once again been rushed into intensive care.

Semper Fidelis?

It's little wonder that in early 1987, pollster George Gallup, Jr., told a meeting of Christian fund-raisers that 42 percent of Americans doubted the honesty of some, if not most, appeals for religious donations.[20]

How well do some of these preachers tread water? Jesus warns us "whoever causes one of these little ones who believe in me to sin, it would be better for him if a millstone were hung around his neck, and he were drowned in the depth of the sea" (Matthew 18:6). The masonry yard must be doing a land-office business in millstones these days.

What used to be looked upon as merely a desirable "Boy Scout" trait, integrity, is now proving itself to be the heart and soul of the whole person.

Oh, how the mighty are fallen! Major Wall Street financiers led off to jail in three-piece suits and handcuffs. These highrollers thought they could rewrite the commandment against stealing. A front-running presidential candidate forced to resign from the race. He mistakenly thought he had "executive privilege" when it came to the adultery command. Two of America's more promising athletes killed by cocaine (in separate incidents). They thought they were mightier, stronger, and more potent than natural laws of survival.

Challenger

Not only can the lack of integrity kill the individual involved, it can also cut down whole groups of innocent people as well.

It was a chilly Tuesday morning, January 28, 1986, when Christa McAuliffe climbed aboard the Challenger space shuttle for her historic mission as the first citizen in space. She was a teacher. I only pray that we learned something about the consequences of getting an "F" in integrity. The weather was cold, but unbeknown to the rest of the nation a group of engineers was fighting back the hot sweat of worried anticipation. Would the booster seals hold in this kind of weather? Was it safe to launch? Knowledgeable engineers and designers said, "No." Influential executives and planners said, "Yes."

Power overruled reason. Integrity was the victim. After seventy seconds of flight, a faulty booster rocket ignited millions of gallons of rocket fuel into a blinding explosion. Debris rained on the Florida waters for a solid hour. At first we believed that Christa and the other six crew members perished instantly at the moment of explosion. Upon examination of the cabin remains, we learned they might have endured almost three and a half minutes of terrifying freefall before smashing into the Atlantic Ocean at 200 miles per hour. I only wish these words about the urgent need for integrity could carry that same force of impact.

Road to Ruin

But only seven people died in this infraction of character. The space shuttle's destruction was dramatic. It was immortalized before the whole world on television. Much quieter is the steady slaughter of *tens of thousands* on the nation's highways. In the months since the Challenger accident extinguished seven heroes, the automobile has done the same for approximately 30,000 potential parents of heroes.

I'm confident that virtually every loss on the road can be traced to some form of loss in integrity. It's an established fact that at least one half of this nation's automobile accidents are caused by alcohol or substance abuse. The other half is always the fault of *someone's* less-than-wholehearted attention to detail, maintenance, or skill. Yes, I too have had my share of fright behind the wheel. And I know it's often the fault of the other guy, or the equipment. But that's my point. If you trace back any cause far enough, you'll find someone who forgot that these glass and steel "things" actually carry flesh-and-blood people. Perhaps I belabor the point. But maybe I can make you squirm enough to want to buckle up. That, too, involves integrity.

Acquired Integrity Deficiency Syndrome

Semper infidelis? Where else could this term have greater meaning than in family, marriage, and sex? Fidelity and integrity have always been an important part of family relationships. Now they, too, are becoming matters of life and death.

Acquired Immune Deficiency Syndrome, AIDS, has infected our headlines for years. Now it's front-page news almost every day. The implications are almost unfathomable—an incurable disease transmitted by the most difficult of human activities to discuss (much less control)—illicit sex. (I realize that contaminated needles among drug users are the second most common form of spreading AIDS. But as a man of the Word, I also realize that the sensual passion to rape one's own veins with a long phallic symbol for the purpose of arousing an orgasmic sensation by injecting narcotics is essentially the same lust of the flesh as illicit sex.)

"The life of a creature is in the blood," we learn from Leviticus 17:11. And now, even more than ever before, we know it's true. Because with AIDS, the "death" of the flesh is in the blood.

If one were "always faithful," would it be possible to get AIDS? Sadly, yes. The infection is too far out of control. The world is simply too far from God.

Through transfusions, pregnancy, nursing mothers, accidental exposure from wound to wound, and other methods, the iniquities of the "fathers" of AIDS can be visited upon another generation.

But not just "unto the third and fourth generation" as sins of old. This contagion is too lethal for that brief a lifespan. In a matter of months, AIDS can reduce a 180–pound athlete to an 80–pound spectator. In a few more weeks—to an obituary notice.

This lapse in integrity will fill whole columns of obituaries. The U.S. Surgeon General has estimated that approximately 179,000 Americans will die from AIDS by 1991.

If you printed two names per line, that many fatalities would require 83 pages of the *Los Angeles Times* listing from top to bottom, six columns across, no pictures, no ads.

And that total of 179,000 deaths by 1991 assumes most of those people who successfully produced AIDS antibodies in their blood would *not* die. The 1987 conference on AIDS in Washington, D.C., introduced evidence that most people who successfully produce antibodies in their blood *will* eventually contract the disease and die prematurely.

Frantic search is under way for better treatments and perhaps a cure. In the meantime, they tell us, the best we can do for ourselves is practice "safe sex," avoid blood-to-blood contact, and practice monogamy.

Indeed monogamy needs practice. Far too many people are out of the habit or never knew how. What are the benefits of remaining "always faithful" to your mate? They used to be little more than convenience, comfort, and consideration. Today those benefits include existence itself.

The Larger Issue

It would be easy to fill this space with many other examples of infirm integrity. The chronology of human failures is endless. But the real question is not, "Who's involved in the latest failure?" It doesn't take much guts to hold up the faults of someone else to hide one's own shortcomings.

The larger issue is, what can you and I do *personally* to avoid our own failures and preserve our ability to serve? When Christ said, "Broad is the way that leads to destruction," He was not calling His disciples to jump on a spiritual bandwagon. He was warning and instructing them in a way of life.

What is *integrity?*

Let's keep it simple. I could give you a long, complicated dictionary answer about how *integrity* means "whole," "sound," and "unimpaired." But that's so much academia. What I'd rather do here is try to breathe some life into these empty syllables. Interact with me as we dress "integrity" up in work clothes and send it out to earn its keep in our everyday world.

Promise

Simply put, *integrity* is doing what you said you would do. "One of the most fundamental acts of a society is promise-keeping," says Dr. Lewis Smedes, former Professor of Theology and Christian Ethics at Fuller Theological Seminary. Here is the bedrock of social relationships. When we can no longer depend on one another to do what we said we would do, the future becomes an undefined nightmare.

Society makes promises to us. Governments make promises to us. Our friends make promises. The church makes promises. All of these relate to the future. Each one says, "When the time comes, you can count on my coming through."

How different it sounds when, instead of talking about reviewing plans and objectives, we picture ourselves as reviewing the *promises* we have made and making new ones—at home and on the job.

To make a promise is a holy thing. In this book, with its simple title, *Integrity*—and as a fellow passenger on the same plane—I am committing a part of my life to you. I am announcing that you have an interest in my future. I am stating that you can expect your life to proceed as you would hope because of my willingness to fit into your needs and desires.

Thus *integrity.* Keeping promises. Doing what you said you would do.

Sixteen References

Ironically, out of sixteen references in the Bible, the first time the word *integrity* occurs it is attributed to a pagan king as protection—against *God's* servant! Genesis 20 tells us that Abraham and Sarah both lied to Abimelech, king of Gerar, about Sarah's identity as a married woman. Therefore Abimelech "sent and took her" (20:2). When God threatened to kill Abimelech if he committed adultery, Abimelech replied, "Lord, will you slay a righteous nation also? Did he not say to me, 'She is my sister'? And she even herself said, 'He is my brother.' In the *integrity* of my heart and innocence of my hands I have done this" (Genesis 20:5, emphasis mine).

God spared Abimelech's life and illustrated three important principles. 1) Integrity can be a life-and-death issue; 2) unbelievers can and do exhibit great integrity; and 3) need it be said even God's servants have feet of clay and often *do* fall painfully short of the ideal?

(If you want to pursue other references, check out these verses that deal with "integrity": Genesis 20:6; 1 Kings 9:4; Job 2:3, 9; 27:5; 31:6; Psalms 7:8; 25:21; 26:1, 11; 41:12; 78:72; Proverbs 11:3; 19:1; 20:7.)

Hidden References

There's an interesting story about integrity hidden in the meaning of its Hebrew spelling.[21]

In the original Hebrew, *thom* signifies "whole" and "complete," thus it is translated as "integrity." But in the plural, *thummim* refers to part of the ceremonial accouterments worn by the High Priest, and him alone. Two special objects are mentioned in conjunction with the priest's decorative breastplate, the Urim and Thummim. "They shall be over Aaron's heart when he goes in before the Lord" (Exodus 28:30). Their exact function is a mystery. But we do know they were important objects because Scripture tells us there were times when a high-level decision could not be made "until a priest could consult with the Urim and Thummim" (Ezra 2:63; Nehemiah 7:65).

Scholars are divided about their exact composition. Some think they were stone objects, others suggest they were another name for the twelve gemstones representing the twelve tribes of Israel. Another feels they were some kind of gold plate. But authorities all agree these items were important.

What does *thummim* have to do with integrity? As the plural of *thom*, this object suggests the perfections or *integrities* required to stand before God and discern His will. No High Priest could enter the Holy of Holies without his heart being covered by "perfections" (integrity). God wanted His priests to understand integrity. He also wants every Christian to be protected with the "breastplate of righteousness" and a spiritual *thummim* as well (Ephesians 6:14).

Integrity in Action

Ideas in theory and ideas in action are seldom the same. But when one follows the other, there is the opportunity for change and growth. I appreciate the following story told by my friend and colleague, Robert Schuller.

Keep on Shining

A judge was campaigning for reelection. He had a reputation for integrity. He was a distinguished and honorable gentleman of no small charity. His opponent was conducting a vicious, mud-smearing, unfair campaign against him.

Somebody approached the judge and asked, "Do you know what your opponent is saying about you? Do you know he is criticizing you? How are you going to handle it? What are you going to do about it?" The judge looked at his counselors and his campaign committee and calmly replied, "Well, when I was a boy I had a dog. And every time the moon was full, that hound dog would howl and bark at the bright face of the moon. We never did sleep very well those nights. He would bark and howl at the moon all night." With that, the judge concluded his remarks.

"That's beside the point," his campaign manager impatiently said. "You've told us a nice story about your dog, but what are you going to do about your critic?"

The judge explained, "I just answered you! When the dog barked at the moon, the moon kept right on shining! I don't intend to do anything but keep right on shining. And I'll ignore the criticism, as the moon ignored the dog. I'll just keep right on shining! Quietly, calmly, beautifully!"[22]

How about you? Just when this darkened world needs brightness the most, many of those around us have chosen to cloak themselves in shadows. You and I can choose otherwise. Obviously we won't attempt to believe we'll live out the rest of our lives in a state of perfection. But we *can* choose to be "semper fidelis" *this day.* Many successful rehabilitation programs teach people to make long-lasting changes by focusing on simple improvements "one day at a time." It might be well to remember that where a lifetime commitment seems overwhelming, "one day" can be manageable. And if you and I can demonstrate integrity in our lives *today,* it will be easier to do so again *tomorrow,* and the next day. But for now, one day is enough.

For today alone, I invite you to join me in an . . .

Integrity Action Plan #1

1. Not focusing on the evil around, but concentrating on the good within.

2. Giving your word and keeping it.

3. Clothing your body and your mind with excellence.

4. Promising to keep on shining.

Such a mutually agreed upon plan could solve the problem of "semper infidelis" overnight *if* this vale of tears in which we live wasn't so fettered by the chains of habit. To change *ourselves* and to appreciate the pulls on those who surround us, we need to understand and respond to the call to action—our topic in chapter 22.

A Call to Action

He looked like almost any other passenger you would see on an airplane, but I should have recognized the difference in his eyes—somehow they really cared. This was one of those long transoceanic flights that ends before it starts because you're crossing the international dateline. I've flown from Los Angeles to Tokyo more times than I care to remember, and assumed this would just be "another one of those flights": grueling, tiresome, and forgettable.

So I was somewhat relieved when this distinguished stranger took the seat next to mine. He looked like someone I could talk to—or simply pass the time in silence, depending on what the long hours invited.

"Hello, I'm Benjamin Alexander," said the stranger-no-more. "You want the window seat?" he offered.

"But you've got the boarding pass for it!" I protested mildly.

"Go ahead and take it if you'd like. I've pretty well seen it all. Besides, I enjoy the sights in here every bit as much as those outside," he said while playfully eyeing one of the female passengers—a beguiling six- or seven-year-old with an enchanting smile.

His voice was kind. Listenable. The sort that might lull you to sleep if it didn't have something unexpected to say most of the time.

"You're Ted Engstrom, aren't you?"

"Yes, how did you know?" I said with a start.

"Well, let's just say I saw it on one of the passenger rosters."

"I didn't know they left that type of information lying around," I countered with a puzzled frown. "What line of work are you in?" From his neat appearance and smooth demeanor, I guessed sales.

"Hydro-electric power. Family business. We've been in the industry for generations."

Without giving me a chance to ask anything more, Ben pulled a newsmagazine out of his carry-on and began settling himself into the seat for taxi and take-off.

"Ding," chimed the intercom—calling us all to attention.

"Hello, and welcome to flight 712 to Tokyo," said the flight attendant stirring everyone into action, stowing handbags and checking seatbelts.

As flight safety instructions about the Boeing 747 drifted through the cabin, my mind turned to the welter of thoughts I had been sifting through on integrity. So I couldn't help but notice that Ben was reading a recent article on broken promises in high places.

"What do you think about all these scandals?" I asked. He lowered the magazine with a sigh and shook his head. Maybe he didn't want to discuss the issues. Or perhaps he would be filled with vituperative remarks about specific people and actions. I enjoy a stimulating conversation. But I've never felt good about gossip. These topics seem to race down the razor's edge between the two. Which side would this newcomer veer toward?

"You're a man of the Word," he said surprising me again. "What do you think about these issues?"

Rarely being at a loss for something to say, I related my disappointment and disillusionment on many of the same issues you and I have shared throughout this book. "How could responsible leaders allow themselves to fall into such irresponsible actions? How could someone expect us to honor their public decisions when their own private decisions are so dishonorable? And more pointedly, how could someone who supposedly lived by the Word of God, flagrantly disobey the instructions of the Almighty?"

I could tell Ben had something worthwhile to say, but he was cut off abruptly by the sudden wails of an infant seated behind us. He changed his thought in midbreath.

"That child back there has much to cry about. She saw her dad for the last time yesterday and her mom is headed home to 'mom.'"

"How'd you know that?" I asked.

"Oh, just the sound of her voice I suppose—and something you said."

"Something I said?"

"Right. Another responsible leader disobeying the instructions of God."

"Huh? What leader are you talking about?"

"Her father. But don't worry, she won't cry for long. She's too young to know what's really hurting her."

This was confusing. Before I could collect my thoughts to piece together another question, the infant fell quiet and Ben handed me a knowing glance.

"Ted," he continued, "I know you've been giving these subjects a great deal of thought. Do you mind if I ask you a few questions about integrity and personal values?"

By now I was so shocked by what he was saying that nothing really surprised me anymore. "Sure, go ahead," I replied haltingly. But then I began wondering if he might know as much about a seventy-one-year-old man seated next to him as he did about a seven-month-old infant fifteen rows away. Who was this man and what was he all about?

"Excuse me, gentlemen. May I interest either of you in a cocktail?" asked the flight attendant. Her warm smile called me back into the real world at 35,000 feet in the sky.

"No, thank you," volunteered Ben. "My friend and I will have juice."

"You seem pretty confident about what I think and want."

"Maybe that's because you seem pretty confident about what you think and want. Tell me this," he continued before I could thank him for the compliment, "what difference does it make if a man drinks himself into oblivion, or sires a half-dozen children by six different women?"

"What kind of question is that?" I thought to myself. "I'll tell you what kind of question it is, by answering it for you," Ben interrupted.

When I told you he ceased to surprise me, I was a bit premature. This remark took me completely off guard. I've been a lot of places and seen a lot of people, but *never* anything like this. In fact I began casting my eyes around the plane to make sure I wasn't in the operating room under anesthesia or something. But I was still strapped in, and he wasn't about to let me go anywhere without hearing more.

"It doesn't make a bit of difference how we conduct our lives today and tomorrow *if* we don't care about the effect these actions may have," Ben philosophized.

"OK," I said to let him know I heard, but didn't necessarily agree. He was obviously headed somewhere with this line of reasoning and I wanted to be near the mental lifeboat if it came time to jump ship.

"You see, people are very anxious to avoid actions in the future if they understand how destructive they are from direct personal experience," Ben continued.

"See that elderly man across the aisle and up two seats? He would never dream of using cocaine. He's watched one grandson and a niece destroyed by the stuff. The outcome just doesn't make sense to him."

"I can understand that," I volunteered.

"But one person can never live long enough to make all the mistakes."

"Now that's something I can 'amen.' You'd have to have at least nine lives, maybe more, to do that."

"Precisely. And then we often have trouble seeing the connection between our actions and our problems. Take that businessman over there for instance—the one reaching for his cigarettes and eyeing the 'no smoking' sign. His actions and his diet are destroying his heart tissue. But he won't admit the connection in his mind till he feels the pain in his chest. And by then it may be too late."

"Well, how does all this tie in with integrity?" I asked with impatience.

"Ted, you've been around long enough to understand the problems a teen will face, and the problems of a young single man, and the problems of a newlywed couple, and the problems of young parents, and the problems of older parents, an employee, a boss . . ."

"Yes, yes," I said cutting him off before he had me as old as Methuselah. "But how does that affect integrity?"

"Let me ask you this. Don't you think you'd have been a much better teen-age student and employee if you understood then what you understand today?"

"Obviously," I conceded.

"And a better friend, groom, father, boss—if you understood *then* what you know *today*."

"Well, most likely," I offered. "But where are you going with all of this?"

"Have you ever tried to impart some of this understanding to others?" he continued.

I could tell he knew I'd written a number of books on many of these same subjects. "I'd want to write down these experiences and tell others about them."

"And that's exactly what we've got here," he said bending down to pull something out of his brief case.

Maybe it's one of my books, I speculated. *He seems to know everything about me. Must have gotten that information from somewhere. But instead . . .*

"It's all right here," he said, dropping his open palm on a Bible. "Here are the accounts of thousands of members of the same family learning about the outcomes of their decisions and passing the wisdom along to newcomers who would never live long enough to relearn everything on their own. And it's authored by someone who's been around long enough to see the outcome of each decision. That, my friend, is the source of integrity."

"Where have you been for the past 1900 years?" I asked him. (And it seemed as if this question caused him to raise one eyebrow almost imperceptibly.) "People have been preaching those words since the time of Christ and we're still making the same mistakes." His observation made a lot of sense, but I wanted to see what else he had to say.

"That's been a problem," he conceded. Then with a sigh of resignation he added, "And we've all paid dearly. That's where the second half of integrity comes into play."

"Second half? What's that?" I asked, knowing full well he was going to tell me anyway. He seemed to pause a long time in reflection. I looked at his eyes and they were moist with remembered pain.

"Someone always has to pay for the mistakes. That young couple behind us took the life of their unborn child rather than reduce their earnings to one income. The man who came onboard in the wheelchair was paralyzed when his grade school buddies dared him to dive into the creek. Without integrity, people perish."

His voice was hushed and the silence grew as loud as the nearby jet engines. About then I began to worry that he was going to say something about me and my own shortcomings. So I quickly formulated another question. But he beat me to the punch.

"Ted, do you know who paid the ultimate penalty so we all wouldn't have to die for our mistakes?"

There was no doubt in my mind that he was referring to none other than our Savior, Jesus Christ.

"That's right," he responded before I could speak. And the answer seemed to mean so much more to him almost as if he knew about the tragedy firsthand.

"Maybe if people really understood the outcome of their actions," he mused out loud, "and could see the pain it inflicts on innocent people, maybe they'd be willing to pay more attention to this matter of integrity. What do you think?"

"I think you're right."

"Then what are you going to do about it?" he slowly added to my surprise.

"Are you Mr. Ben Alexander?" the attendant leaned over and asked, startling both of us. "We have a phone call for you up front by the galley."

We both looked at each other with puzzlement and he disappeared into the galley.

That's the last time I ever saw Ben Alexander. When I became concerned about his prolonged absence, the flight attendant informed me that there was no such person on board, and the seat next to me had been vacant since we left Los Angeles. When I asked the young girl across the aisle, the retired gentleman, and the lovebirds behind me and got the same answer, I knew it was time to look somewhere else for the explanation. Not surprisingly, I spotted a small slip of paper in the vacant seat next to me with these words written on it, "Hebrews 13:2." Ninety-nine percent sure of what it said already, I hurriedly looked up the Scripture. "Do not forget to entertain strangers, for by so doing some have unwittingly entertained angels."

The Message

If you asked me, "Did this really happen?" my answer might surprise you. But before I explain the mystery, there are a few more principles from Ben Alexander and from our previous chapters I want to summarize and tie together.

"What are you going to do about it?" were the parting words from the stranger I entertained. This book is much of my answer. As for me, I'm going to tell people about the importance of looking to the outcome of our actions and avoiding pain toward others.

What about you?

Strange how easy it is for little things to attract our attention and call us to action. The gentle bell aboard a jetliner directs our attention to some forthcoming message: "No smoking," or "Fasten your seat belt." These messages touch on life and death, so we usually respond.

But look at some of the other calls that make us act—telephones, car horns, alarm clocks, elevator chimes, tea kettles, microwave oven timers, to name but a few.

We're eager and willing to be called into action when the outcome is something we enjoy. Why is it that we seldom enjoy the results of "integrity living" as much as we could? Perhaps we simply don't understand the connection between right actions and right results.

Throughout this book, we've seen a lot of people stumble. New disappointments hit the headlines every day. In fact, one of the latest letdowns involved 106 public officials in New York. After a sting operation to uncover graft, U.S. Attorney Rudolph Giuliani made the following statement, "On 106 occasions, bribes were offered or discussed. On 105 of those occasions, the public official involved accepted the bribe. And on the other occasion, he turned it down because he didn't think the amount was large enough."[23]

But is it enough to look at the shortcomings of others, shake our heads a couple of times, and assume we are protected from the same fate? I can say with assurance that the Marines who allegedly compromised the embassy in Moscow had been thoroughly warned. The TV evangelist who locked himself away in a hotel with a young church secretary had certainly preached the Scriptures against adultery. The businessmen who triggered a super bowl of scandal on Wall Street thought they understood all the rules.

If we're going to put out these destructive forces in our lives, we've got to replace them with something else. It's not enough to "mistreat others as we mistreat ourselves"; we must embrace a code of ethics—that kind of "true religion" that transcends our own susceptible reasoning.

As Ben Alexander explained, it's a lot easier to control our present behavior if we deeply understand the future consequences of these actions. How could we let down our friends and family if we actually shared the pain our actions might inflict on them?

Would I betray my mate of many years if I actually felt the pain our children would suffer? Would I steal from the company supply closet if I understood the anguish some widow might experience from the higher prices resulting from my impropriety? Would I gossip about a friend if I saw my careless actions drive that person to drugs and alcohol?

These feelings and these actions make up the very heart of Christianity. The Son of God, the One who was present at the creation of the first human beings, has shared His knowledge of outcomes with men and women for millennia. He then emptied Himself of divinity and became the Son of man for the express purpose of sharing and removing the pain we inflict upon ourselves. This sacrifice paves the way for our life of integrity.

I'm not asking you to become a Christian. I'm only asking you to consider how much better life might be if everyone in our world shared Christ's concern for others.

Think about it for a moment. If this were a pre-Fall Garden of Eden . . . if everyone were a true believer—an uncompromising, caring, loving, self-effacing Christian—you wouldn't have to fear for your life because there would be no hatred and murder. You wouldn't have to be concerned about the breakup of your family because your loved ones would all obey the law against adultery. You wouldn't have to endure the onslaught of sexual temptations because no one would covet your sexual favors. You wouldn't have to lock up your money because everyone would understand the outcome of stealing.

In short, you wouldn't have to fear what others might do to you. Your only fear might be what you could do to yourself.

And that brings us back full circle. Since we can't control others in this present world, the only alternative we have is to control ourselves—and that takes integrity.

The Power of One

Never underestimate the power of one—a power that is tapped by those who gain control over themselves. One girl from Albania improved the lives of underprivileged people in thirty countries. One football player in California tackled the problems of inner city youngsters. One coach in Conyers, Georgia, inspired the whole city· (and much of the nation) to "do what is honest."

Some may look at the trophy winners we showcased in earlier chapters and throw up their hands in discouragement. Too many of us dismiss integrity as something only the superstars can achieve.

But integrity is for *everyone*. One homeowner can write an editor or lawmaker to swing an issue. One consumer can file a class action suit that will benefit millions. One bereaved mother can channel her rage into MADD (Mothers Against Drunk Driving). One teacher can provide the inspiration to motivate students for a lifetime.

On to the Top

Such commendable goals call for an extra dimension. It's been said that nothing worthwhile has ever been accomplished without enthusiasm. I certainly believe it, especially when you realize enthusiasm actually means "God in us."

We talked about the high road to integrity, which leads to the "mountain of God." What better source can we go to for genuine "enthusiasm" toward integrity?

One passage that explains how to arrive at that mountain is found in the Psalms. I share it with you as one of my favorite sources of guidance.

Psalm 15

Lord, who may dwell in your sanctuary?
  Who may live on your holy hill?

He whose walk is blameless
  and who does what is righteous,
  who speaks the truth from his heart

and has no slander on his tongue,
  who does his neighbor no wrong
  and casts no slur on his fellowman,

who despises a vile man
  but honors those who fear the LORD,
  who keeps his oath
  even when it hurts,

who lends his money without usury
  and does not accept a bribe against the innocent.
  He who does these things
  will never be shaken.

Act As If

None of us can live in perfection all of the time. The thought of never offending someone with our tongue, or never taking a second glance at a provocative body, or never padding an expense account, or never telling a half-truth seems overpowering. Fortunately we serve a forgiving God. But as one of my friends says, "Let's not make Him work overtime."

You and I know we are not faultless, but for starters, we can "act as if" what we do makes a difference. We can act as if we believed in telling the truth and keeping our word. We can act as if we wanted to be faithful to our mate. We can act as if loyalty mattered.

You've no doubt heard about cases where people lived a lie so long they started to believe it. Perhaps this marvel can work in our favor. If we act as if we cared for others long enough, maybe, just maybe, the charade would become the reality. Shakespeare tells us, "All life's a stage." Our job is to bring up the curtain on a new act.

What Does the Lord Require?

Here are some themes your new act might contain. We often think we are living up to the standards only to find out something is missing.

I'm reminded of a story about two youngsters who needed to learn more about the art of sharing. "Darling," scolded the mother, "you shouldn't always keep everything for yourself. I have told you before that you should let your brother play with your toys half of the time."

"I've been doing that, Mom," she replied. "I take the sled going downhill and he takes it going up."

Sometimes in the confusion over what is right and what is wrong, it's good to have a yardstick to measure our performance. Here's one I particularly appreciate: "He has showed you, O man, what is good. And what does the LORD require of you? To act justly and to love mercy and to walk humbly with your God" (Micah 6:8). It's up to us to apply the admonitions and see if they don't bring the outcomes we desire.

Do You Not Teach Yourself?

One thing that has weighed heavily on my mind throughout the preparation of this book is the responsibility of God's servants and pastors. The spate of sorry disclosures about sexual misconduct and financial irresponsibility in the ministry saddens me greatly. Elsewhere I've cited the warning from Christ about how it would be better for someone who offends one of God's little ones to tie a millstone about his neck and jump into the ocean. The Bible is filled with admonitions to those who profess to be "wise" and live otherwise.

This passage from Paul conveys the importance of that responsibility:

> Now you, if you call yourself a Jew; if you rely on the law and brag about your relationship to God; if you know his will and approve of what is superior because you are instructed by the law; if you are convinced that you are a guide for the blind, a light for those who are in the dark, an instructor of the foolish, a teacher of infants, because you have in the law the embodiment of knowledge and truth—you, then, who teach others, do you not teach yourself? You who preach against stealing, do you steal? You who say that people should not commit adultery, do you commit adultery? You who abhor idols, do you rob temples? You who brag about the law, do you dishonor God by breaking the law? As it is written: "God's name is blasphemed among the Gentiles because of you" (Romans 2:17–24).

To those ministers who would dare to preach the high words of God and live the low life of heathens I add, "God cannot be mocked. A man reaps what he sows" (Galatians 6:7). "It is a dreadful thing to fall into the hands of the living God" (Hebrews 10:31).

David was a man of God who made a number of human mistakes. We have looked at his indiscretion with Bathsheba elsewhere. He stumbled, but he was always willing to confess his sins and change. His moving words of repentance in Psalm 51 are a powerful tribute to his integrity.

For me, King David represents a clear call to action. There's an interesting reference to David and "integrity" in the New International Version of the Bible. It reads, "I know, my God, that you test the heart and are pleased with integrity—all these things have I given willingly and with honest intent" (1 Chronicles 29:17).

Highest honors are bestowed upon David in the New Testament. "I have found David son of Jesse a man after my own heart; he will do everything I want him to do" (Acts 13:22). Later in the same chapter, Paul explains something about David we all would appreciate hearing about ourselves. "For when David had served God's purpose in his own generation, he fell asleep" (Acts 13:36).

What could be a better epitaph for you and me? "He served his own generation by the will of God and fell asleep." Such is the outcome of walking the high road of integrity.

Ben Alexander

You may have wondered about my experience with Ben Alexander aboard flight 712 to Tokyo. If you asked me, "Did this really happen?" I'd have to say, "No, it did not." But if you asked me, "Did I feel the presence of the Lord during my meditations and writing for this book?" I'd have to say, "Yes!" Paul talks about a trip to the third heaven "whether it was in the body or out of the body I do not know" (2 Corinthians 12:2). For me this was a peak experience with the invisible God of integrity that's more lasting and more meaningful than my encounters with a thousand other visible passengers. And though the event never happened "in the body," the understanding and enlightenment we have shared together in these pages has been unmistakably real.

Before he left to go into action on another "call," Ben asked what I was going to do with this knowledge about integrity and the pain of its loss. I promised I'd write about it . . . in word and deed.

Will you join me in the same? "Those who hope in the LORD will renew their strength. They will soar on wings like eagles; they will run and not grow weary, they will walk and not be faint" (Isaiah 40:31).

Part Six

LEADERS AS MANAGERS

CHAPTER 23

What Good Managers Know

Good managers are not confined to any one field or single occupation. It is a truism of management that a good manager is a good manager wherever he or she may be operating.

Good managers know that the health of an organization is based upon a series of commitments among the members of the organization and between the members of the organization and those outside of it. Commitments often become viable only when they are in writing. At the heart of the old adage "If it isn't in writing, it doesn't exist" is the understanding that commitments must be recorded—they must be observable by a third party. It is not a question of not trusting another's word. Rather, it is a recognition that the life of an organization is an ongoing process. For new staff to understand where their predecessors were going, they must be able to review the commitments made by them. In our computerized world this is recognized as documentation. If someone is going to modify a program, they must understand the program. What is so easily understood about inanimate machines is even more true for people.

A commitment is an agreement on the part of one person to reach a mutually agreed upon objective. An objective, or a goal, is a statement of a future condition or event that includes the time when it will become a past event. In other words, a goal can be achieved. None of us make commitments about the past. All commitments lie in the future. So good managers know that they manage best by seeking written commitments from others.

Good managers know that they have numerous commitments: commitments to themselves, to their subordinates, to their peers, and to their superiors. Obviously, the Christian manager sees all four of these commitments under the lordship of Christ. One's ability to recognize these four types of commitments and to manage them is what differentiates the experienced manager from the inexperienced manager. For these commitments to be managed, they must be first agreed to by the four sets of people involved. Since situations will continually change, these commitments will also need to be reaffirmed with the passage of time.

Commitments to ourselves and our calling will change in the process of time. As one goal is reached, others will replace it. These commitments, goals and statements of faith about our future are the source of our vision and dreams. Therefore it is helpful to put them in writing so we can evaluate our progress.

Commitments to our subordinates will also change as various goals are reached. There will be new plans to be made, and new endeavors to be undertaken. It is to be hoped that we have learned from both our successes and failures and are ready to build on them.

Commitments between peers begin to change as the organization changes with time. A new set of commitments will be required between those who work alongside one another. Organizations are seldom static. They change just as the people in them do.

And in the same way that we expect commitments from our subordinates, so we have *commitments to our superiors*. These, too, will change.

Good managers know that it's seldom possible for a manager or the people working for him or her to fully understand all of the implications of their failing to meet their commitments. It is very easy for the individual to become so concerned with his own situation that he abandons or modifies his original commitments for others he feels are more important. But the ramifications of their failure can ripple through an entire organization. "For want of a nail a shoe was lost, for want of a shoe the horse was lost . . ."

Good managers know that for goals to be realistic they must be backed up by a program or plan for how the goal will be reached. Good managers know that the possibility of things going wrong far exceeds the possibility of things going right. They know that any goal is the result of reaching a series of sub-goals. We call these steps plans or programs.

Good managers know that effective delegation is based upon a written plan. A plan is a request on the part of a subordinate for authority to proceed. It is the evidence that the subordinate knows how to achieve the hoped-for goal and that there is a way for measuring progress. In order to accept delegation four things are needed: 1) knowledge or skill, 2) understanding of what is requested, 3) a belief that it is in one's best interest, and 4) a belief that it is in the best interest of the organization. A plan written by the one who is to accept the task usually demonstrates that all four requirements have been met.

Good managers know that to manage commitments they must build a system of control (including self-control) that will produce timely information as to when there has been an apparent or real change in the commitment. This system must include self-control. When any party to the commitment has been unable to keep it, there must be enough time to enter into a new series of commitments that will benefit everyone involved.

Controls need to be designed as an integral part of a plan. In other words, when a subordinate submits a plan for approval, he or she should, at the same time, submit a plan for measuring progress. Control begins with measurement. Measurement begins with incorporating a system into the plan for achievement, which includes a plan for control.

Since virtually every task can be broken down into a series of events, one of the obvious places to start measuring is at the expected point of completion for each event. If there are ten events that have to happen in order for a goal to be reached, then one way of gaining control is to measure the progress of accomplishment at each of the ten events. Did it happen? If it didn't happen, when is it likely to happen?

Most managers recognize the need to plan for "big" events. Inexperienced managers fail to plan for the "small" events. They fail to realize that almost everything they do is interwoven with everything else. In the long run, planning and small events will more than compensate for the time it takes to do the planning.

Good managers know that management has to do with people. Inexperienced managers tend to think of management in terms of tasks. Good managers realize that an organization is like a body. Its health is dependent upon the health of each individual member. The right person in the right role, given the right tools and the right encouragement and training, is a key to good management.

Good managers recognize that developing an organization requires the development of people. They carry this out through a planned program of selecting the best people they can find, helping them to thoroughly learn their job, coaching them along the way and giving regular personal evaluation.

A Christian organization is one that sees its ultimate purpose as giving glory to God through serving Christ. Good managers in Christian organizations know two more things.

First, they know there is a creative tension between depending on God and depending on oneself, between following well laid plans and following the leading of the Holy Spirit. This tension is never resolved, nor should it be. We are deal-ing with something much greater than ourselves. To quote the words of Bishop Stephen Neill, "The game of life is played between the poles."

Second, good managers in Christian organizations have a quiet confidence that, regardless of what happens, however great the success or dismal the failure, God is at work to do His will. He is the One who is for us.

CHAPTER 24

What Good Managers Do

M anagement theory has to do with organizing, staffing, directing, controlling, communicating, and a number of other functions required by modern organizations of almost any size.

If you have ever had the experience of keeping an hour-by-hour record of everything you did for a week, you have probably discovered that you would be hesitant to submit it as a case study on good management. What managers do every day can best be described as leading others, handling disturbances, acting as a figurehead, disseminating information, acting as a spokesman, negotiating with people, monitoring how things are going, and allocating resources. Many of us feel that practically everything we do is in response to some problem. We see ourselves as continually fighting fires.

The interesting thing is that most managers like it that way. They enjoy the challenge of a new problem every hour or so, the ebb and flow of interruptions, the excitement of changed plans, new ideas. Oh, they would be happy if they had more time. They picture themselves as stretched between conflicting values. They feel guilty about not spending more time with their family and working in their church. They wish they could relax more. But when they do discover some better method of time management, more often than not they spend the time doing more of the same.

Most managers picture themselves as never having enough information. Consequently, almost every decision they face depends upon their ability to internally process whatever data they have with their own experience. Often managers describe the rationale for their final decisions as a "hunch" or "feeling."

On the other hand, management is logical and rational. It seeks to anticipate the need it wants to fulfill, and factually describe that need along with the approaches necessary to meet it. There is a rather tacit assumption that if all the data were available, the solution would be obvious. It is essentially a problem-solving approach. It tends to avoid emotion and feeling, even though it recognizes that since business is carried out through people, "people problems" will have to be dealt with.

The popular management theory of MBO (Management by Objective) is a good reflection of this rational thinking. Overall purposes are formulated by the leadership of the organization. Major objectives (goals) are then assigned to functional units. All of these goals are future events, or desirable futures, that the leadership believes would be desirable in terms of outcome, be it money, product, service or even fellowship. The unit leader then sits down with key individuals and works out their personal objectives, which are supposedly supportive of the organization's objectives. Performance against these objectives (desirable future events) is then the measurement used to manage the operation. Deviation from the anticipated goal is viewed as a need to either modify the plan ("corrective action") or modify the goal.

But the future seldom conforms to our desires, particularly in detail. There seems to be a much greater chance that something will go wrong than right. Consider the baseball batter as an example. His usual "plan" is to get on base, normally by hitting the ball with the bat. But we call those who "fail" six times out of ten (those batting .400), heroes.

It is this unpredictability that challenges the manager. Most managers are attracted to management for this very reason.

Management theory is extremely useful in carrying out any enterprise. Those of us involved in the leadership of Christian organizations ignore it to the peril of the enterprise for which we are responsible. We need clearly stated purposes, well-conceived goals, detailed plans, methods of evaluation and feedback. These are part of the big picture, the framework within which we have to operate.

But we also need people—people who, though they may be concerned with the big picture, are very much involved in the battle at hand. These people know that they are part of an important and meaningful enterprise. But they also realize that to achieve the ultimate purpose, they are going to be faced with a myriad of everyday changes, decisions, frustrations and hardships which are the mortar that makes the grand edifice possible.

The manager of the smaller agency or church or the middle manager of the larger enterprise has three kinds of time: superior time, peer and subordinate time and discretionary time. As far as his or her organizational life is concerned the manager has little or no control over time spent with superiors. The amount of time spent with peers and subordinates may be easier to control depending upon the structural style of the organization. Whatever time is left in the course of a day or week can be used at the manager's discretion. It is only in our discretionary time, the time directly under our control, that we as leaders can devote ourselves to the kind of reflection necessary to give us the big picture we need to intuitively process the data we have when we are faced with those daily fires. It is during this time that we can set our own personal goals and design plans to reach them.

Management theory recognizes this dilemma when it pictures the senior executive as spending a good deal of time in long-range planning, policy making, and in giving general guidance to the "ship." First-level managers are recognized as having very little time to carry out these functions. "Middle managers" fall somewhere in between. Whether you seem to be fighting too many fires or too few depends on where you are in the organizational structure. People at the head of an organization should have more discretionary time than others further down.

If you are a planning type of person, look for someone who is more of a fire-fighting kind of person to help you. If you are spending all your time in the midst of the fray, see what can be done to set aside time for prayer and contemplation of the future.

Don't get hung up on the fact that every day does not go according to plan or that you are not the best time manager in the world. A predictable world would be pretty dull, anyway. On the other hand, dip into the literature that deals with the technique (as opposed to theory) of "time management." A great deal has been written about how to handle mail, interruptions, visitors, meetings, memos, conflicts, and a host of other experiences, more effectively.

CHAPTER 25

Doing or Being

There are two distinctives that should be the hallmark of any Christian organization, whether it is a local church or a worldwide enterprise. The first is quite apparent. It is the *purpose* of the organization. Indeed it is that very purpose that delineates the organization as Christian. The second may not be so apparent. It is the relationships that exist within the organization, how the people within the organization view one another and act toward one another.

The same two distinctives should be the hallmark of any Christian *leader*. The Christian leader is a man or a woman with a Christian *purpose*. A Christian leader is a man or a woman with Christian relationships.

Doing *and* Being

There is always a tension between what we believe we should *do* (our tasks) and what we believe God would have us to *be* (our relationship to others). This tension exists within the Christian organization, and it exists within the life of the Christian leader. We'll briefly discuss both of these situations.

The Organization

Organizations are the outward manifestation of a shared purpose. Any time two or more people agree to work together toward a common goal, an organization exists. All organizations are basically relationships. An organization chart is an attempt to describe these relationships, usually in terms of authority and/or responsibility. How these relationships are structured and how people within the organization view them will determine the character of that organization.

When we look to the New Testament for descriptions of how Christians should relate to one another, we are startled by the tremendous contrast between what our experience tells us an organization should be like and the description of that ultimate organization, the church. Instead of finding a pyramid structure in which those further down on the pyramid are subservient to those above, we are given the model of the human body (1 Corinthians 12). We discover that how this body functions is determined completely by how each member functions. We are told that there are no unimportant members. In fact, our worldly concepts are completely turned upside down as we are told that the "inferior" parts of the body are worthy of more honor. And it is because of this that we are to weep with those who weep and rejoice with those who rejoice (Romans 12:15).

Within this body it is assumed that there is a high level of communication, in that in some sense all members are in relationship to all other members, but especially in close relationship with some. The implication is that members within the organization are to be treated like adults, rather than children, that they are expected to assume responsibility and to carry it out.

Being, Not Doing

It is interesting to note that the New Testament has a great deal to say about how we are to relate to each other and very little to say about the ultimate purpose of this relationship in terms of accomplishment. A startling example is how little the New Testament says about getting on with the task of evangelism. Rather we discover that evangelism will be the natural outflowing of the relationship that exists. Jesus sums this up in his high priestly prayer when he notes that the way the world will come to believe that he is the Son of God will be because his disciples have the same relationship that he has with his Father (John 17:21).

But How?

That's all very well and good, we may reply, but how do you make it work? People are naturally sinful. If we attempt to have an organization in which everybody is running things, people are certain to take advantage of us. How far *should* our responsibility go toward caring for employees? To what extent can we treat people as adults and brothers (rather than children) and expect them to act that way too?

It has been fascinating over a period of years to watch secular management theorists come closer and closer to the New Testament model of the church as an organization. A detailed description of this development is beyond the scope of this book. (See the writings of Abraham Maslow, A.A.C. Brown, Paul Gellerman, Elton Mayo, Robert W. White, Douglas McGregor, Chris Argyris, Frederick Herzberg, Rensis Likert, and others.) However, there is a growing body of literature and experience that demonstrates that there is a direct relationship between the effectiveness—output, goal achievement, success—of organizations and the degree to which individuals within organization are dealt with as valued, mature adults. Note that this does not mean that the organization exists for the benevolent good of the individuals within it. It does mean that in whatever degree possible within the confines of education, experience, and ability, members of the organization should perceive themselves as participating in organization in a way that determines the effectiveness that organization.

How to Begin

Too often the leaders of Christian organizations come to their positions because of qualifications other than those that equip them to be thoughtful managers. And organizations have a history of growing in the same haphazard fashion. Unfortunately, too often when the organization views itself as "successful," it attributes this to the rather nebulous "blessing of God" and consequently fails to analyze what elements God used! The highly educated cohesive core of men and women who have been responsible for the early effectiveness of an organization can quickly become diluted as the organization grows in scope and size. What can we do to rebuild into Christian organizations that sense of "life in the body" that existed in its early days?

Sharing and Accountability

Begin with sharing the goal-setting experience. This is not an easy task. You may discover that people within the organization will have a tremendous "show me" attitude. Their past experience tells them that very seldom are their ideas acted upon. You may also have difficulty with *yourself.* Your sense of leadership may be threatened. You may feel that you are losing control.

Take your time. It takes years to change the character of an organization. As you work with establishing a set of integrated goals at all levels within the organization, expect that it will be one to two years before people really see how they fit in.

Expect and demand accountability, not in the sense of threat for failure to perform, but in the sense that if we really believe in what we are doing and believe we have contributed toward it, we *will* assume that we are accountable for results and will expect that others will hold us accountable. Start "acting as if." Act as if you expected contributions from other members of the organization. Act as if you valued their opinion. Act as if they were adults, not children who need to be told everything that they are to do. Act as if their well being is as important to you as the well being of the organization. Act as if you expect to hold them to account for the goals they have set and to hold you to account for the goals that you have set. Act as if they are important enough so that you need to share with them where the organization is in its progress towards its goals.

Task vs. People

There will be no easy answers. On the one hand, the people cannot be sacrificed for "the good of the organization." On the other hand, if the goals and purposes of the organization are sacrificed for the good of the individuals, then the organization will cease to function.

One of the reasons that the local church is the most complex of all human organizations is that it has set for itself two purposes that tend to oppose one another: the purpose of being a servant to the world in work and witness, and the purpose of building up the individual members of the body in terms of their well-being. This is why we believe that to the degree that we understand how to be effective leaders of a local church, we will learn to be effective as leaders in *any* organization.

The Christian Leader

The Christian *leader*, too, will find the same tension between doing and being in his or her own life. People extend to us the right to lead on the basis of their perception of not only what we have done, but how we have done it, not only what we do, but what we are. The Christian leader must build, develop, and carefully guard his relationships at all levels of life.

The New Testament gives as one of the qualifications of a leader that he must be able to manage his household well. As is obvious from the rest of the New Testament, this does not mean how well he can dictate and control his family, but rather how well he has developed the relationships within his family that are

Christ-honoring and people-honoring. The same principle can obviously be applied to women (Proverbs 31:10).

We believe that the first three levels of Christian priority are first, commitment to the person of Christ; second, commitment to the body of Christ; and third, commitment to the work of Christ. There is no doubt that the New Testament calls us to be willing to sacrifice houses, families, and lands to follow Christ. But the work of Christ will flow forth from the relationships that exist. Too often we have heard Christian leaders say, "What I do as a leader is so important that I must sacrifice my family." If by this he or she means that the work of Christ is more important than the body of Christ, we must protest that this is not the view of the New Testament. The Bible considers our relationships as being more important than our accomplishments. God will get his work done! He does not demand of us that we accomplish great things. He demands of us that we strive for excellence in our relationships.

How This Might Work

Are you a goal-oriented person or a person-oriented (relationship) person? One way to find out is to take a look at your calendar. How much time have you been spending with your spouse, your children, your brothers and sisters in Christ? If you looked at your appointment book right now, would you find dates with your husband or wife, dates with your teenage daughter or son, times on the calendar to be with other people to help them meet their goals? Is your calendar so full that there is no "unscheduled" time when other people can get with you? Is every evening of the week scheduled with "work"? Change your priorities! Start scheduling times for relationships, both with your family, or other members of the body, and with people within your organization. God wants you to have these relationships. (It's OK—really.)

Build Relationships

You might want to consider three different kinds of relationships that are tremendously useful to any Christian leader.

First is the need for a Barnabas, a "son of encouragement," someone to whom you can go, openly share where you're at and seek wise counsel and prayer support. Too often pastors particularly fail to develop such a relationship with a person within their own congregation or fellowship.

Second, build a relationship with a peer group—a small group of men and women to hold you accountable and whom you can hold accountable as fellow members Christ. Find times when you can get together on a regular basis to share your life.

Third, find a Timothy, someone into whom you can build your years of experience, someone that you can help mature in Christ and in his role of leadership.

In all of this, remember the different relationship role that you play. Every leader at some time is a follower. Learning to be a good follower is a major step to being a good leader.

CHAPTER 26

Managing Conflict

How do we manage conflict in a Christian organization? Or should Christian organizations, by definition, be free of conflict? Does the biblical concept of fitting in together disallow the presence of conflict?

What Is Conflict?

Call it "a difference of opinion," or whatever you like, conflict within organizations occurs whenever two or more people disagree on the solution to a problem or the value of a goal. There are two different opinions, two different ideas as to what should be done.

At first, "conflict" may seem like too strong a term. But behind every "battle of ideas" there are usually individuals. And since who we are and what we believe and stand for are intimately entwined, conflict does occur.

How such differences are resolved within an organization says a great deal about the style of leadership being exercised.

Is conflict permitted in your organization? How is it viewed? How is it resolved? How do you as a leader handle differences of opinion with your peers or subordinates? How do you view criticism (which is actually someone holding a different opinion than yours)?

For example, if you, as a leader, are experiencing very little conflict, very little difference of opinion, you have cause to suspect that you have an authoritarian style of leadership. If you seldom hear any criticism, it may well be that people are afraid to share it.

At the other end of the spectrum is the laissez-faire style of leadership that handles conflict by insisting that others settle their differences among themselves and refuses to intervene.

How Do We Respond to Conflict?

How we respond to conflict reflects both our view of ourselves and our view of conflict. It will also depend upon our view of power and its use.

Every leader is empowered because of his or her position. Influence is power. Resources are power. The ability to give directions is power. Prestige and reputation are power. In this sense, power is not a bad word, it is just a way of suggesting that some people are in a position because of a situation or because they have more influence on the world than others.

If we view conflict as a contest in which one person wins and another loses, it may well be we have a need to win so that we can accumulate power. If we view conflict as an arena in which creativity can flourish and new ideas emerge, there then will be less of a drive toward personal power.

When a leader uses the position of leadership to win an argument or to overrule a subordinate, individuals within the organization quickly sense that conflict is being resolved by the use of power. They, in turn, will either attempt to accumulate power for themselves or avoid conflict.

If, on the other hand, they see that differences of opinion are welcomed and that ultimate decisions are made on the basis of available data and an analysis of the overall situation, they are less likely to accumulate power to themselves by becoming winners of arguments.

Conflict and Creativity

There is a close relationship between conflict and creativity. To avoid conflict is to inhibit creativity. When we adhere strictly to the status quo, we usually avoid conflict, but we also eliminate the need for finding new or more appropriate solutions. It is in the press of the struggle for change that the creative juices start to flow.

Almost everyone begins life with a high degree of creativity. Through the process of enculturation we learn to conform, to suppress our creative urges. A few of us fight this push toward conformity and are usually branded different, artistic or even bohemian. The rest of us must wait for a "safe" environment before we will risk being creative. Conflict then becomes a catalyst to creativity. "Iron sharpens iron."

If we were working with unthinking machines or talking about the forces of nature, there would be no need to discuss "conflict." Conflict has to do with people. When an individual or a group sets out to change things, conflict is inevitable. It need not be destructive.

Win-Win versus Win-Lose

Remember the old joke about "Heads I win—tails you lose"? In a trite way it reflects a view of interpersonal relationships. Life is seen as a contest in which some win and others lose. The "winners" get to the "top." The "losers" never make it.

At the opposite pole from such a win-lose picture of life is "win-win." How good it feels to describe a situation in which "everybody wins." For most of us, such experiences happen all too seldom.

This need not be so. There is a style of leadership that actively promotes situations in which both parties win. There are ways of managing conflict that view it as not only useful but necessary, and at the same time insist that it need not be destructive.

Win-Win Management Style

What kind of management style permits creative conflict that produces feelings of "winning" in both parties?

Begin with clear, high performance goals (there is that word again!). If there is no standard against which to measure the usefulness of a decision, the solutions will tend to be subjective and personal. If no one has stated where it is that we are going, there will be little agreement on how we will get there.

Share information up and down the organizational structure. Bad data produces bad decisions which usually produce bad feelings.

Surveys of felt need among members of organizations indicate the need to know what is going on and to feel like one is "in the know." This is usually near the top of the list. What people don't know can hurt them, for when people don't know something they believe is important to them, they will usually find "answers" either from others or from their own analysis of the situation. This usually results in the question, "Why aren't *they* telling me?"

Model appropriate problem-solving approaches. If the leadership makes unilateral decisions or uses its position to win arguments, the rest of the organization will attempt to do the same.

We are not discussing here the question of who must *ultimately* decide. In Harry Truman's words, "The buck stops here." The leader must eventually make what is often a lonely decision. Rather, we're talking about problem-solving, the attempt to find our way forward past a difficult situation in which we need all the information we can get and need to hear as many appropriate opinions as are available.

Model a listening ear. A great deal of emotion is spent in attempting to be heard. If I don't believe you understand my position, how can I accept yours? Too often the aggressive, bright leader will see exactly where someone is going in the discussion and, with a desire to save time (the leader's and the speaker's), will interrupt with a, "I understand, but . . ." Seldom will the speaker feel that he or she has been heard.

Focus on facts, not emotions. This is a key idea. We are all very much aware of how easy it is to carry the day with an appeal to the emotions. Christian organizations and Christian leaders unknowingly become manipulative by appealing to loyalty, "the cause," or biblical ideals that may have little bearing on the problem at hand. The facts, to the extent they are known, paint one picture. But it is not the picture we would really like to see. "Like" is an emotional word, and too often we convert these emotions into rhetoric that has little to do with facts.

Give training in group problem-solving. Many people resort to a bulldozer style of settling differences because that's the only they know.

Most of us assume that the way we feel is the way everyone feels. The way we have learned to handle our problems is probably the way everyone else has learned to handle their problems. It is usually a *learned* experience if there are different styles, different responses for different situations.

Managing Conflict

The business of making decisions in an organization is going on all the time. Many decisions are made by individuals without consulting anyone. Often there is no recognition that a decision *has* been made. But in the midst of all this there will be decisions, debates, problem-solving sessions in which more than one opinion vies for acceptance. The goal of management is to encourage debate but discourage win-lose situations. How is that done?

Insist on facts, or at worst, clearly differentiate between facts and opinion: "Tom, I can see that you really feel very strongly about this. But, would you first list for me all of the facts on which we all agree? Then we can go on to the opinions."

View problems as a deviation from a goal. What is the goal to which this problem relates? The task of the group then becomes to discover solutions that enable the goal rather than enhance an individual: "Bill, I'm not sure exactly what this problem is that you're trying to describe. Help me out here. What is the goal you're trying to reach and what is keeping you from reaching that goal?"

Break down the problem-solving process. Take it one step at a time. Make sure that you and others understand the difference between these steps:

Begin with data gathering. What are the facts? What information do we have? What are additional data that we need to gather?

Once you have as many facts as you can accumulate (or as you have time to gather) move on to the various alternative solutions. Seek as many possible solutions as you have time for.

There will be tradeoffs between these solutions. Some will have pluses as well as minuses. Try to see the positives and the negatives of each solution.

Move on to integrating these various solutions into a working compromise (compromise is not a bad word).

Too often we force agreement on one solution, or a part of a solution, before we have adequately explained and examined alternatives. At other times, we hold one solution over and against another, rather than seek the best features of both.

Seek to strengthen the power of the group. The opposite side of that coin is to avoid enhancing the power of one contestant. Keep asking the question, "How can this problem (conflict) be used to everyone's benefit?" Most of us are familiar with the idea that every problem should be seen as a challenge. Take that a step further: every problem should be seen as an opportunity.

Agree to agree. The primary tool of the labor arbitrator is to obtain agreement from both parties so that mutual agreement is possible and will eventually occur.

Let's not confuse our *theological* positions here. We are not suggesting that we ask people to agree to depart from the fundamentals of what they believe. What we are speaking to here is the everyday business of working out solutions in the organization.

Promote listening. We haven't been heard until the other person can accurately state our view. This takes time, patience, and a sense that the individual is just as important as the issue at hand.

Conflict and the Christian

Conflict, in whatever shape or form it may appear, should be faced and used creatively, and accepted as part of the personal and organizational maturing process. We will always have it, it will always be present, and we must recognize its dangers as well as opportunities.

The two Chinese characters making up the word for "crisis" are "danger" and "opportunity." This is what conflict presents to us—danger in making errors, in how we handle it, and opportunity for moving solidly ahead.

Christians in Christian organizations, and particularly the local church, have a unique advantage in working through conflict. There is a confidence that the God who knows the end from the beginning will bring about equitable solutions as we submit our hearts and wills to him and the leadership of his Holy Spirit.

This is a magnificent "plus" for the Christian. Remember, you and I—plus God—always represent the majority.

Management styles differ from individual to individual and from organization to organization, but for Christian leadership the promised help and guidance of the Holy Spirit can always be asked for, accepted, and trusted. Be sure, early on in conflict resolution, to seek the wisdom, which God promises us in James 1.

Interpersonal Relations

Within an organization the interpersonal relations aspect of conflict is of prime importance. I have discussed this in my book, *The Making of a Christian Leader*:

> The proper handling of troublesome situations demands both tact and the ability to handle people. This requires taking the action needed to deal with basic reasons behind stress and conflict. Problems with people will not become large if you keep them little ones. To do that you must act quickly and directly when the slightest tension begins to surface between individuals.

> Tact may be defined as intuitive perception. It is insight and decorum that is fit and proper in a given situation that helps to avoid giving offense. For example, a tactful person is able to reconcile two opposing views without compromising his own principles. Tact means that a person has a sensitivity to other people; whereas others might wound or hurt, he is able to use the same words or approach with a slightly different emphasis or phrasing that does not offend.[24]

Every human being experiences tension, frustration, and conflicts with other people. If he does not, he is either psychotic or withdrawing from the mainstream of life. A mark of maturity is the ability to handle conflict. This includes the ability to deal with realities as to what can and cannot be changed. A mature executive said to me, "I have learned never to fret over something that I cannot change." Such an approach to life is evidence of stability. The ability to make those necessary compromises with what cannot be changed largely determines whether one will be successful as a social being.[25]

. . . The way a person deals with conflict does denote whether he is a strong, healthy, emotional person, or one who develops neurotic symptoms.[26]

It's Hard Work

But it's worth it. If you and your organization have been operating on the basis of a top-down, do-it-my-way style, it will take some time before people will believe that you really want honesty and openness. If this has been your style, be ready for some painful pricks to your ego.

But if current management research is not enough to persuade you to try some new approaches to managing conflict, read again the twelfth chapter of 1 Corinthians. How surprising that the world finds profitable what the Holy Spirit has been saying to us for almost 2,000 years!

CHAPTER 27

Managing Change

Mrs. Bloomfield had been a member of St. John's Church for twenty-five years. As she walked toward the pastor, who stood waiting at the sanctuary door after the service, it was obvious that she had something on her mind. "Reverend, if Jesus were alive today He would be shocked at the changes in this church!"

There is probably no society in the world that is as accustomed to change as America. We expect change. We assume that tomorrow will somehow be better than yesterday, that new technology will bring "better" things. We expect our children to be smarter than we are. And yet, at the same time, there is the feeling that things have gotten out of hand. Several years ago Alvin Toffler called it "future shock." Most of us by now are sure that we have had enough of it. Mrs. Bloomfield's nostalgia for the St. John's of her girlhood is typical of the middle-class American longing for "the good old days." More and more Christians, particularly when they think about their local churches, are resisting change.

And with good reason. All change is perceived as loss. Even when the change is an apparently happy occasion, like marriage, or moving to a new job, there remains the lingering feeling that something has been left behind, something we can never recapture.

Christian leaders are change agents. We are in the business of leading people to higher ground, to new adventures, to new accomplishments for God. We have been instructed that change needs to be "managed." But too often as we are managing change, we fail to realize that we are responsible for a lot of anguish.

We need the change. We need to move to higher ground. We need to mature in Christ. We need to right the wrongs that are out in the world, to change them for the better. But in the midst of our quest, however noble it may be, we not only need a deep appreciation of how to accomplish our goals, but also how to bring about change in a manner that will produce a minimum of distress.

Change only takes place in people when they are discontent. If we are satisfied with the status quo, why should we change? Skillful union organizers and other mobilizers of public opinion have influenced groups through the discontent of the majority. If one can find enough people who dislike the same thing, then one has a group with a common goal, namely to get rid of that which they dislike. The role of the change agent is then to provide a solution to the common felt need.

But there are also those who are in the business of creating what might be called positive discontent. When the pastor calls us to maturity in Christ on Sunday morning, he or she is creating in us a holy discontent, a discontent with the way we are. We desire to become more than we are. We want to change.

Resistance to change takes place in the same way. If people are presented with new situations that threaten them, the discontentment will be aimed at removing the cause of potential change. The amount of resistance to change will be proportional to the threat to perceive vested interest. It is important to understand that resistance may not be against the change agent or even to the program being proposed. Both may be intellectually perceived as excellent. But however good the program, if it is going to result in what is perceived as changing the way things have always been, it is natural that it will be resisted. Committees or departments can present programs that are obviously beautifully conceived and will in some way produce excellent results for large numbers of people. But time and time again such groups are startled when they present their well thought through plans and are met with cold silence or warm rejection.

The task of the Christian leader is to introduce change in a manner that will challenge and encourage people on the one hand and yet not frighten or discourage them on the other.

We noted earlier that Westerners in general, and Americans in particular, tend to focus on individuals rather than on groups. In few societies are the perceived needs of the individual given so much attention. This emphasis on the individual can blind us to how change really takes place. For a number of years sociologists have been describing the change process within groups of individuals as "the diffusion of innovation." They have recognized that when an innovator poses a new idea or does something differently, there will be some who will see the personal advantages to them very early. These "early adopters" are usually in the minority. A second group, usually a majority, will observe how the first is benefiting from the new idea and eventually become "late adopters." Then there is another minority that never adopts the change. The important idea here is that both early and late adopters accept change because they observe its benefits in others. The notion of the diffusion of innovation gives us some insight into how to plan for change, particularly in volunteer organizations, such as local churches.

There are several things a good manager can do to ensure that new changes are accepted. *First, avoid the obvious to make the establishment of the new program, policy, or procedure the end goal.* Too often people feel that once they have gained acceptance—the policy is approved, the procedure is adopted—the task is then completed. Rather, the end goal should allow enough time to demonstrate that the new change is producing good results. We should include some objective indicators to show us if the change is being successful or effective. What are the qualities we might expect to find? For example, if we are going to institute a new worship service in a local church, what would be the indicators that in six months, the worship service is really bringing people closer to God? Or, if we are introducing a new policy on expense accounts, what will be the indicators one year later that this policy is producing the results we want? To give a third example, if we are instituting a training program to train boards, committees, or departments, how will we know that the program was effective one year after the program has begun?

Why such a long time? While the early adopters may be very enthusiastic about the program shortly after its beginning, the majority of the staff or congregation will withhold judgment, or even have negative feelings toward the program, for a longer period of time. In other words, it is helpful to consider how long it will take for everyone to adjust to the situation.

Second, wherever possible, introduce the change to a group smaller than the entire organization. Find a group that is most likely to accept the idea. Indicate to them, as well as to the rest of the organization, that they are really a "pilot study" group participating in a type of experiment. This not only raises the enthusiasm of those involved, but it also relieves the threat to the rest of the group. After all, if it doesn't work with them, then obviously it won't be imposed upon the rest of the group. People are not threatened by change that is taking place in others. And if they are "late adopters," watching what happens with others will often bring them to a point where they are not only ready to accept the new idea, but are actually clamoring for it.

Third, consider the real losses that are going to result as a consequence of the change. Some people are going to lose authority or responsibility. Familiar patterns are likely to be disrupted, as in the case of change in the worship service. In some cases, benefits that accrue to some people are going to be withdrawn from others. Wherever possible, build into the change plan a way of replacing these losses with some benefit. All change is experienced as loss. But the reason people are willing to accept change is they perceive that the gains, and the feelings associated with it, are greater than the perceived loss.

Fourth, when deciding how to introduce the change, leave as much flexibility as possible for how it is to take place. Quite often there are many different ways of achieving the end goal. By inviting discussion on the ways and means of bringing about change, we give people a sense of participation in their own destiny. One way of doing this is to present several (always more than two) ways of achieving the goal, all of which are acceptable. Now, instead of asking people to accept or reject the goal, we are asking them to choose ways of reaching the goal.

Fifth, build in an evaluation system that will identify the early adopters as well as the late adopters. The reason people are late adopters is that they like stability. If you disrupt that stability, they are going to be hurt in some way. If you can identify those hurts, which may not be anticipated ahead of time, you can often modify your plans to help offset the anguish that people will feel. For example, suppose a new policy or procedure has been introduced that changes the relationships between individuals who previously came in contact with one another on a daily basis. You can suggest that these people continue to get together, perhaps once a week, to discuss how the new policy or procedure is affecting them. This gives them the opportunity to express their feelings and to emotionally disengage.

Finally, when introducing change, it is important to look for a win-win situation. Too often, in trying to overcome the objections of other people, we view them as adversaries who have to be won over or even (if only subconsciously) "beaten." We need to remember that the people we are dealing with are brothers and sisters in Christ, and are members of the same body of Christ of which we are also an integral part. We must try to understand the impact that our actions will have on them and try to prepare them and encourage them. Then the very actions we take will communicate to them that we desire the very best for them.

CHAPTER 28

On Taking Risks

In responding to the generosity of the Philippian church and their concern for his welfare, Paul commends to them their brother Epaphroditus: "Welcome him in the Lord with great joy, and honor men like him, because he almost died for the work of Christ, risking his life to make up for the help you could not give me" (Philippians 2:29–30). Most of us are not called upon to put our lives at risk in the everydayness of our Christian service. On the other hand, most of us would probably be uncomfortable with the thought that we were not willing "to risk all for Christ."

But what about risk when it comes to leading the organization? It is one thing to personally risk our life or our fortune or our reputation. But what about risking the life, the fortune or the reputation of the organization we lead?

I have long since given up the idea that there are standard answers for life's situations. The world refuses to fit into our categories. In a real sense the Bible is not an answer book, but a question book. Asking the right question within the context of the situation is usually the most important thing we can do.

With that in mind, we immediately recognize that there are some people who appear to take too many risks and others who appear to take too few. How do we find the middle ground? What are the questions?

There is a truism which says that organizations are started by a man (or woman), and during their beginnings they reflect that person and his or her life and world view. If they progress, they become a movement. Others are caught up in the directions they are moving. But movements tend to become machines. They tend toward order, discipline, rules and regulations, all of which can make them quite machine-like. When that happens, the organization can become nothing more than a monument to those who began it. In the beginning there was someone who was willing to risk everything to make something happen. In the end there was no one who was willing to risk anything.

It is a fact of life that one of the characteristics of the "natural leader" or entrepreneur is a willingness to take risk. It is also true that managers, particularly middle managers, tend to avoid risk.

Where do we find a balance?

Most organizations are about the business of getting things done. After all, there is a "bottom line" out there! We have work to do!

True. But the Christian counterbalance to the task of doing God's work is the recognition that it is God who is doing the work. He is the One who has prepared all the good works we are going to do (Ephesians 2:10). And He will get it done (in spite of us!). Our local church may disappear from its corner next week. Our high-powered, dynamic Christian enterprise may fail tomorrow. God's work will get done.

Another need for finding balance.

Some say that a lot of life is failure. That sounds like a pretty crass statement, doesn't it? But let's examine it a little. Ted Williams, one of the greatest hitters of all time in American baseball, set a record by hitting the ball four times out of ten when he was at bat. But the other side of that coin is that he missed, he failed, six times out of ten.

How did he become such a good batter? By learning to overcome the mistakes he made when he was not such a good hitter.

Our life situations are similar. Living life is like driving a car. We keep looking out through the windshield of life at the world rushing at us, correcting here, and compensating there. Roads get blocked. We take detours. Tires go flat. Cars need servicing. But we go on. And in the driving there is always the risk that someone else won't stop at the intersection, or for just a moment our attention may be diverted. Both driving and living involve taking risks.

It is not a question of whether we will take risks. Rather, it is a question of which risks to take. To do nothing may be the riskiest thing we can do. The one thing we can be certain of is change, and it hurts to change. It's risky to change.

How then does the organization decide which risks to take? The answer is simple to state and difficult to carry out: Have an extensive program of strategic (or long-range) planning.

Planning is not intended to avoid risk. One way to define planning is "risk taking-decision making." To make plans is to make decisions now that will have an impact on us tomorrow. When we decide, we put the organization at risk.

Perhaps you have never thought about it that way. Perhaps you never realized that when you made plans you were "risking" the organization. But that's a healthy way to think about it. It calls us to consider the consequences of our decisions. It asks the question, "Which is the lesser risk for the desired gain?"

Statistical theory has a concept known as "confidence limits." Confidence limits recognize that in dealing with probabilities we can seldom be 100 percent certain. Therefore, it has developed a way of telling the person interested how likely it is that the data presented represents reality. In its simplest form we hear statements like, "There is a 60 percent probability of rain tomorrow." We hear results of the Gallup poll that may talk about, "The margin of error for these statements is five percent." To put that another way, we can say that we are 95 percent confident that the data is what it says it is.

Now let's apply that to long-range planning and risk taking. What confidence limits do we want to place on a given plan or suggestion for the future? Let's use a fundraising example: What confidence do we have that the suggested program will have the desired result?

We will immediately discover that the answers tend to be quite subjective. Someone may say, "How would I know whether it's 50 percent or 75 percent?" You may not. But you evidently know that it is not 10 percent, nor is it 95 percent. When one begins to compare different possibilities, these relatively crude numbers give us helpful insight.

So our first question was, "What is the probability that this program will produce the desired result?" That can break down into two subquestions: 1) What is the probability that we can do what we say we will? and 2) What is the probability that if the program works, it will produce the intended result?

Again, to use the fund raising example—if our plan to increase the number of contributors to our organization by 20 percent is successful, will that in turn produce the needed income?

The next question of cost-benefit analysis is one that is familiar to most of us: Is the cost of doing the program worth the intended result? Change always has costs. Are we ready for them?

When we have answered these questions, we are ready to look at the risks involved in various programs in a positive way.

But first there is a negative question: For each of the possible approaches, what is the cost of failure, of not achieving the announced result? This question not only helps us choose the program with the least risk for the desired benefit, but it also gives us some clues as to what to do if indeed the program does fail. We need to plan for both success and failure.

A basic element of any planning should therefore be a comparison of the alternatives with some confidence limits on the probability of success for each major program and an analysis of the consequences of only partial success or failure.

The future is never certain. It can be only hoped for at best. The further into the future we move the consequences of our actions and the longer range our planning, the less likelihood there is that we will be accurate. It takes courage to look at the future. It takes even more courage to risk making decisions in the face of an uncertain future where the dangers of failure are known. (It takes little courage to face a future of unknown consequences.)

That is why it takes courage to be a good leader. The effective leader accepts the fact that the future is unknown, attempts to reduce uncertainty by choosing between a number of alternatives, makes a decision and then takes the risk to move out.

In a world where Christ is rarely acknowledged, taking risks can be a gut-rending experience. It's not pleasant to contemplate the results of a bad major decision. One's entire career or future may be riding on the outcome.

This is also true for the Christian. To not be concerned about the consequences of failure would be both unrealistic and a bit foolish. But there is a Christian edge that we need to keep in the forefront of our thinking. We may fail. Our plans may fail. Our organization may fail. But God's work will get done. We need to keep reminding ourselves that the final outcome of God's purposes is never in doubt. The world may judge us as failures, or as Paul put it, "the scum of the earth." But God has a different yardstick. He knows the final outcome. He's primarily interested in the love, the fairness, and the justice with which the game is played.

Martin Luther has been quoted as saying, "Sin boldly!" We will make mistakes, but moving ahead in the Lord's name and for His kingdom is worth the risk. God's work will get done.

CHAPTER 29

Understanding the Dangers

Organizations succeed or fail for many different reasons. When they are young, and the future is bright and exciting, it is easy to miss some of the pitfalls that lie ahead in the road. But the mature organization is not without its hazards. In many ways the dangers that it faces are more subtle. They are often the result of success rather than failure. In what follows we have attempted to list ten dangers for the Christian organization. You can use the checklist at the end to help you discover whether you may be facing any of them.

It has been well said that an organization begins with a *man*, becomes a *movement* that develops into a *machine* and eventually becomes a *monument*. How do those things happen?

Settle for the Status Quo

How easy it is for the Christian agency to be willing to settle for the status quo, to struggle to "keep things as they are." But it is impossible for any organization to stand still. They will either progress or retrogress. God's work demands that we move forward. This is true in our personal life. It is just as true in our organizational life. Once we settle for maintaining things as they are now, at that moment we begin to slide toward ineffectiveness, a slide that becomes steeper the farther we go.

One of the clues that we are settling for the status quo is lack of internal tension within the organization. This naturally leads us to the next danger.

Eliminate Creative Tensions

The organization that has "made it" tends to resist creative tensions. We like to settle for peace and calm. Creative people have new ideas. They want to change things, to make things better. But new ideas bring with them a conflict of interest, and conflict of interest brings internal tension. When a new idea is offered, too often what we hear is, "You have done things wrong," rather than "Here's a better way."

The result of eliminating creative tension is that we often fail to face up to the situation around us. An example of this might be how we handle the world economic scene with its increasing inflation. If we do not go through the struggle of creatively addressing ourselves to the tensions this is going to create in our ministries at home and abroad, many organizations will find themselves in deep difficulty down the road.

Don't Plan in Depth

Almost every organization does some planning, but if we fail to plan our ministries in depth, as well as breadth, danger lies ahead. In other words, it is too easy for us to look for quantity and size as a primary result of our planning, rather than quality and meaningfulness in the program and ministry God has placed before us. These need to be placed in priority. Quality is far more important than quantity. Size must always be secondary to the effectiveness of the ministry we perform under God.

Discriminating between breadth and depth is not easy. That is why there is a real danger here. We may have a great desire to expand our ministry throughout and beyond our community or to the rest of the world, but if the quality of ministry that we are performing at the place we have begun is not being continually strengthened, then we may discover that we have overextended ourselves.

Stop Listening

A subtle danger for experienced Christian leaders is a failure to really hear and listen to younger colleagues, to give them a role in participatory leadership. Younger staff members have a great deal to contribute. Often we are so certain that we have "been there" before that we do not hear them. This is even truer of our usual attitude toward younger women staff members. Those who are older and who provide leadership need to have an open heart to what younger colleagues may say as God speaks to them. After all, it is self-evident that tomorrow's leadership rests with them. If we want to insure the continuation of a solid ministry, then we need to invest ourselves in developing leadership. Part of the investment is to have the time and the skill to listen.

Depend on Past Successes

How easy it is to place our confidence in what the organization has done in the past, or even in what it is doing now, it is easy to bask in the accolades of others who tell us what a great job we have done. But our dependency is not on what we have accomplished in the past or what we are doing now; rather it should be on the work and ministry of the Holy Spirit. How wonderful it is to cast ourselves upon him and believe that he will lead us on a miracle basis.

How do you do that? We are the first ones to admit that it is a paradox. On the one hand, we are responsible for God's work. On the other hand, God is doing it all. But when we place our confidence in what we have done in the past and fail to balance this with complete confidence in what God will do in the future, danger lies ahead.

Depend on Our Personal Experience

This is a corollary to depending upon the organization's experience. Too many of us are ready to depend upon our own brain power, expertise, and experience, rather than to depend upon God. Obviously, God has gifted those in the church, and these gifts need to be utilized and sharpened. But it is God who "works in you to will and to act according to his good purpose" (Philippians 2:13). We must constantly be reminded that it is "'not by might nor by power, but by my Spirit,' says the LORD Almighty . . ." (Zechariah 4:6).

Another way of saying this is there is a danger of our attempting to take back what we have given to the Lord, to take back the management of our lives into our own hands.

Neglect the Highest Good

Here is a danger of which we are all aware but too seldom face. It is the danger of becoming so busy in what are genuinely good and fine works for the Lord that we neglect the highest good, which is our worship of God through all of our service. We need to saturate our hearts with God's Word. How easy it is to become so busy about his business that we forget God's desire is for us to know him.

We need to remember that it should be "my utmost for his highest."

Forget Unity

Christian organizations have both the promise and the demand of a special kind of unity. We are related to one another as the different parts of a body. This relationship is not an option. It is a command. The maintenance of this type of Christian unity takes skill and perseverance. Too easily we forget that the primary way the world is going to know that we are Jesus' disciples is by the love we have for one another. And the world will believe Jesus is the Christ when they see that we have the same type of oneness with the Father that he had (John 17).

Unity is not the absence of healthy conflict caused by creativity and differences of opinion. Unity finds its first dimension in the allegiance we have to our Savior. It finds its expression in our recognition that each of us has gifts that help us to function as parts of this body. Part of our task is to affirm one another's gifts and to respect one another's roles. This is a primary task of Christian leadership.

To Lose the Joy of Service

How quickly those who are in the work, who are on the front line of service, can lose the real joy of that service. Paradoxically, the further we proceed in positions of leadership and authority, the greater servants we should become. The highest role of leadership is that of servant. It is said of our Lord that he came not to be ministered unto but to minister.

Christian leaders, like all leaders, need to be undergirded with authority and perquisites of office. However, if these are seen as being the just due of the *individual*, rather than the accoutrements of the office, we can come dangerously close to believing that we are the ones who should be served.

The servant role ought to mark us. This kind of ministering service brings the deepest joy, gratification, and satisfaction.

Forget the Bottom Line

Accountants like to call our attention to the "bottom line," the final statement of what is left over after outgo has been balanced off against income. The bottom line in Christian service is the complete honoring of Christ and offering to the world the knowledge of the Savior. Every organization needs to know what is its "bottom line." Everything must head toward this objective.

A "Danger Ahead" Checklist

Here are ten questions that relate to the ten dangers we have given you. Note that none of them are bad in themselves. In fact, they may be very good. However, if you check three or more of these as being characteristic of your organization, perhaps it is time to evaluate. Perhaps you have already succumbed to some of the dangers we have outlined above.

- Our organization chart hasn't changed in the past twelve months.

- I haven't been faced by a new creative idea in the past two weeks.

- We have no way of measuring the quality of our programs against a set of standards.

- Most of our executives are fifty or over.

- There is a great sense of satisfaction in the organization and all that God has accomplished through the organization in the past.

- Most of the leaders of the organization have a real sense of being on top of their jobs.

- Few of the leaders in our organization are what one would call real Bible students.

- The average person in our organization would question whether we have true biblical unity.

- Most of our leaders think that the primary function of leadership is to lead.

- We seldom ask the question as to whether the ministry we are performing is there for the *primary* purpose of honoring God.

CHAPTER 30

You and Your Board

Almost every organization has, or should have, a board of directors. For no matter how competent the leaders of a Christian organization or a local church may be, there is always the need for a "disinterested party" who can stand back from day-to-day operations and exercise wisdom and judgment on behalf of the organization and its leadership. God does his work through men and women!

When Do You Need a Board?

There is a tendency to believe that only growing or larger organizations need a board. Just the opposite is the case. The small, struggling organization desperately needs the kind of assistance a good board of directors can bring to it.

Types of Boards

There are a number of different kinds of boards, and all have their role. A *board of reference* may be made up of men and women whose names will authenticate the work of an organization. Normally they have no other function than to be aware of the organization's overall purposes and goals.

A *board of advisors* is usually made up of people competent in the same field as the organization. With no legal responsibilities for the organization, they serve because of their interest in the general purposes of it. They give mostly technical assistance.

The board we wish to discuss here is a *board of directors*, a group of men and women who have legal responsibility for the organization.

The Purpose of the Board of Directors

The board of directors serves three general functions: first, it serves as a board of review. Second, it serves to install or remove top management. Third, it serves a function in public and community relations. For the Christian organization there is a fourth dimension, that of spiritual leadership.

In its *review function* the board should help set policy to insure that the organization is carrying out its objectives, to make certain that the organization has developed strategies, that it is doing long-range planning, that it is handling its investments well, and that it is maintaining a good *esprit de corps*. In many ways the board is just someone that the management can talk to. Normally a board of directors will carry out its review functions by being actively involved in a number of committees, such as finance, audit, and personnel. The latter generally reviews the salaries of top leadership executives.

The board of directors has an important role in the *installation and removal of organizational executive leadership*. This is probably the most difficult function the board has to perform, yet the most important. For a failure of leadership will almost always result in the failure of the organization.

The third major function of the board is that of *public and community relations*. The board can carry out many tasks that the executive members of the organization might find it difficult to. It can supply contacts for the organization and help to establish working relationships with other groups.

The role of *spiritual leadership* is very difficult to define. Perhaps the only way to express it is: find Spirit-filled men and women through whom God can operate.

Selecting the Board

For a board to play its role and carry out the functions we have described above, its members need to be carefully selected. There are a number of questions to ask as we go about this process:

How large should a board be? Probably the smaller the better. The size should be determined by the number of people available to constitute a quorum, the frequency of board meetings, amount of representation of different constituencies that is needed, and the amount of work the board will have to do to carry out its function. Perhaps for most Christian organizations, from five to fifteen is a good rule of thumb.

Who should be selected to serve on the board? Certainly go for the best men and women you can find. This is particularly important when originally constituting a board. Start at the top. The willingness of new members to serve on the board will be greatly influenced by the caliber of the people who are already board members. This speaks strongly to the need to search for, cultivate, and eventually attract community and Christian leaders. On the other hand, we do well to avoid Christian "celebrities." People who are very prominent in their own right may bring a constituency with them, but remember, they will take some of it away when they leave! Board members make an impact when they join the organization—and they make an impact when they leave!

Look for enthusiasm and a desire to serve, balanced by an ability to make a good contribution. The people you want will usually be committed to other important activities. They will need to be convinced that they can make a contribution to your organization and that what your organization is doing is important. Once they are convinced they will normally be enthusiastic.

What should be their spiritual qualifications? We need men and women of spiritual maturity. This does not necessarily mean mature in years, though normally the two will go hand-in-hand. We need men and women who are well-spoken-of by others, people who have demonstrated an ability to manage their own Christian affairs. Find ways to observe and evaluate as much as possible in this area. Remember, we are not only concerned with whether people are able to express themselves in godly terms. We want to know how such godliness has been worked out in the day-to-day business of living and carrying out the work of an organization.

Should they be insiders or outsiders? In other words, should the board include members of the paid staff? Most American organizations vote yes. But make sure that the balance is maintained. A ratio of one insider for two outsiders is perhaps a good suggestion.[27]

What kind of a mix of different people should be on a board? Think about what kind of a mixture of ages, sexes, professions, experience, Christian background, connections, and prestige you would like to have. Perhaps you need to give consideration to ethnic representation. However, avoid tokenism. Too often women or minority groups are brought on a board not because of what they contribute but only because of the people they represent. Make sure that they, too, have gifts to provide and roles to play.

As you think about the different people for the board, think about how they will work together. You're not always looking for agreement; rather you want a balance of viewpoints. Make a chart with the kinds of people you want listed down one side and the types of jobs or roles you want them to fulfill on the board across the top. Try to analyze what kind of person would best fit each role.

Who should choose the board members? In the case of the self-perpetuating board, the existing board will elect new directors. In the case of a local church, the ecclesiastical tradition and the practices of the church will be followed. However, for the nonchurch Christian organization, many times the recommendation of the management will be carefully considered. Often the top management or leadership will propose board members and do the research necessary to bring them up for nomination. Consequently, the chief operating officer of any organization does well to cultivate and maintain a background list of people whom he or she feels would be outstanding members of the board. Many times it is a good practice to select the board of directors from an advisory board. Indeed, some organizations make this mandatory.

To keep the board vital, you might want to consider a rotation system, with a prescribed time off the board before reelection.

Board Operation

Committee work within a board is important. It expedites the work and keeps members involved. Be sure areas of committee assignment fit the experience and interest of the individual members.

Accurate corporate minutes are vital. Be certain to have a capable secretary or at least staff assistance for the secretary if needed. After all, the minutes of the board meeting are essentially the formation of corporate policy.

A strong chairman is needed, not to be the decision-maker or the one to exert undue pressure, but one who would guide the board meeting carefully, secure input from all participants, note the sense of the meeting, and seek to head toward consensus. The chairman is the key to a successful and harmoniously functioning board.

Preparation for board meetings should be done well in advance. An agenda should be prepared and background reading should be provided. Recommendations that will be made by the leadership to the board should be spelled out as much as possible in advance. If the board is to develop confidence in management, then the management must do its homework. Since good board members are likely to be busy in other activities, meetings of the board should be planned at least three meetings ahead even if this stretches out two years in advance. In this way board members budget their time accordingly.

Supporting the Board

Orient and educate new board members to how the organization rates. Each organization has a special jargon of its own. Provide them with as much background information on the organization as possible without overwhelming them with too much material. If there is a house publication, make sure they read this. Send them a policy manual if you have one and the minutes of previous board meetings as well. Shortly before the first meeting which they are to attend, contact them personally either by phone or mail, welcoming them to their position and explaining in detail how their first board meeting will operate and what their role in it will be.

It is the executive's responsibility to keep board members well informed regarding the organization's activities. The board should not only read such material carefully, but also respond with suggestions and encouragements. An uninformed or poorly informed board member can cause unnecessary problems and difficulty in a board session. This requires a constant and very specific flow of information between meetings.

It is the responsibility of the executive to keep in close touch with the board and to provide them with everything they will need to function wisely. Don't overlook the need for board members to get to know one another. Provide opportunities for socializing and mutual support. Many local churches have a practice of taking the board on a weekend retreat as part of the first meeting after election of new members. Organizations that may only have quarterly or semiannual meetings need to think of similar ways of bringing relationships closer.

Don't overlook the *cost of supporting a board*. Consider it as a well-warranted expense. Usually your board members will be giving you their time at no cost. However, you may need a policy that covers some or all of their travel expenses. It may be advisable to spend money on the setting in which the board meets. These are problems that need to be discussed within the board, but it is the role of the executive to bring them to the board's attention.

One of the most effective things an executive can do to support a board is to make sure it continues to work on the organization's long-range plans. After all, it is only as the board has a clear understanding of where the organization has been, where it is now, and where it intends to go, that it is able to give wise judgment. Good planning is the context within which good decisions are made.

Whether it be the pastor of the church or the chief executive officer of the Christian organization, each needs to take a personal interest in the board members. Seek out opportunities to have a luncheon date with them. If they live in different cities, make sure they are contacted if you have occasion to be in that city. As you see that they have special skills, contact them for personal advice. At the same time, let them know that you are open and available to help them if they see occasions where your knowledge and experience can be useful to them.

How to Avoid the Rubber Stamp Board

This is a question I have been asked a number of times. Many Christian leaders feel frustrated because instead of giving policy guidance, their boards seem content to go along with whatever leadership suggests. What can be done? This process cannot be accomplished overnight. It may take as many as three to five years before you can develop the kind of a board really needed to make the organization function effectively. But by setting out a description of the kind of a board you need and then working to fill openings that come, you can have a sense of moving toward your objective and eventual success.

If you are in the process of forming a new board or expanding a present board, then the suggestions above should move you a long way toward avoiding a "rubber stamp" board. On the other hand, if you already have a board that is giving you inadequate input or direction, there are a number of things you can do: first, analyze the skills and capabilities of the present board. Second, try to define specific job descriptions for members of the board. Third, consider a rotation system or an expansion system that will permit you to bring new blood onto the board. These three moves will many times encourage present members who are really not willing to become involved to gracefully move off the board.

The board of directors has a tremendous impact on the potential of any organization. The time and energy invested in clearly defining roles, carefully selecting members, and supporting the members once they are selected, will produce long-lasting dividends.

CHAPTER 31

Murphy's Law for Managers

People have always attempted to make some sense out of God's universe. With the advent of Newtonian physics, we began to describe the world in terms of "laws," rules by which we could bring some consistency and predictability to life. We have learned the hard way that the "laws" of one generation often become the laughingstock of others. But still the search continues.

Perhaps the failure to find ongoing consistency in the material universe is what one day encouraged Mr. Murphy to postulate his now famous law: "If anything can go wrong, it probably will."

Think of all the possible failures. Consider all of the possible mistakes. They will happen, so says Mr. Murphy.

In more recent years a Mr. O'Toole has framed O'Toole's Comment on Murphy's Law: "Murphy was an optimist."

We suspect that Murphy was a young man when he framed his law (and O'Toole was even younger). For as we get older, we learn to accept the fact that not only will things go wrong, but there is much to be learned from such occasions.

Why is it that some people seem to get things done with ease and little fuss, while others apparently encounter nothing but failure? We suspect it has something to do with the age at which they learned Murphy's Law and began applying it to the storing up of "experience."

Why do things go wrong? It sounds overly simple but it boils down to when, where, what, and how.

The desired event didn't happen when we needed it, or what we wanted wasn't where we wanted it, or the thing that was produced was not what we wanted or we didn't know how to do it or did it incorrectly.

From a management viewpoint there are two kinds of time: *elapsed time*, the time that goes by on the clock or the calendar, and *work time*, the time when we are actually engaged in work. We can seldom do an hour's work in an hour. During that hour there will usually be interruptions. Although the amount of time spent at the task (work time) may actually add up to only an hour, when we look at the clock, we discover the time allotted (elapsed time) has exceeded the hour.

Experience teaches us to leave room for the unexpected or to isolate ourselves in order to minimize interruptions.

It's surprising how often the right thing manages to arrive in the wrong place. Shipments of material are held up. People who have needed skills are at another location. The "right" solution is applied to the wrong problem. All of the elements or parts needed are available, except for one. For example, preconference planning for a major consultation is complete, but someone forgot to ask whether there was a public address system available.

Experience anticipates the possibility and starts asking in time to correct the error. It remembers the things that went wrong before and makes checklists that others can follow.

How many times have you ordered something only to have something else delivered? How often are you faced with, "Oh, I thought you meant . . . "? The task gets done, but it has the wrong outcome. Murphy's Law strikes again.

Experience tells us that we can't be certain someone really understands until they are able to explain to us what we said. The best plans are not the ones we create, but the ones that others create and the leader approves.

How one does something has to do with procedures and methods. This is where we find "human error." Most of us think of applying Murphy's Law in this area. Interestingly, human error is the easiest kind of problem to overcome. If you know what it is you want to accomplish, and you know how long it will take, chances are great that you can find someone with the adequate skills to accomplish it.

Experience knows that resources, such as money or people, are part of the solution, not the problem.

An Italian economist by the name of Pareto observed some time ago that 80 percent of life's problems are caused by 20 percent of life's events. Salesmen find they get 80 percent of their orders from 20 percent of their customers. Managers discover that they need to spend 80 percent of their time on 20 percent of their problems. Pastors may discover they spend 80 percent of their time with 20 percent of their parishioners.

Murphy's Law helps us to recognize that something can go wrong with almost anything, but it does not follow that everything will go wrong all of the time. In fact, a little reflection will cause us to see that we are all used to living with a great deal of "failure" each day. We accept the fact that the greatest baseball player of all time batted only .400. (He "failed" six times out of ten!) We leave ourselves enough time to get to work, recognizing that we might get caught in a traffic jam.

If we live in a world where anything can go wrong, and if Pareto is right that 20 percent of the "failures" will consume 80 percent of our time, then it follows that what we need to do is to identify the disastrous 20 percent.

The task for the executive is to know what 20 percent to focus on. Another name for such an approach is "Management by Exception." Don't be concerned about the things that are going well. Look for the weak points.

But how does one do this? The answer lies not only in hundreds of books on management practice and theory, but in a good deal of experience (!) that has to be lived. But there is a simple outline of steps that perhaps will increase the chance of discovering the key 20 percent. It follows the same outline as the problem: when, where, what, and how. They are questions which need to be asked when we plan, when we evaluate, and when we replan.

The next time you have to estimate the amount of time needed to prepare for a sermon, design a program, or carry out a task, begin by asking (yourself or the person responsible), "How long will it take?" Write down the answer. Next ask, "What's the fastest we could possibly do it?" Write that down. Finally ask, "If everything goes wrong, how long will it take?" Write that down.

When you analyze the three answers, chances are that your original time estimate will be more optimistic or pessimistic than the final one. Use your best judgment to decide which is the best guess. Keep track of how long each part of the task takes. You'll discover one usually takes longer. You now know the Pareto 20 percent for the *time* dimension.

The "where" question is usually applicable to only part of a task. It assumes that you are faced with a problem of geography. Find those things that have to come the furthest distance, either in number of stops or actual miles. For example, a special printing job being done by an out-of-town contractor. Those are the 20 percent for "where?"

Letting others know what you want is a matter of clear communication. What individual or organization is least likely to understand what you have asked for? For example, making arrangements in a country that has few English speakers, or dealing with people you have never met can be a potential problem. These are Pareto's 20 percent.

One of the advantages of spending a lot of time planning is that you can look at a number of alternative ways of doing things, and select those that are optimum for your task. If you discover in your planning that there is only one way to do something, there is no other alternative, that's your 20 percent. For if that one fails, you have no way out until you do find an alternative.

How dull life would be if everything happened as anticipated! How wonderful to know that God can take our "mistakes" and work them out for good. Joseph must have certainly felt that Murphy had been around! His brothers sold him as a slave. His master's wife tried to seduce him. Those he befriended in prison forgot him. We can learn from Joseph's response to his brothers: "You intended to harm me, but God intended it for good."

My friend Ed Dayton would like to suggest a new "law" which hereafter will be known as Dayton's Law: "At least 50 percent of the things you plan will probably go right. Rejoice."

CHAPTER 32

Enthusiasm–The Secret Ingredient

We live in the age of high-speed information. But we're saddled with an organizational structure straight out of the Roman Empire. This is a major dilemma in the church. God inspired a system of elders and ministers ideally suited for the day of foot traffic, horses and sailing vessel. Today He relies upon our faith and ingenuity to make it work in a time of jet travel and satellite hook-ups.

This split has been a source of great frustration to many of today's young leaders. The very leaders who possess the imagination and enthusiasm to overcome these problems are all too often turned off by the necessity. Now more than ever before, our church needs the optimism, energy and entrepreneurship of today's young thinker, who is almost always enthusiastic. And much enthusiasm is needed in the work of the Lord!

Enthusiasm—"infused with god." What could better explain this word that derives its meaning from the Greek roots EN, meaning "in," and THEOS, "god"? We all recognize enthusiasm when we see it. But how does it work? And why? These answers often remain a secret. The dictionary uses lower case *g* in spelling the word *god*. Al Capone was enthusiastic. But there was certainly nothing capital about the god infusing him.

How can you and I become infused with the true God in a manner that will propel us toward lasting success? Let's examine this important ingredient along with a recipe for using it effectively.

Sky High Enthusiasm

I remember traveling aboard a DC-4 in 1953 to an evangelism conference in Ireland. Engine problems grounded us in Gander, Newfoundland, for 24 hours.

But did our group sit around waiting and relaxing? No! In those 24 hours we organized a public meeting in the airport for hundreds of people. The Palermo Brothers were singing and several of us preached and testified. We probably had three hours of meetings right there in the airport, and the people were entranced by this group of young men and women who were sharing their faith in Jesus Christ.

Then a radio station came out and taped some of the things we were doing. The next day as we were flying out of Gander, the pilot came on the intercom and said, "I have something I want you folks to hear." And he turned on the Gander radio station. There was the service we had the night before outrunning us through the airwaves as we headed toward Ireland for the next "infusion."

Amazing! These enthusiasts never missed an opportunity. They weren't going to just sit around the lobby; they wanted to have a meeting. They wanted to share, to testify. They were filled with "theos" and wanted nothing more than to share it with others. The more enthusiasm they gave away, the more we all possessed.

That reminds me of another airborne incident in 1958 on our way back from Sao Paulo, Brazil. Everyone was so excited about the miracles God had performed at our Congress that we all got together in the back of the chartered DC-4. Spontaneously, we started singing, rejoicing, testifying, and celebrating the eminently successful campaign. Soon the captain sent word back saying, "The ship is out of balance. You'll have to return to your seats." Apparently, that which lifts your spirits doesn't always do the same for an aircraft. But it's times like these that help you feel the influx of something more real than the physical.

Forget the 95 Million if You Can't Evangelize Sixty

One evangelist discovered that Christians have a lot to learn about enthusiasm for taking the gospel to secularized people. Here are some telling excerpts from Jim Petersen's book *Evangelism As a Life-style*.

> In 1963 my family traveled by ship from the United States to Brazil. There were 120 people on board. Half were tourists and half were missionaries—including us. Sixty missionaries and sixty tourists! A one-to-one ratio for sixteen days. Since there isn't much more to do aboard ship other than walk, read, or converse, I couldn't imagine how any of those tourists could get through the trip without receiving a thorough exposure to the Christian message. More ideal conditions for evangelism couldn't exist.

During the first three days my wife and I spent our time relating to the other passengers. Conversations were unhurried and soon we found ourselves deeply involved in discussing Christ with our new acquaintances.

On the third day I thought that if the other fifty-eight missionaries were doing what we were, we would have a serious case of overkill. I decided to check with the others about coordinating our efforts. My first opportunity came when I encountered six missionaries sitting together on the deck. I joined them and expressed my concern that we get our signals straight so we wouldn't overwhelm the passengers.

I had totally misjudged the problem. When I explained what was on my mind, the six just looked at one another. Apparently, it hadn't occurred to them to talk to the other sixty passengers about Christ. Finally one said, "We just graduated from seminary and didn't learn how to do that sort of thing there." Another said, "I don't know. I have sort of a built-in reservation against the idea of conversion." A third said, "I've been pastor for three years, but I've never personally evangelized anyone. I don't think I know how either."

I remember saying that if we, in sixteen days and with a one-to-one ratio, couldn't evangelize sixty people, we might as well forget about ninety-five million Brazilians. Perhaps it would be just as well if we would all catch the next boat north.

What was missing? Jim Petersen's book recounts how he motivated the other "evangelists" to begin fulfilling their purpose by sharing the spirit that burned within him.[28]

Thus we discern several valuable lessons about enthusiasm. Like a childhood disease, you get it from somebody who had it before. Classes, books, buildings and job titles won't automatically infuse you with God—unless they drive you into contact with a real live "carrier." We also discover that enthusiasm is contagious. Once infected you can pass it along to others with ease and joy.

Enthusiasm for Dollars

An associate of mine tells the story about his wife, who had lost a contact lens. She looked all around the bedroom for it. But the more she looked for it, the more frustrated she became. "Why do these things happen to me? Here I am in a hurry and now I've lost a contact lens! Where is it?" Then she told her husband about the problem.

One of the first things he wanted to know was, "How much is it going to cost me to replace this thing?" Upon hearing the figure of $25, he went into the bedroom with a different spirit of enthusiasm. Within minutes he had located the missing lens.

"How come I looked all over for this thing and couldn't find it? Then you walk in and practically pick it right up. What's the difference?" asked the woman.

"Well, you were looking for a contact lens," he explained. "And I was looking for $25."

The power of enthusiasm!

Poor Eyesight, Rich Vision

"I had only one eye," she writes, "and it was so covered with dense scars that I had to do all my seeing through one small opening in the left of the eye. I could see a book only by holding it up close to my face and by straining my one eye as hard as I could to the left." And so begins an amazing story of enthusiasm and perseverance as recounted in the Dale Carnegie classic, *How to Stop Worrying and Start Living*.

Borghild Dahl was virtually blind for half a century. Yet she saw enough to behold the power of enthusiastic determination. She refused to be pitied, refused to be considered different. As a child, she wanted to play hopscotch with other children, but she couldn't see the markings. So after the other children had gone home, she got down on the ground and crawled along with her eye near to the marks. She memorized every bit of the ground where she and her friends played and soon became an expert at running games. She did her reading at home, holding a book of large print so close to her eye that her eyelashes brushed the pages. She went on to earn two degrees: a B.A. from the University of Minnesota and an M.A. from Columbia University.

Borghild started teaching in the tiny village of Twin Valley, Minnesota, and rose until she became professor of journalism and literature at Augustana College in Sioux Falls, South Dakota. She taught there for 13 years, lecturing before women's clubs and giving radio talks about books and authors. "In the back of my mind," she writes, "there had always lurked a fear of total blindness. In order to overcome this, I had adopted a cheerful, almost hilarious, attitude toward life."

Then in 1943, when she was 52–years-old, a miracle happened: an operation at the famous Mayo Clinic. She could now see 40 times better than she had ever been able to see before.

A new exciting world of beauty opened before her. She now found it thrilling even to wash dishes in the kitchen sink. "I began to play with the white fluffy suds in the dishpan," she writes. "I dip my hands into them and I pick up a ball of tiny soap bubbles. I hold them up against the light, and in each of them I can see the brilliant colors of a miniature rainbow."

As she looked through the window above the kitchen sink, she saw "the flapping gray-black wings of the sparrows flying through the thick, falling snow."

She found such ecstasy looking at the soap bubbles and sparrows that she closed her book *I Wanted to See* with these words: "'Dear Lord,' I whisper, 'Our Father in heaven, I thank Thee. I thank Thee.'"

Dale Carnegie ended his chapter of this story with an obvious admonition. "Imagine thanking God because you can wash dishes and see rainbows in bubbles and sparrows flying through the snow. All the days of our years we have been living in a fairyland of beauty, but we have been too blind to see, too satiated to enjoy. If you want to stop worrying and start living, count your blessings—not your troubles."[29]

Recipe for Success

These accomplishments by Borghild Dahl demonstrate the power of our secret ingredient. But what's so secret about enthusiasm? Unlike the formula for Coca-Cola that's locked in a safe and known to only a handful of specialists, everyone sees and understands enthusiasm. But every good cook knows it's one thing to gather up ingredients and quite another to stir them together into a delicious, taste-tempting treat. As you examine our recipe for success, keep in mind that having a cookbook on the shelf doesn't put the meal on the table. You've got to stir up some action.

Recipe for Success

A. Gather these ingredients

    1. A worthy goal

    2. Facts, information, knowledge and experience

    3. Good health and a positive outlook

    4. Determination

     5.   Tenacity and perseverance

     6.   Ingenuity and creativity

     7.   Prayer

   B.   Now put them all together with:

   Enthusiasm

The reason this last ingredient is secret is the simple fact that enthusiasm is not a separate ingredient of itself. Rather it is a companion of all the others.

We can't accomplish anything unless we attack it with enthusiasm. We can't be placid and settle for the status quo. That's unacceptable. It's not even biblical. Things cannot remain as they are. The world sorely needs "change agents" to affect a real difference. And that takes enthusiasm. You and I need to make people restless. That's the purpose of preaching—to make people dissatisfied with where they are by helping them understand there's something better beyond. To the new generation of leaders coming along today I say: Come share some of your enthusiasm for life with our joy for the afterlife.

Enthusiasm Training

Is it possible to learn how to increase our enthusiasm through merely studying a book? I cannot guarantee that reading the pages of this book will infuse you with God and His power. But I can guarantee if you do those things that enthusiastic people do, you will benefit. And one thing enthusiastic people do is improve themselves through study and training in the fields that are important.

I believe the most successful leaders place personnel development among their highest priorities. Millions of dollars are spent each year in industry for management development and training programs. But still there appears to be a shortage of strong leadership potential. There may be two reasons for this.

One is that promotion is emphasized far more than development; the other is that development is frequently not supported at top management levels. Without realizing it, leaders often doom the ultimate success of programs because they show too little active interest, though they may give token consent or encouragement to their key people. These factors are equally damaging to the development of Christian leadership.

Trained with Enthusiasm

A few Christian leaders have the mistaken assumption they don't need to be trained. After all, they're led by God Himself. What can mere mortals teach them? Consider that a number of people in the Bible were trained for leadership even though they had received a call from God. The best example is probably the disciples, who were trained at the feet of Jesus for three years. In His high priestly prayer to the Father before His death, Jesus alluded to those things He had passed on to the Twelve in order to perpetuate His work on earth. "I have passed on to them the message you gave me. They accepted it and know that I came from you, and they believe you sent me" (John 17:8 NLT).

A prophet of God in the Old Testament period was specifically called to enunciate His truths to the world. Yet under Samuel's direction an actual school—the school of the prophets—was set up to train these leaders (see 1 Samuel 19:18–20). It was here that David no doubt found refuge from Saul who at that time wanted to destroy him. During the time of Elijah and Elisha such training schools were located at Gilgal, Bethel, and elsewhere (see 2 Kings 2:1–3; 4:38; 6:1). According to Jewish tradition, these schools trained students throughout the long history of Judah to fill the office of prophet. There were many of these seers or scribes, for the Old Testament frequently alludes to prophets in the plural.

Such schools were the forerunner of the Jewish rabbinic centers following the return of the captives from Babylon under the direction of Ezra, Nehemiah, and Zerubbabel. The theological schools of the early church were a direct outgrowth of this concept, and the modern seminary is the extension in our time. (I only wish there were more than the 100,000 students enrolled in seminaries out of 12,000,000 American college students today.)

The purpose of the schools was always threefold: to develop, train, and educate men in the leadership functions necessary to perpetuate God's work. We may safely conclude that spiritual gifts can be developed.

Other biblical references demonstrate the need and justification for developing gifts within people to place them in positions of leadership. Moses trained his successor Joshua. Joshua was discovered in the battle against the Amalekites; Moses saw his potential immediately and groomed him to become the undisputed leader of the people. Numbers 27:16 states that God would give His people direction through the appointment of a man. But the calling required training and supervision. For many years Moses shared his leadership responsibilities with Joshua.

Training was an important part of the formation of the early church and the work of the apostle Paul. Remember that the training of people was the key for the rapid expansion of the church in the first century. Paul trained Timothy, Barnabas, Silas, and John Mark. He was also responsible for the growth of Sopater, Aristarchus, Secundus, Gaius, Tychicus, Trophimus, and others whom he mentions in his Epistles.

Paul could have appealed simply to his special gift of apostleship and let it go at that, trying to do all the work himself. But he wisely followed the course of preparing others and helping to establish those with whom he shared the gospel.

Our missionary and evangelical enterprises are doomed today in the Third World if our leaders, both from the West and in the developing nations, do not develop leadership among Christian nationals. Thank God, this seems to be an increasing emphasis in these younger churches in the Third World. People like John Haggai and my World Vision Indian colleague, Dr. Sam Kamaleson, are making a tremendous impact in this ministry.

Dr. John Gardner makes a poignant observation in his book, *Excellence*. "The society that scorns excellence in plumbing because plumbing is a humble activity, and tolerates shoddiness in philosophy because it is an exalted activity, will have neither good plumbing nor good philosophy. Neither its pipes nor its theories will hold water."[30]

I have known executives who approach golf, skiing or tennis with more intense effort than they approach their task as leaders. Excellence requires more than reading a book on management principles. Professional expertise demands that we take continual action for improvement. And that requires enthusiasm.

Such reluctance is due in part to a false perception of success. To succeed is to "sell out" in the eyes of many Christians. Yes, Christ warned us that we cannot serve God and money. But He never told us we cannot use money. In fact, He later admonished, "use worldly wealth to gain friends for yourselves, so that when it is gone, you will be welcomed into eternal dwellings . . . So if you have not been trustworthy in handling worldly wealth, who will trust you with true riches?" (Luke 16:9, 11). I happen to agree with Hendrik van Loon when he says, "In history as in life, it is success that counts."[31] But our success must always be measured by God's yardstick.

Ordway Tead in his helpful book *The Art of Leadership* examines the various methods of giving expression to leadership training. He provides five methods of instruction that may be adapted to unlock enthusiasm in a potential leader.

Methods of Leadership Training

1. Experience in a leadership situation under some supervision

2. Progression from small to larger leadership situations

3. Apprentice courses of practice and study

4. Conference study of methods by groups of leaders

5. Systematic personal conferences of trainer and leader.[32]

Development is fundamental, and it has to be measured or quantified in some way. If potential leaders have not learned to use effectively the material being taught them, the training program must be revised. Several criteria can measure this factor, although admittedly it is not easy. Ordway Tead offers five suggestions that help quantify the impact of enthusiasm.

Evaluation of Leadership

1. The volume of work done by the group the individual leads. It may be possible to measure this in terms of volume or cost per unit of man hours.

2. The quality of work done by the group. Sometimes this can be done by inspection, sometimes by studies of attitudes of clients, colleagues, customers or the public.

3. The stability of membership in the group. If there is a marked tendency for people to enter the group and then quickly resign, that is a bad sign. Figures of "labor turnover" are used in many organizations to discover such a tendency. And figures of the number of individuals who have stayed with the group for a given number of years can further show how stable the group is.

4. The number of complaints or grievances that is brought to the responsible directors of the group.

5. The opinion of the members of the group as to their own state of mind in relation to dealings with the leaders.[33]

With this understanding of the relationship between leadership training and enthusiasm, here are several helpful steps suggested by my friend Frank Goble in his book *Excellence in Leadership*.

As An Enthusiastic Leader . . .

- I will reserve the following dates and times for an improvement program.

- I will schedule a meeting with my staff to plan an organizational improvement program. Who? When? Where?

- I will start holding regular meetings with my staff as the first step toward adopting the coordinated team approach at all levels under my jurisdiction. Who? When? Where?

- I will attend some seminars. Which seminars? When?

- I will start reading leadership literature. What? When?

- I will start a leadership library. How? When? Where?

- I will obtain and display some signs to remind me and my associates to do things in a professional way.

- I will analyze my own use of time. This is how I will proceed:

- I will seek a qualified consultant to help improve personal and organizational effectiveness. Who? When?

- The area which shows the greatest possibility for improvement is:

- I will start there. What? How? When?

- I will do the following:

  This checklist is a tool to identify those areas needing improvement. The list can and should be expanded and adapted to your individual needs.[34]

Enthusiasm Overview

1. Look to the examples of yesterday for ways you can share your enthusiasm today.

2. Discover the enthusiastic joys of personal evangelism.

3. Let the personal triumphs of others inspire you to new heights of enthusiasm.

4. Cook up the Recipe for Success often—with bushels of enthusiasm.

5. Be willing to learn from others through formal and informal training.

6. Take positive steps for putting your enthusiasm into action for improvement at home, on the job and in the church.

7. Look on the kaleidoscope of ethnic diversity in our land as a continual reminder of how much we need *enthusiastic* participation in service to the Lord.

I've characterized enthusiasm as the secret ingredient for success. It's secret only because it becomes, through second nature, an unnamed part of everything a successful leader thinks and does. We've seen the rules, the examples and the checklists for enthusiasm. All we need now is the determination and the will-power to put this information into action.

Part Seven

LEADERS AS DECISION MAKERS

CHAPTER 33

Decision Making

M any years ago a Christian leader wrote a letter to some of his followers in Corinth reflecting back on his decision not to visit them:

> When I planned this, did I do it lightly? Or do I make my plans in a worldly manner so that in the same breath I say, "Yes, yes" and "No, no"? But as surely as God is faithful, our message to you is not "Yes" and "No." For the Son of God, Jesus Christ, who was preached among you by me and Silas and Timothy, was not "Yes" and "No," but in him it has always been "Yes" (2 Corinthians 1:17–19).

Paul faced all the demands for making a decision. The situation demanded action. He was under time pressure. He lacked complete information. There was uncertainty which suggested a risk in making a decision. There were possible costly consequences if he made the wrong decision. On the other hand, there was the possibility of good benefits from an effective decision. Lastly, there was the possibility of two or more alternative actions.

Good decision making is the hallmark of effective leadership in an organization. But good decision making from a Christian perspective requires an additional dimension. It is this additional spiritual dimension that can give the Christian executive the confidence he needs to move ahead with a decision while others stand and vacillate.

There is a close relationship between decision making and problem solving. Usually both start with a statement like: "Something needs to be done!" The steps in the process are not difficult to describe:

1. *Identify and describe the situation.* Gather as many relevant facts together as possible.

2. *Line up alternatives.* These may range from taking no action (a decision in itself), to a number of possible actions.

3. *Compare the various alternatives.* There will usually be advantages and disadvantages to each.

4. *Calculate the risk of each.* Since you usually will not have enough information to make a perfect decision, face up to the possible consequences of each alternative.

5. *Select the best alternative.* If alternatives have been adequately compared and rated as to risk, many times the best one will be self-evident.

Your first reaction may be that anything that complicated just isn't useful. But our mind is able to comprehend and digest so many things in a brief moment. The process by which comprehension occurred just takes longer to describe.

Many times our ability to understand a situation is half of the solution. Gather as many facts as possible. There will never be enough, but within the time demands of the decision, take time to organize the data that is available. When this is done, describe the situation as accurately as possible.

Data gathering is a skill that needs to be developed. Find out what the key sources of information are. Decide if others should be called in to contribute information. But remember that you're asking for data, not opinions on what decisions should be made.

From the data that you have gathered, list possible alternatives in a way that will permit you to visualize them all at one time. If you are working with a group, it is very helpful to write the data (problem description) on one piece of paper and then to list the alternatives on another.

There will be cases when the alternatives for a decision are either yes or no, go or don't go. However, try not to be satisfied with only two alternatives. Seek wise counsel. Ask several people for possible alternatives based upon the data that you have.

Since we can never completely predict the future, almost every alternative will include some factor of uncertainty. Find some way to compare alternatives. Some factors you might want to compare are: the risk involved, the cost of the alternative, the people available to implement the decision, the past effectiveness of using this type of alternative, the amount of time that this alternative will require, and how it will be received within the organization.

A list of assumptions that you are making for each one of the alternatives may be a key to which is the best. It is surprising how often people arrive at the same conclusion for different reasons. Therefore, a side benefit of listing your assumptions is your ability to communicate to others (and yourself!) the base upon which you are building your reasoning.

How much time you take in this process will, of course, be dictated by the urgency of the decision you face.

The major difference between problem solving and decision making is that in problem solving we assume there is a right solution. The problem has an answer. But decision making almost always includes an element of risk. We don't have enough information. We are not sure of the future. We don't have enough time to gather all the data. Therefore, try to develop your own method of rating the risk of each of the alternatives. Perhaps something as simple as a grading scale of 1 to 10 will be of help. Look back at your previous assumptions and see if they help you in assessing the penalties for making the wrong decision.

Many times the correct alternative is self-evident as we compare and rate the risk of each one of the various alternatives. But there are many times when it is very difficult to choose between alternatives. What do we do then?

Sometimes we can combine alternatives. This can be done by taking parts of two different alternatives or perhaps trying both of them. For instance, one might be a short-range solution to the need you face while the other might be a longer range solution. Don't be afraid of a compromise. Inflexibility in decision making tends to destroy effective leadership. Often all you can do is make the best out of a series of bad situations. Intuition or hunches will also play a major role in selecting the "best" alternatives. Here is where the spiritual dimension really matters. Pray about the alternatives. Seek God's promised wisdom.

Many times how a leadership decision is announced and implemented is just as important as the decision itself. If it will have a major impact on the life of the organization, consider the timing of the announcement. Perhaps it should be postponed until just the right set of circumstances present themselves. When you make an important decision, take a little time before announcing it. Sleep on it. God may have other plans!

The manner in which the decision is announced is of tremendous importance. If it is presented as "I'm sorry, fellows, but this is the best we can do in this lousy situation . . .", then you can expect the same response from your subordinates as they communicate the decision throughout the organization.

The individuals to whom the decision is announced can make a big difference in its reception. Many times it is a good idea to privately lay some groundwork ahead of time with those who are going to have to implement a major decision or will be affected by it.

Once a decision is made, don't look back or second guess yourself. Expect and demand commitment to the decision, on your part, and on the part of those who are going to be working on it. Don't seek popularity in decision making. Leadership can be a lonely business. Be consistent in applying the consequences of your decision. Don't vacillate.

Murphy's Law says that "if there is a possibility of anything going wrong, it probably will." What may have been a very good decision three weeks ago, in the light of subsequent events or new data, may appear to be a very poor one. This means that important decisions should have a built-in feedback process that will let you know as soon as possible if things are going sour. At this point, it is not a question of who's at fault, but how to turn things in a more positive direction. In a sense, you are faced with a new decision: what to do with the bad one you've made! It may be that the decision was right, but the planning was poor. Perhaps the wrong individuals were given the assignment to implement. Perhaps a new and better alternative has appeared, one which is distracting people from the original course of action. Go through the same process of decision making you went through before: identify the situation, line up alternatives, compare alternatives, calculate the risk, select the best new alternative, implement a new and revised decision.

It is here that the Christian executive or church leader has the advantage over his or her secular counterpart. Each one of us as children of God can be assured that God is working all things together for good on our behalf. But those of us who are privileged to work as part of the organizational life of His Body have the right to assume that this applies equally to the organizational task. This does not mean that we should be casting blame for failure on the Lord. Nor should we discount our own role in any "successes." It does mean that that extra dimension can produce decisions which can turn the world upside down.

CHAPTER 34

The Tragic Choice

Leaders are constantly involved in choosing. We normally call it decision making. What is actually happening most of the time is selection from a number of possible alternatives. This versus that, or often, this versus those. Indeed, a primary skill of the manager is to make decisions, to make them in a timely manner, and to make a sufficient number of right ones so that the good of the enterprise is maintained.

We all want to make right decisions. There is something in us that would like to believe we are making the right choice. However, too often there is a built-in assumption that we are choosing between "right" and "wrong." This is seldom the case. If we are dealing with strictly technological matters, there may be a right way and a wrong way. But most decisions involve people. And when people are involved, there is seldom a choice that is right for everyone.

John Carnell pointed out that the ultimate problem of choosing is what he called "the tragic moral choice." So often in life we must choose between the lesser of two evils. Carnell illustrated his point with the awful question, "When someone puts a gun to your baby's head, and says he will shoot her if you don't allow him to violate your wife, what do you do?"

Perhaps that seems a bit extreme. Perhaps we are not faced with many moral choices, but consider some of these:

1) A committed Christian brother who has worked for your organization for ten years is causing dissension because of his attitude. The morale of the rest of the organization is endangered. You have tried to counsel with him. You know that he is going to have difficulty getting another job. You also know that if you don't

separate him from the organization you will be unable to continue your ministry. What do you do?

2) You and your staff are financially stretched to the limit. You have been attempting to carry out a vision you have for the future. You find that you are faced with the choice of using resources you have set aside for the future or watching some of your staff disintegrate under the pressures. It appears to be a question of the people now—or the ministry in the future. What do you do?

3) Your church or organization is involved in a ministry that is attempting to speak prophetically to some of the social sickness you see around you. However, your financial support is coming from a constituency who are really part of the problem. If you speak as clearly as you believe you should, you are going to alienate those who support you. If you don't, you feel that you will violate your conscience. What do you do?

G. N. Tyrell helps us here by understanding life as being made up between "divergent" and "convergent" problems. Most of life is not made up of problems that can be solved technologically (convergent). Rather, "Life is being kept going by divergent problems which have to be lived and are solved only in death." There are few neat answers, but there are some lessons to be learned from organizations that have handled the ongoing problem of choices between wrongs.

How can we handle these types of tragic choices?

1) *Recognize* that there are probably no easy answers. If there were, you wouldn't be needed as a leader. The task of the manager is to make choices in the difficult situations.

2) *Gather all the information that time allows.* Often this will not be very much. One of the first questions to ask is, "How long do I have to solve this problem?"

3) *Are there policies, procedures, or rules that cover this problem?* Completely? Partially? What do they say?

4) *Consider the known impact on everyone and everything that is involved.* By "known" I mean what you believe to be true.

5) *Consider the possible impact.* Here we are dealing with speculation. It is often futile to play the "What if . . . ?" game. However, by exploring possible implications of choosing one thing over another, we are sometimes helped from falling into a pit that we might not otherwise recognize. One way to discover the impact of a choice is to ask if it affects long-range plans or our short-range plans.

6) *Ask if there are ethical and/or moral questions involved.* Sometimes there won't be. Other times they will be disguised. Think about the second and third order impacts as you look for these. If this happens, that will happen, and then what would happen?

7) *Ask if it is possible to reverse the decision once it's made.* Don't fall into the trap of thinking because you made one decision you can't change it. Very often we can decide to change a previous decision.

8) *Ask what advantages there are of having to make a choice.* For example, if you must make a change in the organization, can you use this opportunity to make some other changes that would not have been possible until you made this one? In other words, is it possible to make a feature out of the failure that you seem to face?

9) *Do you really have to choose?* What will happen if you don't make a decision? Perhaps this isn't a problem for you at all.

Finally, to quote St. Augustine, "Love God and do as you please." God expects us to have courage in making leadership decisions. If we are continually turning over our lives to His control, if we are attempting to live a life of love, and obedience, then we should expect God to honor the decisions we make.

CHAPTER 35

Making Critical Choices

For all of my adult life, I've carried a pocket memo pad with me everywhere. In it I record not only things to do but also stories of people who have faced critical choices and either caught a wave that led to success and joy or sank into the shallows of failure and unhappiness. Many of these stories find their way into my "Eclectic Notebook" for sermon illustrations and editorial anecdotes.

Each one of us is forced to make decisions constantly. Those signposts appear all the time. My old coach never failed to get a warm response when he said, "When you come to a fork in the road *take it!*" Following are stories of men who came to that fork. Some made good decisions, some made bad choices. All of the choices had far-reaching consequences.

The Fatal Gambling Debt

At the start of the Second World War, a young man enlisted quickly with enthusiasm to fight in this noble war. However, he soon found himself on a station in a lonely, frozen wasteland peering into a radar scope for most of the day and playing cards at night.

The subtle temptation of gambling began to eat away at the young soldier's heart, promising something for nothing—great riches, really, if only he could master his technique and make the stakes high enough.

The more he played, the deeper he sank into debt and the higher his stack of IOUs rose. Soon it was obvious even to his artificial optimism that he would never in the foreseeable future be able to pay his debt to the soldier with whom he bunked.

Alone on his watch one dark night outside a Quonset hut he observed a shadowy figure entering a sensitive area in which receipts of the PX were stored. Although he couldn't see who it was, he learned the following morning that someone had stolen a large sum of money there. The angry commander announced that he would find out who it was if it took him the rest of the war.

The gambler saw his opportunity. Rising to his feet he said, "Sir, that won't be necessary. I was on duty and I know who entered the PX."

A murmur arose among the soldiers as their compatriot prepared to finger the thief. The gambler turned and pointed to his roommate. "That's the man," he said.

There was no proof whatever that the accused man had entered the PX, but the soldier on watch said he saw the accused (to whom he owed a small fortune) so the suspect was court-martialed. That one decision gave him his freedom from a gambling debt but sent an innocent man to prison.

The soldier, now free from his gambling debts, was unable to forget the injustice. It ruined his later marriage and his business and eventually led to suicide.

The Man Who Said He Would

A young farmer living in the Midwest was in line to inherit a picture-perfect farm with black loam that had grown tall corn and waves of golden grain for several generations of his family. He wanted to marry his high school sweetheart so she could share his life on the family homestead. He would propose, he decided, the day after high school graduation. His dreams were wide and his love strong for the girl with the dancing eyes and bright smile who had stolen his heart.

High school graduation day came and as he had determined, he asked for her hand in marriage. She accepted and a wedding date was set.

The next morning as the girl was traveling to an interview for a job in a nearby town, she was nearly killed in an automobile accident. A drunk driver had crossed over the center line and hit her head-on, emerging from the tangled steel with only bruises.

For five weeks the girl lay in the hospital recuperating from lacerations, broken bones, and a damaged eye whose sight would never be restored. And when she got the news that she would walk with a limp, she feared that the young man who so recently had pledged to be at her side for a lifetime might be unwilling to keep his promise.

She needn't have worried. The young farmer kept his promise, standing strong like the oak trees on the back forty. He made her his wife and they can look back on three decades with their four children and thank God for a commitment to each other that has yielded unspeakable joy.

When It Happened to "Her"

A physician in a small Colorado town wasn't as loyal. He, too, pledged his love to a beautiful woman who owned a real estate agency. She regularly worked late and arrived home well after dark.

A rapist watched her for a long time until that fateful day when he attacked the woman. Things were never the same again.

The physician took the news hard, forgetting that his wife was the one who was violated. He couldn't look at her without thinking of what had happened to his bride. Intimacy vanished. Quarrels replaced the serenity of their home. The very sight of his wife began to fill the doctor with disgust. He made excuses for working late and canceled their weekly Friday dinners at the country club.

There was no turning back when the physician made his choice. He would leave his wife and put behind him the memory of the rape—the "violation." Her crying and pleading were to no avail. His decision held. The doctor is now in his third marriage and the children of his current "blended" family make no secret of their eagerness to leave home for good as soon as they come of age.

The Detour to Death

In the autumn of 1987, a middle-aged truck driver began to feel aches and pains in his joints. As he herded his eighteen-wheeler down the highways of the land, slicing through cities and rolling across the prairies with his 40,000–pound payload, he found that he was stopping more often at rest stops for quick naps and some exercise.

A physician diagnosed the trouble as early arthritis and prescribed a powerful steroid. It was the kind of medicine that, the trucker learned later, should not be taken for more than six months. This doctor had made the fateful decision to keep the trucker on the drug for more than three years.

The end of the prescription was also the end of the line for the man who wanted nothing more than to stay in the driver's seat and enjoy the romance of the road. But a doctor's inappropriate decision sentenced the trucker to live with bones so brittle that he could break a rib merely by turning over in bed. His active life is over. He spends his days hobbling around in the home of his parents, trying to decide if it would be appropriate to bring suit in a court of law for the mistreatment that has plunged him into despair and shortened his life expectancy.

A Policeman's Close Call

Two San Francisco police officers had worked all night on a case and were exhausted. It was 4 a.m. when the lieutenant approached the driveway of his associate and prepared to say goodnight.

"By the way," the captain said, "you talk a lot about being born again. What does that mean?"

Oh no, the lieutenant thought. *I'm exhausted and it's four in the morning. Couldn't this wait?*

But the curious officer pressed him. In the dim light of the squad car the lieutenant gave his partner God's simple plan of salvation through Jesus Christ and hoped the man would be satisfied, get out of the car, and let him go home to get some sleep. Instead, the captain pressed him further about the eternal matter. He was eager to respond, and the lieutenant almost missed what followed.

"You can give your life to Christ right here in this car," said the lieutenant. "You don't have to wait."

"I'll do it now, then," said the officer.

There in the wee hours of the morning, he made that most critical decision of all—that eternal decision to become a follower of Jesus Christ. Not twenty-four hours later the captain suffered a brain hemorrhage and fell into a coma while on duty. He never regained consciousness and entered the presence of the Lord a week later.

The lieutenant found himself in New Mexico later that year, speaking at a retreat for police officers and their families. At a meal with the parents of an officer the conversation turned to police work in San Francisco. The wife of a policeman spoke of relatives in the city and lamented the tragic death of her nephew through a brain hemorrhage. "The saddest part is," she said, "that nobody in our family can determine whether or not he was a Christian."

The lieutenant asked her to give him the name of the man and a brief description. After she had, he recognized that her nephew was the man he had led to Christ in the squad car that dark morning before sunrise. He related to the happy woman what had happened and assured her that she would meet her nephew in heaven.

"I Don't Know Why I Did It!"

A young man in Fresno, California, took summer employment as a truck driver to haul fruit from the San Joaquin Valley to Los Angeles. He and a buddy in another truck repeatedly made the two-hundred-mile run together so that they could help each other in case something mechanical went wrong.

One day at around sundown, one of the young men caught up with the other driver and started to pass him in a tunnel under a railroad track. Just as he was side by side with the other truck and inching ahead slowly, he suddenly braked and dropped in behind. At the other end of the tunnel a heavy caterpillar tractor on a trailer was stalled in the darkness without any lights. Because the passing driver decided for some unknown reason to put on the brakes and get behind the other driver, the man up front who spotted the machinery first was able to swerve into the left lane and avoid hitting the enormous equipment.

As they came out of the tunnel, the first driver pulled over to the side, his hands and legs shaking from the close call. As his buddy drove up behind him he called, "Why did you drop back?"

"I don't know," the second driver said. "Something told me to do it."

"That saved my life," he said. And after some moments of reflection and discussion of the fateful decision they went safely on their way, never to forget the close call in an underpass where a critical decision made all the difference in the life of a truck driver.

He Went Out and It Was Night

An evangelist with an effective ministry for three decades, including two terms as a missionary with his wife and children in the Philippines, found himself involved in sexual misconduct. The misstep took place far from home during extensive itinerant ministries. When the sin was uncovered and confessed, his wife and children were willing to forgive him.

He arrived home in late afternoon to the warm greetings of his family. His wife cooked his favorite food and encouraged him to stay with his family and put the terrible sin behind him.

The evangelist looked at the opportunity squarely but he remembered his new ties whose allure he could not resist. While the food was being put on the table he slipped out a back door with his suits and personal effects and drove away, never to return. The moment of decision came and went, never to return. He has since remarried and has lost the love of the bride of his youth and of his children. He made a critical choice and is suffering today because it was the wrong one.

"Here I Stand!"

Just before the 1949 Los Angeles evangelistic crusade that brought Billy Graham to national prominence, the evangelist was at Forest Home conference grounds in the San Bernardino Mountains about eighty miles east of Los Angeles. There he wrestled with the question of biblical authority. Was the Bible the Word of God? Did it perhaps merely *contain* the Word of God? Was it written by men or God-breathed? Could it be trusted?

In that forest of scraggly pines, cedars, and oaks the young man of thirty years cast aside all doubt; in a critical prayer he determined that he would go to Los Angeles and preach God's Word with authority. And the rest is history.

By Faith He Understood

Two police officers in a New England city were dispatched to apprehend a criminal reportedly cornered in the house of a seaside neighborhood. The two officers had worked together on the same beat for many years and had learned to trust each other. After talking to neighbors they located the house in which the fugitive was hiding. The older officer crept to the back while the younger officer, at a signal, kicked open the front door and yelled for the criminal to freeze.

Just as the young officer spotted the criminal it appeared to the cop he was reaching out for a gun, so he was just about to squeeze the trigger when he heard his fellow officer scream, "Hold your fire!" From the vantage point of the rear entrance, the older policeman could see that the criminal was reaching not for his gun but for a bar of soap that had shot out of his slippery hands when the sudden entrance of the officers had surprised him.

Because the young officer trusted his superior he made the critical decision to hold his fire and the criminal was brought alive to face his accusers.

"The Lord Will Provide"

A Chinese missionary working with his wife among the impoverished community of fellow Chinese in Calcutta, India, often had to make decisions by faith to carry out his programs of mercy and salvation. He and his wife were people of faith who had proven God many times.

One of their proposed projects was a Christian school to help educate children from homes of abject poverty and thus reach into their homes with the gospel. The missionary selected a site and began the process of finding a builder who would erect the Christian school for Calcutta's ragamuffins. The cost would be $15,000 and the money would have to be paid within thirty days.

"You may start pouring cement," the missionary told the building contractor. "God will provide."

Half a world away, the pastor of a large church was embarking on a trip for a missionary medical group on whose board of directors he served. Friends in that church who knew of the Chinese couple serving in Calcutta were exercised to collect funds through a special offering. The church added a small amount, bringing the total to an even $15,000. The pastor tucked the check into his suit pocket, boarded his flight, and was off on his trip that would eventually lead to Calcutta.

When the missionaries met him at the airport in Calcutta he was hospitably cared for in their humble apartment. As they sat talking that night the pastor inquired of their work and was told about the school project recently undertaken by faith.

"How much do you need to start the project?" the traveler asked.

"The builder wants fifteen thousand dollars," the missionaries explained. "We have already begun to build."

"How will you get the money?" the pastor asked.

With a smile of confidence the Chinese man replied, "The Lord always provides the funds for the projects we dedicate to Him."

The pastor reached into his suit pocket, pulled out an envelope, and handed it to the missionaries. "Indeed, the Lord has provided," he said.

Their rejoicing was great that evening. And the next morning they called the Christians of their congregation together for a special celebration. The critical decision to move ahead by faith for the building had been the right one for Christ and His kingdom and the poor people of Calcutta.

Let God Be God

A Southern California businessman incorporated his building maintenance business in 1970 and sold franchises all over North America. One of them in Toronto started well, then fell on hard times because the franchisee went heavily into debt with one customer who couldn't pay.

The day grew closer when the franchise would either have to stop going into debt by servicing the struggling corporation or continue to provide the service with hopes that the company would be able to pay their entire bill without dragging the service company down with it.

The cut-off day arrived. Early in the morning the Toronto franchisee phoned the head office in California to get his orders. My friend had spent long hours on his knees in prayer. At 8:30 a.m. he was ready with the answer.

"Wait a little longer," he told the franchisee. "Continue to service the account. We're standing behind you in this decision. God will fight for us."

It was the right decision. Not long afterward the delinquent company paid its bill in full and the franchise continued to enjoy solid financial growth.

Choosing Death on an Icy Lake

Each summer, a staff member at Hume Lake Christian Camps sings to the young campers a song he composed on his guitar. The scene is the Roman Empire just before Constantine when the persecution of Christians was outrageously commonplace.

In the song, the decree goes out to Rome's military contingents that all soldiers are required to participate in a heathen ceremony praising the emperor. "Forty brave soldiers for Jesus," the song says, stood to reject the emperor's decree, announcing their allegiance instead to their Savior and Lord, Jesus Christ.

Furious, the emperor had his troops build a bath house on a frozen lake to which the forty soldiers would be forced to march naked across the ice. When they arrived at the bath house, the emperor reasoned, all forty would gladly participate in the pagan sacrifice to their earthly ruler and save themselves.

Only one soldier stood guard that night when the "forty brave soldiers for Jesus" took off all their clothing as commanded and started the march across the frozen lake to the bath house. The guard watched in awe as the Christians willingly walked barefoot and naked on the frozen water, singing songs of praise to the Almighty God as they went. At the bath house, they lined up outside, still refusing to enter and participate in the ceremony.

The eyes of the guard at the water's edge were riveted to the men as he marveled at their bravery and noted their resolve. Suddenly he saw one of them break ranks. The traitor turned to enter the bath house to recant his faith, and to obey Caesar. But the heat inside the bath house overcame the shivering body of the traitor and he died instantly.

"Thirty-nine brave soldiers for Jesus" continued to sing songs to God and to worship the Creator as the soldier on the shore watched with increasing awe. Suddenly he laid down his sword, took off his helmet, his uniform, and finally his boots and under garments as well, then he started running across the ice. The thirty-nine soldiers cheered and embraced their brother in Christ and froze to death that night with the hymns of Zion on their lips.

"Forty brave soldiers for Jesus!" the story ends; nothing could change their true hearts. Only for truth would they stand there and die, only for life would they perish. That was a critical choice that they would have eternity to enjoy.

Short of the Goal

The head of a restaurant chain headquartered in Atlanta has taught thirteen-year-old boys in his church for more than three decades. The boys know they have a friend in their teacher and often make bold to ask for favors. Now and then a former student who turns sixteen will come to his teacher for a loan to buy a car.

In one case, the teacher said he would lend a boy $500 if he would listen to a series of six cassettes issued by the church denomination's publishing arm. Near the end of the last tape, the teacher interrupted the tape by inserting his own voice with this message:

"Steve, if you have listened this far, I congratulate you and want to give you the promised loan to help you buy a car. Phone me right away."

Each week the teacher would ask, "Have you listened to those tapes yet?" and Steve would mumble something like, "A little bit," or "Yeah, I listen to one when I get home from school in the evening . . ."

Finally the day came when the boy announced to his teacher that he had listened to all the tapes.

"Did you hear anything unusual on any of them?" teacher asked.

"No, not really, but I listened to the tapes," Steve insisted.

"Were you awake when you listened to them?" teacher asked.

"Oh, yes sir," Steve replied.

After taking the cassettes back, the teacher told the startled boy about the message he had superimposed on the last tape. "I'm sorry, Steve," he added. "I would have been glad to help you but you didn't keep your promise and you weren't honest with me. I hope this will be a lesson you will remember always."

Little Missteps, Big Pains

Life is full of pesky decisions of seemingly little consequence but which can yield enormous aggravation.

I thought of this when a friend called to say he had worked like a slave revising ten chapters of a book, only to pull the plug on his computer at the end of the day to move a piece of furniture and lose the entire record because it had not been saved.

I think of the friend who changed the oil in his car's engine, then forgot to replace the drain plug and poured five quarts of fresh oil right through the engine, and into the grass. To make matters worse, he then drove off without lubrication and was stopped dead by an engine whose innards had totally congealed, requiring the purchase of a new engine.

Another friend had what he called "the chance of a lifetime" to interview the great literary master C. S. Lewis. "Now make dead certain," he told his staff, "that I have a tape recorder that's working."

He had a tape recorder that was working, all right, but the staff had forgotten to put in the carrying case a take-up reel for the fresh new tape. In those days before the convenient cassette recorders, a reel could not be used if it had no empty reel to take up the tape that had passed through the recorder head. My friend wrote as fast as he could on his tablet, but there is no record today of the master's voice on tape.

A builder on the central coast of California invited his son to join him in a manufacturing venture. The son did everything right except to have an attorney remove liability through a properly drawn agreement. Because these few lines were missing from the contract, my friend lost his entire retirement of more than $800,000 and had to reopen his construction business and forget plans to enter into a lighter schedule of fewer demands.

A medical worker accidentally increased an immunization dosage for a child to three times what it should be. Her father sat in the doctor's office for a long time, coaxing his daughter to drink what was actually a lethal concoction. When his daughter died, it was almost too much for the father to bear, knowing that he himself had held the poisonous dosage and encouraged his daughter to drink it. He died of a heart attack several months later.

The Sony Corporation laughed when upstart VHS companies challenged its Beta-Max video cassette recorders and players, but in a few years Beta-Max had disappeared from the shelves as VHS systems took over.

Computer corporations smiled when Bill Gates quit Harvard University before graduating to get into his entrepreneurial company he called Microsoft.

They aren't laughing now. Today the young man is worth billion of dollars and Microsoft's software drives nearly 90 percent of the world's personal computers.

Big networks were not worried when Ted Turner bought up small television stations to run movies and then expanded into the news gathering business. Today his Cable News Network (CNN) dominates the world's news gathering industry and is seen and heard by heads of state and commoners around the globe.

Who could have imagined how big Amway (for "The American Way") would eventually become back in 1960 when two men from Michigan started offering biodegradable cleaning materials? Many who made the critical decision to join Amway have made substantial profits.

After the June 17, 1972, Watergate burglary, President Richard M. Nixon called it an issue that would be of interest to people in Washington but that most people in America wouldn't care much about it. Two years later he became the only Commander in Chief in the United States ever to resign.

When You Can't Decide

Not all decisions are clear-cut. The school to attend, the best car for the money, the community to choose when you relocate your family, the employment choices available . . .

More often than not, however, help is available for the asking. Sometimes it requires many prayers, lots of digging, many letters, phone calls, and personal visits with the people who can help.

An associate working late at work one evening was told by his boss to lie when his wife called and to tell her he was in a meeting. In reality, he was out spying on his wife because he didn't trust her. What should the associate do?

A lawyer took the case of a teenager in New England who was accused of murder. As the lawyer looked into the case, he found that evidence led to the clear conclusion that his own son was the murderer. What should he do?

As we face each critical choice, usually we know what we *should* do. The critical part is having the will to do it. A pastor of mine once said, "Most of my unpleasant work would be unneeded if the people of my congregation just did what they *ought* to do."

Nothing lasts forever. Making the right choices today will yield blessings without number both in our lifetime and in that great day which is still to come.

The day of the Lord will come like a thief. The heavens will disappear with a roar; the elements will be destroyed by fire, and the earth and everything in it will be laid bare. Since everything will be destroyed in this way, what kind of people ought you to be? You ought to live holy and godly lives. (2 Peter 3: 10–11)

CHAPTER 36

Knowing Where to Draw the Line

Every organization has its own style, its own way of doing things. Much of how it carries out its day-to-day business is based on a set of rules, many of which are never put down in writing. Some of these might be classified as traditions: Who gets copies of what memos? What are the rules about entering someone's office with or without speaking to his secretary? Who takes the lead in inviting whom to lunch? Is it all right to make personal phone calls on church or company time? Who pays for them? Does everyone take the same amount of time for lunch, or is it all right for some people to take a greater amount of time?

Where Do You Draw the Line?

How do we sort out which rules apply to whom? The Christian organization has a particularly difficult time in answering the question. On the one hand is the responsibility of individuals to fulfill their roles according to the expectations and requirements of the organization. On the other hand is the commitment the members of the organization have to one another, a reflection of their common commitment to God in Christ.

After all, Christianity is all about how we live. After the external foundation of the first eleven chapters of Romans, Paul exhorts us to God-honoring relationships, relationships so personal that we are described as "all joined together to each other as different parts of one body" (Romans 12: 5, GNB).

"Love must be completely sincere. Hate what is evil, hold to what is good. Love one another warmly as Christian brothers, be eager to show respect for one another, Work hard. Do not be lazy. Serve the Lord with a heart full of devotion. Let your hope keep you joyful, be patient in your troubles, and pray at all times.

Share your belongings with your needy fellow Christians and open your homes to strangers" (Romans 12:9–13, GNB).

How Do We Interpret This for the Organization?

As we have pointed out before, for the local church, the question is never resolved. It can never be a question of the local church before the individual or the individual before the church. Somehow we have to find a way of meeting the needs of both. And yet for the organization created to work outside of the structure of a local fellowship, it seems obvious that the organization has been called into being to do something. If it fails to do this, it loses its reason for existence.

But the dilemma remains. Are some people given more freedom than others? Do some have more prerogatives than others? What is best for the organization? What is best for the individual? Where do you draw the line?

Pieces of the Puzzle

It is a complex situation. We can only make a start at laying out some of the factors:

For example, in the state of California the law states that there are two classes of employees: exempt and nonexempt. An exempt employee does not receive overtime pay since it is expected that this person operates at an "executive level." It is assumed that this person will keep working until the job is done. On the other hand, the nonexempt employee must be paid on the basis of a 40-hour week. If this person is unable to finish his work during the day, and he is asked to keep working, he must be paid an additional amount.

But is this the only distinction between these two groups? Is there no difference between a person who enters the organization as a junior clerk and another person who has faithfully served the organization for ten years and is now a senior secretary? Should not the older employee receive more "benefits"? But, how can we treat each person as an individual and still be "fair"?

What right does the organization have to motivate its employees to do much more work for the same salary because they are engaged in the "cause of Christ"? The leaders, or senior executives may have founded or joined the organization because they believed in the cause of which it was a part. On the other hand, that junior clerk who joined the organization two weeks ago may have only been looking for a job and liked the idea of working in a "Christian environment."

What can the Christian organization expect of its staff that a non-Christian organization cannot? On the other hand, what should Christians expect of the Christian organization over and above the non-Christian organization?

What about the differences in pay? Should the leaders of the organization be paid the same salary as the most junior person who started two weeks ago? If this is not the case, should salaries in Christian organizations be the same as those in non-Christian organizations?

Working on the Puzzle

Ultimately, each organization will have to answer these questions for themselves. But there are some factors which need to be understood. These are not answers, just data to help reach your own (probably temporary) solution:

- There is something in human nature that says the wants of yesterday become the needs of today. What starts as a "benefit" given by the organization soon becomes a "right" of the employee. For example, one year an extra half day is allowed the staff before a holiday because of a special situation. The following year it is "suggested" that this would be nice to do again. By a third year it is "understood" that an extra half day will be given each year.

- There are few secrets within an organization. If a benefit is given to one person, it will soon be expected by others.

- There is no longer a willingness on the part of Westerners in general, and Western Christians in particular, to walk to someone else's agenda. Young men and women today feel that they have the right to ask "Why?" Older leaders have a particularly difficult time with what they regard as either rebelliousness or laziness on the part of young people. Whether these changing attitudes are right or wrong is not the question here. It is important that we understand the changing culture within which we live.

- There is a growing Western tendency to view the work one does to "earn a living" as only that. If this interferes with "my life," it is the former that must change. In other words, employers are being asked to shape their jobs to the individual lifestyle desired by the individual.

- How this jibes with the Protestant work ethic, which most of us have come to believe is fundamental to our effectiveness, remains to be seen. Some Christians view this change with a great deal of alarm and concern, while others see it as a rightful return to priorities that make the value of persons more important than the value of accomplishments.

- There will always be a "generation gap" in the ability of an organization to explain itself and its actions to its employees. The young church secretary, fresh out of school and buried under what appears to be an ever-increasing stack of letters, may never understand why the pastor spends an hour and a half at lunch. It is always difficult to see the beauty of the top of the mountain when one is buried at the bottom.

- Everyone has three kinds of time: leader-imposed time, over which we have no control; peer-imposed time, over which we have little control; and discretionary time, that which is left over. It is in the nature of task-oriented organizations that those at the "bottom" have very little, if any, discretionary time, while those at the "top" have a great deal. However, this idea is not understood and little appreciated by many people.

- There is a great difference in the value of the individual's time at the ends of the organizational spectrum. The chief executive's time may be worth (to the organization) $100 per hour while the junior clerk's may be $5 per hour. Salaries seldom reflect (particularly in Christian organizations) this difference. But again, this difference in value is not understood by most people.

- As a result of this difference in the value of time between individuals, most organizations have perquisites that are designed to give organizational leaders more time, or more effective use of their time, These vary from assigned parking spaces to longer vacations. The apostles evidently faced the same kind of a situation. We read in Acts 6:2: "It is not right that we should give up the preaching of the word of God to serve tables . . . we will devote ourselves to prayer and to the ministry of the word."

- This is seldom understood by younger members of an organization. Some leaders easily succumb to the idea that they should be willing to do anything that any member of their organization can do.

- Some organizations see all staff members as joining a cause. As a result, there is a tacit assumption that since everyone is equal in the sight of the Lord, that everyone is equal. Others require only the leadership to hold the vision. There is a great difference in these two kinds of organizations.

What Should the Staff Member Expect of the Christian Organization?

A defined ethos: Are you a movement or a company? Are you starting out on the assumption that before a person joins your organization he or she must be as completely dedicated to the cause as its leader? Or are you satisfied to have some members who are just "employees"? Your staff needs to know before they join the organization.

Dedication to the task, demonstration by the leadership that they are about the most important of all businesses, God's business. This will work itself out in many different ways, but it must be there.

Persistence, a doggedness about getting the job done.

A clear statement of purpose and goals, with a good understanding of how individuals at different levels relate to those goals.

Christian ethics: "Love is patient and kind; is not jealous or conceited or proud; love is not ill-mannered or selfish or irritable; love does not keep a record of wrongs; love is not happy with evil but is happy with the truth. Love never gives up; its faith hope and patience never fail" (1 Corinthians 13:4–7 GNB).

Good stewardship, the thoughtful concern about how finances and individuals are used. There is nothing more devastating to the staff of a Christian organization than to believe that the Lord's money is not being used wisely and well.

Openness, an earnest attempt to spell out the boundaries of its methods of operations and its expectation of individuals.

What Should the Christian Organization Expect of the Christian?

Diligence and competence in work, a desire to do better. This may be bounded by the forty-hour week or by job descriptions. We are not speaking here of how long a person works, but the attitude with which they approach the task.

Uprightness and integrity in the use of time, company supplies and equipment, expense accounts, and level of conversation. How easy it is to fall into the trap of, "Everyone else does it, why shouldn't I?"

Continual effort to maintain Christian attitudes. Calmness. Reluctance to take vengeance. Little complaining and chronic griping. A level of trust toward one another.

Warm and responsible interpersonal relationships, a sensitivity to the use of power or position, an avoidance of exploiting people, a sensitivity to the suffering that goes on around us and a willingness to help in time of need at the point of felt need.

A response to the organization norms. Conformance to the rules.

How to Draw the Line

Decide if you are a "movement" or a "company." A movement needs to clearly define the goal to which it is calling its members.

Realize that in our modernizing society, *we are always in the process of change.* Rules and norms appropriate two years ago may no longer be appropriate today. Dress code is a good example. In 1970, we worried about dresses too high above the knee. In 1976, we were concerned about dresses too close to the floor.

Stay abreast of secular standards in your community, everything from changes in the cost of living to appropriate dress.

Spell out rules and norms in writing to the best of your ability. Even for the small organization a staff handbook covering things like the organization's history, statement of faith, basic objectives, financial policies, requirements and procedures, salary administration, hours, attendance, benefits, vacations, holidays, anything that has become a uniform policy, is helpful.

Train your supervisors regarding what it means to be a good supervisor and the inevitable tensions of living and working.

Be open to question and challenge, but be consistent in response. Have times to regularly remind the staff of the rules, perhaps coupled with a time for seeking suggestions or improvements. For example, in our own organization, we periodically have staff retreats in which we invite the staff to submit anonymous written questions on any subject they like. We make a point of reading *all* the questions in attempting to answer them.

Attempt to explain the difficulty in applying uniform rules and regulations and the need for flexibility. Be flexible where needed. At the same time, be ready to announce your mistake if you have gone too far in giving benefits to one person that you are unable to give another.

Keep the cause to which Christ has called you clearly before all members of the organization. Report on successes and failures. Share in prayer.

Part Eight

GENERATIONAL LEADERSHIP

CHAPTER 37

You As a Young leader

I am at that point in my life where I feel comfortable looking back down the road I have traveled. It has been an exciting life. If I had to do it all over again, I would—gladly. Perhaps I should have taken more time to smell the flowers and listen to the birds singing along the way, but the tasks, responsibilities, and opportunities have been fulfilling. Many men and women have been my teachers. I am grateful to them all. For those of you who are beginning this exciting journey, or have the opportunity counsel young leaders, these seem to be among the things that stand out as important to me.

School and Society

Each of us is the product of our parents, our school, and our society. This is so obvious as to be forgotten in most instances. Of these three, I would like to focus on the impact of our schooling and our society—our culture—upon us.

We in the "Western" part of our world are the most educated of all people. I recognize that a high percentage of our readers have had sixteen years of school, many much more. Our society handles this long period of schooling with the (hidden) idea of postponed adulthood. A man or a woman is only considered an adult when he or she has left school and taken a full-time job. Even if he or she is married, in the classroom and the school one is still treated as preadult.

This you-are-not-an-adult conditioning elicits the expected result: men and women in school typically don't act like adults. It's amazing how many young adults, who in three weeks will graduate from seminary to accept a pastorate, live out the same rituals of dress, horseplay, and college humor. There is much talk about the heavy grind of college and graduate study. Three months later all this is left behind, and the new Christian leader is wondering how he even thought that forty hours a week of classes and study could have been a hardship.

The result of this postponed adulthood and its accompanying structured school life is a naïveté about how difficult the task of leadership really is. Since many of us have not yet had the experience of managing ourselves, we have little insight into how to manage others.

The Public and Private Sectors

We are also living in a society that increasingly lives a compartmentalized life, dividing it primarily into private and public sectors. What we do "on the job" is differentiated from what we do with "our own time." This is a natural response to an increasingly complex society. As time seems to compress itself and the number of new things to be learned or handled multiplies, we long to find some place to hide, a place to hang loose and "be ourselves."

The result is that life becomes more and more fractured. The pressures of society push us to compartmentalize life. To use the technological skills we have mastered to earn a living seems cold and mechanical. "Do not fold, staple or spindle," we cry. The difficulty is that we quickly set the different compartments one against the other.

The Christian is unique. He or she believes that there is ultimate purpose and meaning to life: "The chief end of man [and woman] is to give glory to God and enjoy him forever." As Christian leaders we need to bring our relationships into our task. We need to strive for integration, for wholeness.

The Normal Phases of Adult Life

In her book, *Passages*, Gail Sheehy points out that there are normal phases of adult life quite as distinct as the normal phases of childhood. We move from one phase to another in a series of "passages." People are different at differing times in their lives. They do respond differently, see things differently, at different ages.[35]

When we are young, we *refuse* to compromise. As we grow older, we realize we *have* to compromise. Perhaps in our thirties, we *learn* to compromise. By forty, we are *willing* to compromise. Sometime in life we (it is to be hoped) learn that compromise is what life is all about. We learn that often our "ideals" were less than ideal when placed alongside those of others. "*Our* goals" turn out to be more desirable than "*my* goals."

The idealism of youth is the bedrock on which the wisdom of maturity is built. Nothing wrong with that. But age does make a difference. The young Christian leader may not experience this, but it needs to be respected in others.

Paradox

Our society is oriented toward solutions. Our technological cement gives the illusion that we have much more control over destinies than we actually have. Too often young Christians fail to live in the light of the paradoxes of life so clearly stated in the Bible. The ultimate paradox, of course, is God's sovereignty and our freedom. Both are true. God is sovereign. His will *will* be done. Yet, men and women are free. We are responsible. "Logic" says those two ideas cannot coexist. Maturity discovers that we can live and work as though both were true.

Learn early to live in the light of faith.

Courage

To exercise good leadership is not easy. To assume a position of leadership often isolates one. There comes a time when *you* must decide, often for an unpopular position. So it takes courage.

But it is easy to confuse courage with dogmatism, an unwillingness to listen or to bend. Single-mindedness can lead to narrow-mindedness. In his book, *The Courage to Create*, Rollo May points out that it doesn't take a great deal of courage to move ahead on something in which you have complete confidence. True courage moves ahead in full knowledge that failure is possible.[36]

Love

Jesus tells us that the basic test of our commitment to him is our love for one another (John 13:35). Love has to do with relationships. There are some people who are so consumed with tasks and accomplishment, that they have little time for relationships. But love, without focus, without shared purpose, can become ingrown.

Love with abandon, but love with purpose.

Education

Your education has just begun. Ahead lies the "School of Hard Knocks." But for the effective leader of the future there will also be more, and often continuous, training. Build it into your goals.

Almost everyone is surprised by that first job after leaving school. No matter how well the organization explained it, the position seldom is what we expected. Time and again recent seminary graduates have complained, "I'm not using 10 percent of what I learned!" Be patient. You will. Not all of it, but a great deal. A good education teaches us how to *learn*. Once that is mastered, the whole world opens up.

Again the paradox: the more we learn, the more humbled we are at our own ignorance. And yet, with this comes a sense of completeness. Count on it.

Learn from Your Seniors

All of us have so very much to learn from others. Young executives need to recognize that there are few things more valuable than the experience we gain and garner in living our lives. Find ways to spend time with those who have been down the road a bit farther and who know something of the pitfalls as well as the "freeways" which can be traversed. Don't be afraid to ask counsel and advice (older colleagues are almost always happy to give it!). Find ways to seek out time with your superiors and others who have moved on ahead; their counsel and advice can be tremendously profitable and oftentimes extremely redemptive.

Watch for Models

How grateful we can be that the Word of God has provided us with various models for living, most perfectly exemplified in the model of our Lord Jesus Christ. In our ministries we need to look for models among our colleagues and fellow staff members. We believe the apostle Paul had this in mind when he wrote, "Dear brothers and sisters, pattern your lives after mine, and learn from those who follow our example." (Philippians 3:17 NLT). Those of us in leadership positions have a special opportunity—and a special responsibility—to point to others, through our example, toward greater fruitfulness and deeper commitment to our Lord. Our organizations ought also to seek to model for others. In our particular ministry, we constantly remind ourselves that we should strive to be examples of Christian excellence as leaders of other Christian organizations visit us to find out our management systems, procedures, and policies. Our role as models—whether on a personal or organizational level—should never be reason for pride, but rather, for profound gratitude. We should watch for models and learn all we can from what they have to show us in behavior, actions, and attitude.

Be a Reader

Be as widely read in as many disciplines as you possibly can. If you don't enjoy reading, cultivate the habit. Read contemporary literature; read literature that pertains to your area of concern and work; read much in the area of devotional materials; read management and leadership books and articles. Build shelves in your library for devotional material, reference material, management and leadership material, and other particular disciplines and interests that you may have. Read! It is one of the best ways to grow!

Learn from Failure

We need to recognize that in what we often call failure, we can learn the very most. Most failures can and ought to be learning situations. There is nothing wrong in failing or in making a mistake. Let's just be certain that we don't make the same mistakes twice or three times, and thus fail for the same reason. When you fail, pick yourself up, dust yourself off, and move ahead to build upon the experience. Don't bemoan the fact of failure, but ask the Lord to again use this experience redemptively in your life ministry.

Purpose

Christian leadership demands a purpose. Under the Lordship of Christ, we need to decide why we are here and where we are going. Doubts will come. In a world where the chances of things going wrong far exceed the likelihood of things going right, we can easily resign ourselves to failure. That is why we must continually reaffirm our purpose.

Prayer

Who can explain it? We have direct access to the Maker of the universe. He has gone before and follows behind. Call on Him, counsel with Him. In His Word, God continually invites us into His presence: "Call to me . . ."; "We have one who speaks to the Father in our defense—Jesus Christ, the Righteous One" (Jeremiah 33:3; 1 John 2:1). God's way of working is in answer to believing prayer!

Believe

Ours is the God who is *for* us! He is not playing games. Daily trust your life to Him. "The steps of a good man [woman] are ordered by the Lord" (Psalm 37:23 KJV). I have selected Psalm 32:8 as my life verse: "I will instruct you and teach you in the way you should go; I will counsel you and watch over you." Try it; it works!

CHAPTER 38

When It's Time to Retire

One of the facts of life in the Western world is retirement—the idea that at some particular time or age a person should leave his or her vocational or organizational responsibilities and "retire." Fifty years ago many people looked upon retirement as one of the goals of life. At the time it was seen as a just reward for a long and hard career. Visions of quiet days idled away by gentle streams or pleasant vistas were seen as very alluring.

Whether you are beginning to contemplate retirement yourself or whether you are a Christian executive who needs to help other people prepare for retirement, there is much more to the process than at first meets the eye. What you might have considered as primarily a question of finances or retirement plans out to be one of life's greatest transitions for many people.

We would like to consider retirement from the perspective of impact on the individual and steps we might take to make the transition an effective one.

All of our advertising keeps bombarding us with the idea that to be young is good and to be old is bad. If the same form of advertising was applied to the idea that to be white is good and to be black is bad, civil rights advocates would rise up in indignation all over the country. Perhaps one day the Gray Panthers will have their way with the media! Meanwhile, better face it, the emphasis on youth is probably not going to go away very soon.

Our society continually tries to brainwash itself to avoid the fact of death. Rather than death being viewed as a final climax to the productive life and an entrance into the presence of the King, death is seen as something to be avoided and glossed over. Old people are viewed as a sign of approaching death. Many people avoid them.[37]

The Organizational Security Blanket

Few of us recognize the sizeable feeling of security we gain from working within an organization.

First, it gives us a sense of place. We know who we are. We know where we fit. Have you ever noticed how people tend to introduce you? "I'd like you to meet Mr. Brown. He's with Christian Life International."

Second, it gives us leverage in the world. The organization will stand behind us in terms of credit ratings, social support (such things as life insurance and other fringe benefits), and in a host of other ways that we might never think of (passes to certain functions, an ability to travel, expense accounts, and so forth). When was the last time you combined a business meeting or trip with a social event?

Third, organizations give us a goal orientation. We share a common task with others in which we have a common responsibility and for which we feel a common drive. This gives us something to look forward to, as well as a feeling of accomplishment.

Fourth, a role in an organization gives us prestige, not only with our neighbors, but with ourselves. It's nice to know this building, this project, these people are what they are because of what we have been able to do (even with the Lord's help!).

Fifth, organizations give us an opportunity to help others, to feel responsible, to feel that we are needed.

Sixth, organizations permit us to relate as professionals to others. A pastor will naturally join a pastoral association. The Christian executive will look to others in a similar field, people with whom he or she can exchange information or with whom he or she may join a technical society.

The day you retire from an organization many of these things are removed. Now you are one individual "against the world." Your mobility may be greatly reduced, your sense of direction may be gone. Your feeling of self-worth may be greatly diminished.

Be Prepared

How do we cope with such a radical change? The first thing to do is to recognize that it does lie ahead. Be prepared.

In many ways, preparing for retirement is much like preparing to enter a new business. This is particularly true for the individual who has worked as part of a large organization. There is a whole list of questions to be faced:

1. What will you do for the remaining years of your life?

2. Where will you live?

3. What will be your relationships with your children?

4. What kind of environment should you be in?

5. What kind of lifestyle would you like to have?

6. What kind of lifestyle will you probably be forced to have? What will be your standard of living?

7. Can it (retirement) be postponed?

8. Can it be hastened?

These questions are an attempt to anticipate the kind of future we would like to have, to take the steps that will move us in that direction.

Have a Goal!

One of the most deadly enemies of life is a lack of purpose. Too many people set a goal to begin retirement, but no goal as to what they will accomplish or become as a result of retirement. Goals are powerful motivators. At 63 we need goals for 70. At 68 we need goals for 75.

Is there a book that you've always wanted to write? By beginning to gather background information on it and putting it aside while you're yet an active member of an organization, you will have a head start when you finally have the time to do the writing. Is there a new skill that you wanted to acquire "when you had the time"? Start doing research now on what schools might be available. You are going to be a different person than you are now. Although in many ways you are going to have physical limitations you did not have when you were younger, in other ways you will have experiences and capabilities to make you much more "valuable." Where do all of these changes fit?

Solutions

View this as a career change. In the same way that you would investigate your potential role in a new organization, investigate this new role you're going to play in society.

Consider what God has made you, what he has allowed you to become. If, as a Christian, you view your chief purpose to bring glory to Him, what is it He has taught you about yourself, others and the world that you might now use in some new and fresh way?

Analyze your lifestyle and standard of living; what is there about your present lifestyle sustained by the fact that you work for an organization? What part of it will have to change? What are your likes and dislikes? Perhaps you'll discover that there are a number of penalties to working in your present situation which may disappear when you retire. Perhaps you will have new interests. You may want to consider visiting the local university to take something like the Strong Aptitude Test which would give you some additional insight into things you would really like to do.

Plan financially. Many financial services companies will help you work through an analysis of your situation and then give you a picture of the possibilities of having the kind of future financially you would like to have. Their objective, of course, is to sell financial services, but it is worth the effort to begin to ask yourself some questions as to the level of income you expect to live on and whether any retirement plan that your organization has, social security, plus whatever other financial resources you have are going to be adequate. Investigate the many savings plans and retirement accounts available for self-employed people or for wives, plans that help you to postpone income tax costs until you are in a lower tax bracket.

This may also have something to say about your learning to be a manager of money. It's surprising how many of us who have been working on a salary all of our lives have really become used to letting our salaries control our expenses. Even men and women who do an excellent job of managing the finances of their companies often are poor personal finance managers. Perhaps you need to get some outside consulting help here.

Plan for it just as you would plan for entering your own business, for in one sense that is what you're doing. One solution many people have found worthwhile is to launch their own business. Perhaps there is a business you can start now, even while you are still working for the organization from which you will retire. This should be openly discussed by all concerned.

Try to "test it out" or prepare for it before it happens. Both the individual and the organization should consider ways of gradual transition rather than an abrupt change. For example, if you were going to get involved in your own business, perhaps you should gain your organization's permission (if needed) to start experimenting with a business like this now. Most businesses, crafts or hobbies have their own newsletters and journals. Go to the local library and find out what they are and then start subscribing to them.

Build bridges for the future by planning how the skills you have and will have in the future may be used by others. Take some of the aptitude tests and other tests available to help you over your particular talents and what you like to do. You may be amazed at the possibilities of a whole new career. Don't overlook the possibility of doing consulting for other organization similar to yours. This could be accomplished either by short-term visits or with perhaps two to three months spent as facilitator. The latter role is particularly useful in assisting other local church congregations.

Build up contacts and friendships for the type of life you are going to lead. If you are thinking of moving into a retirement unit, develop friendships with people living in such places. Find out the pros and cons. If you are a person who has always enjoyed being with people younger than yourself, perhaps you find it distressing to join the ranks of "senior citizens." On the other hand, many people enjoy the company of people their own age. Some people advocate moving into a retirement community even before one retires so that one can begin to establish lasting friendships. Many times people who postpone leaving a home they had lived in for many years find it increasingly difficult as the years go by.

The Advantages of Age

Old age has a lot of things going for it: wisdom about world and how things work, a broad knowledge of its different aspects, the "experience" of having made mistakes, a greater tolerance for others which results in a greater ability to love and understand. Many people become more patient as they grow older, although it is a well-known phenomenon that as we approach the end of life, we tend to exhibit many of the personality traits we may have covered up during early and mid-life.

Weigh the advantages of advancing years. Your lifetime of experience may be exactly what's needed to move another person along the road of increased effectiveness.

The Role of the Christian Organization

Most Christians do respect the wisdom that comes with years, so at least we have some advantage over the non-Christian. However, as a Christian executive responsible for people who are approaching retirement in your organization, how much can be done to pave the way, so that "retirement" becomes a milestone along the way and not the entrance to nonpersonhood?

First, and most obvious, is the need for assistance in financial planning. An organization can take the lead in helping its staff think through their financial situations and to the extent that is possible, provide them with a retirement plan to meet their needs. It is surprising how many Christian organizations have retirement plans about which the employee can only learn with a great deal of digging. Any retirement plan should give the staff members a yearly report on his or her anticipated income at the time of retirement.

Second, provide awareness of the problems of retirement. It is all too easy to lull ourselves to sleep by imagining how great it's going to be not to *have* to work, rather than to realize that is at the very core of life.

Third, consider retirement education, starting no later than five years before the mandatory age for retirement within your organization. This might take the form of encouraging staff members to take applicable courses in nearby schools, to provide them with literature from some of the senior citizens' societies like the American Association of Retired Persons.

Fourth, consider ways of continuing to employ key people who have passed the mandatory retirement age. There are a number of ways to do this. Many seminaries renew the contract with their faculty on a year-by-year basis. Others find new consultative assignments for their retirees, many times rehiring the individual as a consultant. If it fits in with the plans of the employee, many times there will be specific assignments he or she can continue to do on a part-time basis.

Fifth, consider whether mandatory retirement is really to the advantage of your organization. There is a good deal of discussion about this subject, and we realize that there are many pros and cons. Some people feel that older people need to be moved along to make room for younger people. Contrariwise, a growing organization often needs all the mature leadership it can find.

Sixth, make sure you are not building a financial trap for yourself in the name of Christian commitment. For example, most churches now realize that by giving their pastor a parsonage, they have kept him or her from accumulating equity in a home for retirement years. If low salaries are part and parcel of your organizational structure, then perhaps you need to consider a retirement program that provides an unusually high percentage of retirement income.

Part Nine

LEADERS AT HOME

CHAPTER 39

The Executive and the Family

It is our profound conviction that there are three levels of priority for the Christian, and the relationship between these priorities is of prime importance. These priorities relate to the whole structure of our relationships, including our relationship to our family.

Our first priority is obviously God through Christ. The Bible leaves no room for disagreement here. Our commitment to God must be ultimate (Matthew 22:36–37).

The second level of priority is not so universally appreciated. The Bible calls us first to a commitment to God, but second to a commitment to one another. The biblical concept is that the work of Christ is carried out by His church, not by individuals (Ephesians 4:12). Indeed, the New Testament focuses primarily upon the relationship of believers to one another and to the world, rather than to the work they are to carry out.

A third level of commitment is to the work of Christ. And yet it is clear from Ephesians 4 that this work is to flow forth from a unique combination of gifts given to individuals for the building up of the body of Christ.

What effect does success have on a person? As an individual rises to a place of leadership in an organization and becomes conscious of making significant contributions to the growth and welfare of the organization, the work can become more and more exciting. Past successes generate enthusiasm for new ventures. We can easily become stretched beyond our own capabilities. Fatigue, and its accompanying sense of despair, can drive us on to new endeavors, rather than warn us to slow down. Beware.

Success can also produce tension between a husband and wife. Are both partners going in the same direction? Is the wife or husband of the Christian executive called to the same work? Traditionally, when a pastor has been called to a church, the congregation has assumed the wife was part of the package. The wife was seen as an extension of her husband. This view is more and more being rejected by younger wives. On the other hand, organizational wives are often viewed as a source of discontentment and potential gossip. How is your partner viewed? Where does he or she fit into your success?

If you are one of those men or women whose life is completely centered around the work to which God has called you, then we would suggest the need for an ongoing reevaluation of your commitment to the body of Christ, and particularly to your family. Use those same skills that have brought you success in your organization to evaluate the health of your family. Here are a number of areas that you may want to consider.

1) *Your appointment book.* Most of us put down in our appointment books those engagements that have the highest priority in our lives. Are your spouse and your children down in your appointment book? If your wife and your children analyzed the way you are spending your time on the basis of your appointment book, would they feel that they have a significant priority in your life? Have you taken your teenage son or daughter out to lunch recently? Perhaps your schedule is full this month, so plan ahead!

2) *Your understanding of your call.* Have you shared this with your family? They need to understand what it is you do and why you do it. It is amazing how many children have misconceptions of their parents' work. Have you let your children spend the day with you at work? Have you ever walked them through your organization's facilities and explained to them how things work? What about taking your children on a business trip? If you are a person who is required to do a considerable amount of traveling, what about saving ahead so that your wife can accompany you on some of these trips? She can see what you do first hand, meet some of the people you go to see, and experience some of the travel stresses you have.

3) *Times with the family.* Too many executives take their work into their homes with the result that the "work" is quickly viewed by the children as competition with them. Many executives and pastors encourage people to contact them at home, with the result that the family can develop a "them and us" mentality. This is a particular problem for the pastor. Careful attention must be given to protect times with the family.

Once this time is secured, it needs to be quality time. It is all too easy to be in each other's presence without really experiencing each other's person. This may require considerable advance planning for such things as an evening of games, a day away at a park or beach, or some other mutually enjoyable experience. Take a look at your children's calendars. Are there going to be special times like ballgames in which they are participating or other events that they would like you to attend? Older children in school or away from home still need you too, even though at times they may not seem like it.

4) *Family devotional time.* This is an area that can quickly be neglected by the Christian leader with "greater" responsibilities. It becomes especially difficult when times of family worship and prayer are viewed as something "we have to do because of Dad's work." Visit your local Christian bookstore for help here. Don't assume that because you're an effective pastor or because you're a well-known speaker you have insight into what would be appropriate for children and families. Many good books are available to give you creative ways to make these times fun and worthwhile.

5) *Vacation times.* In the type of merry-go-round world in which we live, our only defense against the unbearable number of demands placed upon us is to start planning into our lives those things which we believe would be honoring God and healthful to ourselves and to our families. Compare your calendar with your spouse's and children's. What do they tell you about the way you're spending your time? When can you set aside extended time to be alone with you family and build into each other's lives?

A Christian executive shared with us his frustrations of being so involved with his work that his family always suffered. No matter how hard he tried, he arrived home each evening still full of the day's problems. He tried the suggestion of leaving his worries on a "Worry Tree" in the front yard. It didn't work.

Finally, he sensed the Lord was telling him he was going about it in the wrong way. Rather than empty his mind of his concerns, he saw that he should fill it with thoughts of his family. His drive home was about five miles. He picked out conspicuous landmarks along the way and associated them with specific members of his family. As he passed each one he tried to imagine what that family member would have been doing that day, what special concerns he would have, or what she would like to discuss with him that evening.

By the time he walked up the front path his mind was full of his family. Now the cries of "Dad's home" began to take on new significance. As he expressed it, Dad was really home, and the family knew it.

The most important part of God's creation is people. Relationships are what life is all about. No matter how high our spiritual calling, the basis of our effectiveness is our effectiveness as members of the mystical body called the church, and the love we have for one another. If you are looking for a measure of your effectiveness, check out the love life within your family.

CHAPTER 40

When Did You Leave Your Family?

Ironically, one of the last dangers you encounter as an effective leader is the peril of becoming too involved—too committed to the task at hand rather than the duties at heart. Once you've proven to others how well the organization gets along with your leadership, you must then prove to yourself and your family how well it gets along without your leadership.

What good is a leader who steers the organization toward success but runs over friends and loved ones in the process? What good is a leader who propels the group to new heights of achievement and leaves the family behind? These possibilities are all too real. That's why every arriving leader needs to consider the question, When did you leave your family?

Not long ago the pastor of a large Los Angeles area church was interviewing men for his staff. He asked when they would like to take a day off during the week. He got several different replies: "Oh, it doesn't really matter." "I never take a day off." "I don't really need any time off." The pastor hired none of them.

Then he interviewed another young prospect. "What day of the week would you like off?"

"Well, I surely don't want Monday off. After the Sunday crunch, I'm in no shape to enjoy the next day. Let me have Thursday off. That's the best day of the week for me." That young man was hired.

Many ministers work 12 to 15 hours a day, and some rarely take a day off. What is so meritorious about working seven days a week and never taking off any time to rest and be with your family? God condemned the pagans of old for sacrificing their children on what they considered a religious altar. Does He feel any different about us today?

Marijuana Low

It was a cold, rainy night. My son Gordon, then 21 years old, finally came home around 1:00 a.m., after a long night of smoking marijuana with his friends. I was livid, embarrassed, distraught, and afraid. How could this young man whom we loved so much do this to his mother and me? It wasn't fair; it wasn't right. It was happening to other parents, but who would have ever thought it would have reared its ugly head in the Engstrom family?

We couldn't understand why. But this particular evening I held my peace, even though I had a mind to give Gordon a tongue lashing he'd never forget. I listened to him as he shouted that most Christians were phonies, the church was filled with hypocrites, and there were at least a hundred ways to God. And on and on he went.

The more I listened, the more something began to happen inside me. After a while, I no longer saw a son whose head was clouded from the effects of pot. Instead, I began to hear him. Even though I didn't—and don't—approve of anyone's using drugs for recreational purposes, I knew that much of what Gordon had to say was true. The distance between us was real.

I can remember a hot tear falling on my cheek, then another and another as Gordon spoke. I knew in my head he was also talking about me. I only tell you this story to say that although that winter evening in January 1968 was difficult, humiliating, and upsetting, I think it may have been the first night I really listened to my son. In a fresh, new way, I was establishing a real relationship with Gordon—one that had been sacrificed in my rush to serve the families of other people. In serving others, I had left my own family behind. And now I was going back to meet this one beautiful and important member.

When did you leave your family?

Help Unmet

Bill Edwards was 38 years old. He had a pretty wife, two beautiful children, and was considered one of the outstanding pastors in the city. Bill and June were married while Bill was still in seminary. Their first child was born during his senior year. June never completed her college education but took a job to help Bill through seminary. Bill became an effective preacher and was greatly respected by both his assistant and the congregation. He worked hard on his sermons for a growing congregation. But because of a misplaced priority, Bill's wife left him at the height of his career.

Why? What went wrong?

Of all the human relationships described in the Bible, the highest and most significant is the one found in marriage. The apostle Paul could only compare it to the relationship of Christ and His church (see Ephesians 5:22–33).

The disruption of this relationship creates tremendous spiritual repercussions. Peter tells us troubles in the relationship can even interfere with our prayers (see 1 Peter 3:7).

If you're married, is your ministry as a leader built upon the foundation of a strong marriage relationship, or does your work move forward in spite of your relationship with your spouse?

You may respond in your own defense, "But this is the work God has called me to! My spouse understands that. That's one of the sacrifices we are making together."

Perhaps. But perhaps that is your view of the situation, and although it may be outwardly shared by your mate, inwardly—consciously or unconsciously—your loved one may feel quite differently.

I think two of the most important decisions a person makes in life are: first, the decision to accept Christ as a spiritual mate, and second, the decision to accept another human being as a physical mate. Here is something to be prayed through to make sure this is what you want to live with. I have seen so many leaders who have been irreparably hurt because they didn't have a mate who was supporting them. I have seen couples, each with his or her own personal agenda and ambitions. They were not a team. Each was pulling in different directions.

The teamwork of a husband and wife in the ministry is terribly important. This is not to say, for example, that a man and wife should have a comparable prominence in the public setting. But each needs to be fully supportive of the other. The most successful leaders I have seen are those who had good, solid, successful marriages, whether it's a Billy Graham or Cliff Barrows. And I've seen others who have struggled. One of Satan's most effective traps is to bring discord to a marriage. But the emergence of this problem only underscores the need for those who serve the bride of Christ to respect, love, and cherish the one they have married.

Homebound Sabbatical

I'm impressed by the example of my friend, James Dobson, founder of Focus on the Family. At one point in his career, Jim took seven years off with no speaking engagements in order to spend time with his daughter and his son; he wanted to be home with his family. After the seven years came to an end he gradually began to appear in public rallies. Dr. Dobson saw the need in his life and met it. That's a rare insight today.

New Directions

Ever since World War II, we've seen a sustained effort to diminish the importance of morals and family relationships. But this new morality is not new—it's older than Noah's ark—and it is not moral—it's contrary to everything that perpetuates a stable society. Leaders who face the twenty-first century still need the value system and priority structure that has proven itself for centuries.

I confess that my family life is not what I enjoyed as a youngster growing up. Even when we started raising our family, it was much different. For example, the day of the family devotion is almost past. Dorothy and I have only recently, in the last several years, resurrected our devotional life together. We've had our own personal devotions, but once again we're reading and praying together.

In this American Christian society we seldom talk together as families. We have different meal hours, and we eat sitting in front of the television set. Many parents are so preoccupied with their favorite TV show they don't tuck their kids into bed anymore. And what ever happened to family vacations?

Even the church divides the family. Rarely do you see everyone sitting together in the church service. There's a junior church, senior night, Sunday school, and nursery school. Then we try to patch it all back together with an occasional "family night."

First Things First

How do you sort it all out? Where do your Christian priorities lie? How does one find a balance between commitment to the Lord and the family? We can answer these questions by first understanding the meaning of *priority*.

Some view priority in terms of putting one thing before something else. Others may think of ranking items.

Priorities have both a *when* and an *if*. All priority questions are first about *when*? We are faced with whether we are going to do an activity first, second, third, or perhaps never. By assigning such time ratings to events, we essentially put them in terms of priorities—what we are going to do when.

This comes from our need to choose the future over the past. Priorities should be determined by what lies ahead rather than what lies behind. Over the Archives Building in Washington, D.C., is the Shakespearean phrase *What Is Past Is Prologue*. This says it well.

Here is a list of questions you might want to consider in establishing priorities:

1. How urgent is it? When must it be done? Does it have to be done right now, today, soon, or someday? When you ask this question, you may discover that something doesn't have to be done at all!

2. How important is it? Very important? Quite important? Somewhat important? Not so important? Note there is always a tension between the important and the urgent. But it is the urgent things that keep getting in the way of the important things, is it not? We are always faced with those things that have to be done "right now." The urgent often turns out to be the enemy of the important.

3. How often must it be done? Is it something that's done every day? Only occasionally? Or just sometimes? This will give us some insight as to how dependent we are on this event's occurrence.

4. Can someone else or some other organization do it just as well? The answer might be no, perhaps, or yes. If the answer is yes, perhaps we should not be involved at all, but should turn the idea and suggestion over to some other committee, department, or organization.

5. Is it part of a larger task to which we are committed? Very often we can get involved in goals that are attractive for the moment, but that really have nothing to do with our organization. This is probably the most subtle trap of all. How easy it is to get involved in interesting projects that really do not relate to where we hope our ministry is moving!

6. What will happen if it's not done at all? What will happen if we abandon this whole goal? Disaster? Trouble? Difficulty? Nothing? If nothing will happen, perhaps we have a clue that we shouldn't be involved in it in the first place.

7. Is this the best way? There will always be alternatives. But after we have decided upon one, we need to ask this final question.

There are many priority questions for you as a leader. For the Christian organization there is the question of which purpose—of all the possible ministries with which we could become involved—is the one God wants for our organization?

Once we become involved in a ministry, we face the question of a choice between goals. Thus, of all the things that we could do to carry out the ministry, which seem most important to us now? Which should be postponed? Which should be abandoned? We can also think of priorities in terms of allegiance. What claims the highest priority in our lives?

The primary question should always be: Will this bring glory to God? Then we need to consider:

1. We can't minister to everyone. To whom do we want to minister?

2. We can't do everything. What must we do first?

3. We can't be everything. What is most important to me at this time?

Because both needs and situations change, these questions must be asked again and again. The cycle continues. We will face new problems and receive new information about the world in which we are working. Thus, we need to review our priorities continually.

Posteriorities

You have undoubtedly already learned that organizations have a tremendous amount of natural inertia. Once individuals have been assigned to a task, and suborganizations such as boards or committees or departments have been formed, the groups tend to generate lives of their own. It is easy to stop asking, What is the goal of the Christian Education Committee this year? and start wondering, What should we do this year?

What we all need are posteriorities, statements of things that we are not going to do this year. Picture an organization as an alligator—it has a great tendency to grow a very large tail. Periodically someone needs to chop off the tail, so the alligator can keep moving! Perhaps we need a committee to decide each year which 10 percent of all the things we did last year we are not going to do again this year.

With this understanding of the process, I'd like to recommend these priorities for serving the family of God and man:

1. God first

2. Family second

3. Fellow Christians third

4. Work of Christ fourth.

Workaholism

One of the devil's favorite elixirs for blurring priorities and dissolving family unity is workaholism—especially in the church. Studies today cite that members of the clergy occupy one of the most stressful positions in the American labor force.

As a pastor you may be convinced you are married to the church. But let me bring you in on a little secret: the church is already married. That's what the Bible says. In the New Testament the church is pictured as the Bride of Christ. The minister must heed the instruction of Scripture. "But if any provide not for his own, and specially for those of his own house, he hath denied the faith, and is worse than an infidel" (1 Timothy 5:8 KJV). There is no exemption from family obligations and responsibilities.

Such a provision indeed may include much more than physical or financial support. If the pastor is overworked, why not reset priorities and share with the congregation the decision to place the family above the church? People in the pews will accept the pastor even more readily for this humanness. They face the same problem and will appreciate this example of guidance and courage.

Pastors, when on a vacation, shouldn't preach! They should provide for a change of pace by doing things that are not part of their regular routine. It is vital to give the mind and body a chance to regroup and recharge itself.

Many pastors, without necessarily intending to do so, convey the view by their own work habits, or by preaching, that church work must always have the highest priority in the lives of everyone. If not, people are often made to feel guilty because they have a split commitment. The message comes through, "Ye cannot serve God and mammon." This obviously is true, but the truth gets garbled through misinterpretation and false priorities.

One family was seldom seen in the evening service at church. On several occasions the pastor heard family members being put down indirectly with such remarks as, "My, Bob and Jane, we missed you last Sunday night." Little did people realize that this wise pastor had given counsel to the family. Bob traveled a great deal during the week on his job. As a result he saw very little of his family.

One day, feeling guilty, he stopped by the pastor's study. "Pastor, I know I should come to the evening services, but I feel the need to be with my family on Sunday evenings."

The pastor wisely advised him to stay home. "Bob," said the minister, "stay home as long as you use the time to be with your family." That minister had rightly resolved the issue without creating any guilt for his friend.

Dr. C. Peter Wagner, former professor of Latin American affairs at Fuller Theological Seminary in Pasadena, California, confessed in a published magazine article to being a converted workaholic. He says that some time ago he had an excruciating headache that lasted for 70 days and 69 nights. He sought spiritual counsel and looked to the Bible for help. He related the following:

> During the ordeal I was under excellent medical treatment. I put myself under the care of a highly competent chiropractor, consulting also with a medical doctor to be sure I was not missing any better option. The chiropractor studied a series of X-rays and used a combination of unintelligible polysyllables to describe what was wrong with my muscles, bones and nerves. Three or four visits per week to his clinic, exercise and diets eventually corrected certain structural defects. But my problem went deeper.[38]

After much soul-searching and spiritual examination, Wagner came to the conclusion that his problem was really very simple. He had been working too hard!

He continued:

> Simple? Who ever heard of God punishing someone for working too hard? I was always taught that work was a virtue. Would God be angry with someone who gave too much to the poor?[39]

Wagner resolved such questions in his mind and came to realize, before it was too late, that there is a price one pays when the addiction to work sets in. He was one of the fortunate ones. Today the term workaholic is a daily vocabulary word to him.

Wagner goes on in the article to show how he had fallen into the typical trap of most workaholics, the praise that goes along with hard work. The usual pattern, he confessed, was hearing people comment, "I don't see how you possibly get done all that you do." That, he says, is the supreme pat on the back for the workaholic, and since such a person craves to hear it as a reward, the workaholic will work all the harder to get it. Wagner confessed this pride in productivity.

> Wasn't I proud of propelling myself out of bed and into high gear at 4:30 every morning? Wasn't I proud that while my neighbors were sleeping at 5:00 a.m. (imagine!) I was out in the street run-

ning a mile? Wasn't I proud of the number of books and articles I could get published in a year? Wasn't I proud of my ability to bring work home and continue through the evening with only a brief interruption for dinner? Wasn't I proud of foregoing vacations year after year so that I could produce more? Wasn't I proud of the number of miles I could travel and speaking engagements I could handle without a break? Wasn't I proud of dictating fat envelopes of tapes on airplanes and shipping them home to my secretary? Wasn't I proud that when I would land in some exotic country I would invariably choose to work rather than take in the tourist attractions?

Without the headache, I never would have realized what harmful effects this was having on me. I had developed strong guilt feelings about doing anything that would interrupt work. I could not stay in bed more than six hours, would not watch television, could not plan days off or weekends without productive work, and felt uncomfortable when I would go for a drive with the family. I envied some of my friends who could function on only four hours of sleep. But even worse, I found myself judging others for spending their time in such unproductive ways. Imagine, watching the movie on an airplane rather than dictating letters! Through it all, of course, I easily rationalized it as "serving God," a simple process for a clergyman, but handy also for almost any Christian workaholic.[40]

One of the most important words in our English language is balance. Extremes or tangents in any area of our lives may well create confusion and distress. Balance is one of the basic keys the workaholic needs to restore. In the Gospel of Luke, the apostle, commenting about Jesus' childhood, wrote, "And Jesus increased in wisdom and stature, and in favour with God and man" (Luke 2:52 KJV).

Notice that Jesus dedicated His first years to living a healthy, balanced life. Physically, intellectually, emotionally and spiritually there was growth because all levels of His life were integrated, thus, balanced. He combined all the basic elements needed for a disciplined and well-rounded life. He wants to do the same for us. Dr. John R. W. Stott states it plainly in his book, *Balanced Christianity*: "It seems that there is almost no pastime the devil enjoys more than tipping Christians off balance."[41]

Serve the Family by Serving Yourself

Workaholism is only one way to leave a family behind. Over and above the obvious tragedy of divorce, there are many other ways for a leader to turn away from the followers.

Most of these estrangements trace back to one familiar cause, self-neglect. People are not a consumable product; they are a renewable resource. But all too often we act as if we could spend our entire life breathing out power without ever stopping to inhale strength.

What kind of strength does a leader need?

Recreation is one strength we need. We get so busy that we don't take time for physical exercise. For me it's golf. For others it may be tennis. Others enjoy running. I think these are scriptural. Paul talks about fitness in running and racing. We know our bodies are the temple of the Holy Spirit. What kind of structure can a leader build with weak materials?

Then we need *friendships*. What happens when a leader turns away from lasting friendships? Ours is a mobile society, and it's harder to build friendships on the move. But effective leaders need many friends. I've had the privilege of meeting with a group of associates and close friends for over two decades. Every May, Dorothy and I meet with six of these couples for a weekend together someplace across the country to renew our warm fellowship and acquaintance. For us, anything less would be a form of abandonment.

We need to be *reading*. Millions have left the enduring words of a book for the flickering screen of a television set. But advice, orders, instruction, warning and encouragement all wait on the printed page. I love to read, and I love to encourage others to do the same. For example, I've willed my set of the Harvard Classics to one of my grandsons who's an avid reader. But first I'm going through them over the next couple of years myself. I've got the whole set, and I want to see what great writing is. Why be one of those who would leave the collective wisdom of the entire civilized world waiting in the next room for an entire lifetime? Leaders are readers; and readers are leaders.

We mustn't neglect *fellowship*. To neglect fellowship is to neglect the lifeblood of leadership. Why should anyone follow a leader without knowing positively that that person really cares for his or her needs and well-being? And how can a leader communicate such interest without fellowship? Maybe it's the plain, old-fashioned ice cream social experience. Perhaps it's a formal gathering. Maybe it's a large group, or a small face-to-face encounter. A leader in touch is a leader involved is a leader in control.

And don't forget *dating*. Date your spouse. Never forget to fill his or her life with fond memories. Take a trip. Go shopping. See a good play. *Forget that you're a leader and be a lover.*

These may seem like harmless electives in life. But when a leader ignores the fuels that regenerate personal effectiveness, that leader is walking away from a primary responsibility to self. And you cannot leave yourself without leaving the family that relies upon you.

If you can leave these priorities, there's another related danger. When did you leave your first love? Remember the clarity of your call to be a servant, a witness, a pastor or an evangelist? When did you leave that driving desire to give your best to God? It doesn't happen overnight. It's a gradual thing we all have to guard against.

Family Members Left Behind

If the shepherds have difficulty in keeping their family priorities in line, what of the sheep?

Today, it appears that we have a strong bent towards institutionalizing our elderly. We've put the pain aside so we don't have to make priorities out of less than productive members of our family. What a tragedy!

Family decline has become a virtual cliché in modern society. But what are the implications for the future as the years go by and our population ages? The realities of this situation—both for today and for tomorrow—should motivate all Christian leaders to keep their own houses in order.

Life expectancy in 1900 was 47. Today, it's 72 for men and 77 for women. The United States now has 30 million people age 65 and older, 2.5 million of whom are age 80 or more according to Stanley Brody, a gerontologist at the University of Pennsylvania. About 12 percent of the population will be older than 65 by the year 2000 with approximately 5 million of these more than 80 years old.

Although many senior citizens are not significantly disabled, one out of six—more than 5 million people age 65 or older—needs help with such daily activities as bathing, cooking, dressing, grooming and stair climbing. About 1.5 million have five or more of these limitations and require long-term care.

The rapid increase in this functionally limited population has created what experts on aging call "parent care." Many seniors' children in their 40s, 50s and 60s face the dilemma of paying $35,000 a year to place a parent in a qualified nursing home, of putting the parent in a substandard nursing home, or of absorbing the emotional and economic costs of caring for the parent in their own homes according to Robert Binstock, a Case Western Reserve University gerontologist. Many families are quietly going broke.

The average nursing home patient is an 82–year-old widow who has three or more chronic disabilities. The most common are heart and circulatory diseases, arthritis, rheumatism, and diabetes.

A National Academy of Sciences report says 50 percent or more have some mental or behavioral problem, attributable to Alzheimer's disease, depression, or psychosis. Many are so demented they cannot express pain or complain of thirst or hunger. Others are isolated by deafness or blindness.

Women in these institutions outnumber men three to one.

In trendsetting California, only 15 percent of those in long-term care are able to walk on their own; 79 percent need help dressing; 86 percent, with bathing, 39 percent, with feeding; and 29 percent, with toilet functions.

Seventy percent of the patients do not have a spouse, and at least one-fourth have no relatives whatsoever. Of those three-fourths who do have relatives, more than half of them received no visitors in a one-year period.

As the years glide into the future, these trends will only intensify. The need for correct priorities starts right at home with a leader's own family members.

Priority Primer

1. Take care of your own life before you offer to take care of the lives of others.

2. Serve your own family before serving the family of others.

3. Answer the Seven Selective Questions when placing first things first.

4. Use "Posteriorities" to sort out what you don't want to achieve.

5. Work at ridding yourself of workaholism.

6. Remember the importance of recreation, friendships, reading, fellowship, dating, and other true priorities.

7. Prepare now to give priority to aging members of your family.

Throughout this chapter we've examined the importance of well-placed priorities. This skill—the ability to balance the needs of God, family, friends, strangers and self—is one of the final touchstones of a true leader. For without it, leadership is reduced to little more than an endless stream of cold, unfeeling orders.

When did you leave your family behind? No matter what the answer may have been, last year, yesterday or an hour ago, the one reply I'm most anxious to hear is something similar to "Never again!" Without the strong support of our family and friends, you and I cannot face the years ahead with confidence. But with that support, all things become possible. I sincerely hope you are well supplied with this source of strength as we contemplate a scenario for the twenty-first century, the subject of the Epilogue.

The Future:
A Scenario for the Twenty-First Century

W hat I've shared with you throughout these chapters is a prelude to a far more important race. The ideas, the experiences, the Scriptures we have shared about leadership all have the potential for helping you lead into the future.

Maybe those of us passing the torch of leadership and those who seize it can run with greater determination if we consider a dark scenario. What would be the consequences if this torch should fall to the ground, its light going out forever? Let's contrast the sinister outcome of failure with the joyous outcome of success in this team effort of passing humanity's most important torch.

Shove Thy Neighbor

Without the light of a divine Father who created all men as brothers, the plans of Hitler, Idi Amin and Colonel Kaddafi all make sense. "Why put up with anyone who thinks differently? My way is best, so let my enemies perish," they reason. The Khmer Rouge found it convenient to shove their uncooperative neighbors out into the killing fields. There are those who would do the same in South America, Central America, the Caribbean, Eastern Europe, South Africa, and elsewhere.

What kind of light is needed in these shadows?

I was impressed some time ago by two African friends of mine who so beautifully exemplify the power of unity. One is a white South African and the other is a black Ugandan. They are Bishop Festo Kivengere of Uganda, and Michael Cassidy, a native of South Africa, the founding head of *African Enterprise*. They work together, in spite of the intense friction between white South Africans and black Africans. Yet these men are close friends and they have enjoyed highly successful joint ministries in many parts of the world. I have had the privilege of being with them on many occasions as they ministered together in services and meetings.

I recall one evening when I served as the master of ceremonies at a well attended dinner. Mike and Festo shared in the program. I was sitting between them. Mike's water glass was empty. He was about to get up to speak. He asked Festo if he might drink the rest of Festo's glass of water. Without either of them thinking twice, Mike finished the water from Festo's glass! For me that symbolic act said it all. They are truly brothers.

This type of relationship is not natural for us human beings. It has to be taught, modeled, and spotlighted with the torch of truth.

Through a Glass Darkly

Paul mentioned that even Christians "see through a glass, darkly" (1 Corinthians 13:12 KJV). But what of the godless world?

In 1775 Patrick Henry proclaimed a belief that went down in history beside his other sentiments about "liberty or death." When asked of the future, he replied, "I know of no way of judging the future but by the past." Certainly that is the case for all who reject divine revelation about the future. Isaiah spoke of sinners who "stumble at noon day as in the night" (Isaiah 59:10 KJV).

God plagued the Egyptians with physical darkness to remind them of their spiritual confusion. He promises to do the same thing once again in the modern world. "And the fifth angel poured out his vial upon the seat of the beast; and his kingdom was full of darkness; and they gnawed their tongues for pain" (Revelation 16:10 KJV). This is physical darkness. Imagine the pain of spiritual blackness.

But with the beacon of God's Word we know the joy, the clarity and the confidence about our future. "Then your light shall dawn in the darkness, and your darkness shall be as the noonday" (Isaiah 58:10 NKJV).

How could we ever let the light of the gospel grow dim?

Disunity

Christ warned against the danger of division. "If a house be divided against itself, that house cannot stand" (Mark 3:25 KJV).

Modern humanism, New Age secularism and scientism run wild today along with heresy and other spiritual infections. Such ideologies affect the body of Christ by creating disunity, disloyalty and rivalries among Christian brothers. And they exact their toll against the effective carrying out of the Great Commission. Add to this the lack of clear definition by some evangelical groups and agencies as to goals, strategies, methods, and programs that need to be employed to fulfill Christ's command, and the problems become further exacerbated.

Other divisions arise over diverse understanding about the end time. Obviously there are differing views among believers as to eschatology. But certainly there is no reason for Christians to despair because ominous clouds envelope our world and threaten total destruction. The increase of evil need not darken our spirits either, for God's righteousness will prevail. "Where sin increased, grace increased all the more" (Romans 5:20).

The Christian accepts the darkness of world conditions, but at the same time is able to relax about the future because the Word of God clearly reveals that God is in control of history and truth. The Word clearly teaches that righteousness will triumph. The book of Revelation closes on a victorious note. This does not mean mankind will escape severe judgment, but we know God will vindicate Himself and His faithful followers.

Though great upheavals may sweep the religious world, the biblical Christian has marching orders that must not fail. We cannot escape the truth. God has commissioned us to preach the gospel to the end of history as we may know it. This is part of His plan; for God wills that no individual should perish. It is encouraging to know God is raising up vast numbers of Christians who can, by virtue of His power within, be instruments of hope and salvation amid confusion and despair.

My eschatology is broad. I believe the Lord could come very soon, and I often pray, "even so come, Lord Jesus." But whether it's 1 year, 10, 100, or even a 1,000, our job remains unchanged. We all have but one lifetime to serve the Lord.

The Power of Unity

As Christians our hope for the future is unity. This was never more evident nor more clearly manifested than during the days of first believers. Truly this was one of the remarkable features of the early Christian church at Jerusalem. This was true in spite of the great diversity among them. Unity was there because of daily vigilance. The early Christian leaders constantly exhorted the Christian community with this urgent need.

The early church expressed herself in the prevailing view that there was only one church or body of Christ. Diversity of gifts was recognized, but these believers viewed all Christians as one with each other. This enabled them to minister effectively—so much so that Luke records in Acts 17:6 that they "turned the world upside down."

In Acts this unity was expressed in various ways. It was clearly seen by the depth and warmth of Christian fellowship, both at worship and in their homes. It was expressed by sharing with those less fortunate. The early church welcomed outsiders and outcasts. Their homes were always open to their brothers in the faith.

Some of this may have been a carry-over from Jewish tradition and culture. From childhood, believers were taught a strong social consciousness. The Torah laid great emphasis upon welcoming the stranger and sojourner. The early church was bound together into closely knit families of spiritual fellowship that continually reached out to the needy. The effect of this unity of fellowship was a mighty force for carrying out the church's mission of evangelization.

This emphasis on unity did not cease with the book of Acts. It was also stressed by the Apostles in their writings. But it is nowhere better expressed than by the term that Paul often used, "We are laborers together with God" (1 Corinthians 3:9 KJV). He was talking about partnership. The apostle addressed himself to this issue on many occasions (see 1 Corinthians 12:15–16, 21).

This same unity has preserved the church through Roman persecution, the Dark Ages, industrialization, world wars and the space age. It can also preserve us against the gates of hell, better known as the nuclear age. But the burning question every torchbearer for Christ must answer is, How many unreached peoples will suffer because of our inability to reach the world soon enough?

Are we Christian evangelists doing enough to support each other in the common effort?

Equality, support and mutual acceptance mean we in the West cannot think quite so much of the senior/junior relationship we often adopt when considering fellow Christian workers from other nations. We must use our gifts to supplement and complement each other. This may not necessarily be two people working together. It could be a whole body of leaders and members of the congregation who share in mission, contributing their various gifts. One might have the gift of teaching, another the gift of evangelism, another the gift of administration, another of giving help and support. Whatever the gift, all contribute meaningfully in a partnership that is coequal, even though individual talents and gifts may differ. It would be wrong to attempt to qualify the gifts God has given to us and say one gift is stronger or more important than another. Partnership means everyone who shares in the ministry of evangelism or church growth makes valid and acceptable contributions to the joint ministry according to individual callings.

It is an attractive model to see an African, an Asian, and a European working together in evangelism.

The Mongolian Connection

Several years before attending the International Congress on World Evangelization at Lausanne, Switzerland, in 1974, I had heard a student of world missions say that to our knowledge there were no Christians in Outer Mongolia in northern China. The statement of this fact impressed me, and I began praying for people in that part of the world. I had never prayed for them before, having never really thought about that great sweep of land south of Asiatic Russia being in need of the Light.

At the Lausanne Congress each morning in the large auditorium nearly 4,000 delegates from 150 different nations shared in a Bible study for about 30 minutes. Each day there was a different leader from a different part of the world who brought the Bible message from the book of Acts, illustrating how God had mightily worked in that first century church. One morning the Bible lesson leader might be a European, the next an African, another day an Asian, the next a Latin, until all people had been represented.

Following each of these messages we, as delegates, would gather in small groups of 8 or 10 throughout that great hall to counsel and talk together concerning what we had heard. Then we prayed together for 20 or 25 minutes.

One morning, as my wife, Dorothy, and I were seated in our group, I noticed a distinguished Chinese gentleman. We began getting acquainted in our group and I asked this man for his name and where he came from. With a smile, he said, "I am the only delegate here in this Congress from Outer Mongolia." Immediately I reached across the back of my chair and hugged him. I must have frightened him by such emotion, and I'm certain he didn't know what was happening. Then I told him I had been praying for people in Outer Mongolia and I was thrilled to meet someone from that country. He showed me his Bible, which was in the Mongol language with Chinese characters. He was extremely proud of it because there are very few Bibles available in his language. I asked him what his present responsibilities were. He told me he was living in Kaoshuong, in southern Taiwan, and that he was producing a 15–minute radio broadcast each day that was being beamed shortwave from Taiwan into Outer Mongolia. I could hardly believe my ears!

I asked him, "Are there many Christians there now?" He replied, "Oh, yes. There are literally scores, and more people are being converted to Christ all the time." We talked further and he shared with me his anticipation that there would soon be a strong moving of the Spirit of God among his people.

What a thrill for me! Here I thought the people for whom I had been praying were locked behind tightly closed doors. God was so gracious to give me some confirmation of answered prayer by allowing me to meet the only delegate from Mongolia among those thousands of delegates from around the world! Here he was—a fellow torchbearer—in our little group of 10 who prayed together that morning!

And now the Presbyterian and the Evangelical Alliance Mission radio stations in Seoul, Korea, are beaming the gospel daily by shortwave into Mongolia as well.

This revelation was not the only fruit of that conference in 1974. What was perceived as a single conference of evangelists has now blossomed into a full-fledged international movement, the Lausanne Committee for World Evangelization. It has already has become one of the most influential Christian movements of the twentieth century.

In January of 1987 I had the opportunity to attend a planning conference in Callaway Gardens, Georgia, with Dr. Leighton Ford, Chairman of the Lausanne Committee for World Evangelization. Leighton Ford is a close friend and colleague, a man of intelligence, integrity and prayer. His perspective about the organization and his vision for the future are extremely inspirational. For that reason, I would like to share a portion of Dr. Ford's remarks with you. They demonstrate a widening of the trail we all can use in carrying our torch to the world.

The New World

We need God to do a new thing because we are facing a newer world.

It will be a *larger* world. If you are 50, the world has doubled in your lifetime. By the year 2000 there will be one and one-half billion more people. India will be the biggest country with more than all of

Africa and Latin America.

It will be a *developing* world. Eighty percent of the population will be in developing countries by 2025. Sixty percent will be in Asia.

It will be an *older* world. By 2025 there will be one billion people over 60—one in every 7.

It will also be a *younger* world. Sixty percent are now under 24. Half of Latin America is under 18. Mexico City has a population under 14 equal to New York City. There is not a Third World city with a median age over 20.

It will be an *urban* world. Mexico City will have 31 million by the year 2000. By 2000 there will be 22 mega cities, with ten million plus.

It will certainly be a world of *conflict*. Fifty percent of our scientific minds are engaged in so-called "defense." Many fully expect a nuclear terrorist incident or one between the new nuclear nations by 2000.

It will be the world of the "*information era.*" A world divided not between haves and have-nots, but between knows and know-nots. We can now send the Encyclopedia Britannica across the Atlantic six times a minute. If the auto industry kept up with computer information advance, a Rolls-Royce would get 3 million miles a gallon, would cost less than $3 and you could put six on the head of a pin. Jean Pierre du Prie, an information specialist, said, "The more we 'communicate' the way we do, the more we create a hellish world. Ours is a world about which we pretend to have more information, yet one that is increasingly void of meaning."

And it will be a different world in *religion*. Islam is growing 16 percent a year; Hinduism is growing 12 percent, Buddhism 10 percent, Christianity 9 percent. There are now more Muslims than Baptists in Britain. Yet David Barrett speaks of the era of "universal response" and "global access."

By 2000 the number of missionaries from Africa, Latin America and Asia may exceed North America's.

Yet the younger churches may well need revival and renewal from nominalism.

North America and Europe will be seen increasingly as spiritually bankrupt for all our success, technology, and Hedonism.

What Do We Need Most?

I asked a younger pastor in Minneapolis: "What do your people most need to be mobilized for world evangelism?" He pondered a moment and answered quietly: "a staggering view of God." As we face this great, growing, suffering surging world; as we face the vast dimensions of world evangelism; as we face the programs before us in the next several years, I am convinced that only a "staggering view of God" will be enough to take us through.

As our Lausanne Sr. Associate, Ray Bakke has traveled the cities of the world, and has asked the leaders in his consultations to list the obstacles to reaching their cities with the gospel of Christ. Inevitably, he says, seven of the ten reasons are internal to the church—not external to the world—lack of vision, lack of prayer, lack of unity, lack of talent, leadership, too busy to spend time with non-Christians—these are the typical problems.

As Archbishop William Temple said years ago, "The evangelization of those without cannot be separated from the rekindling of devotion of those within."

Judgment must always begin with the house of God. Twelve years ago the Lausanne Covenant called us not to be triumphant, but to be penitent. The Lord complained in Isaiah 42:19, "Who is blind but my servant? or deaf as my messenger that I sent?" Then he said that he had "poured out his anger" upon his people who had not followed his ways.

Perhaps our greatest need today in the church worldwide is a recovery of true, biblical holiness. Robert McShane said, "My people's greatest need is . . ." What would you say? McShane said, "my personal holiness."

In Scripture God says, "'Be ye holy as I am holy." He doesn't ask us to be strong as He is or all-knowing as He is. He does ask us to be holy as He is. The pursuit of holiness, I think, is a neglected priority in our Christian mission strategy.

So what a tremendous reassurance when the God who pours out His anger on our disobedience also promises to pour out His spirit for our obedience. Isaiah 44:3: "I will pour water upon him that is thirsty, and floods upon the dry ground: I will pour my spirit upon thy seed and my blessing upon thine offspring."

I am afraid too many of us, especially in the West today, want a Christ without a cross, a Savior who will fulfill us, but not call us to suffering. Yet we are called not just to receive Jesus as Savior, but to follow Him as Lord and the way of the cross.[42]

I am grateful to Dr. Leighton Ford and the Lausanne Committee for their tireless efforts in setting the pace for this torch relay of world evangelism. They are helping thousands of believers and thousands of congregations multiply the power of individual faith.

When Men Prayed and the World Was Changed

It happened during a very dark period in American history, the Great Depression. A group of laymen in Charlotte, North Carolina, became deeply burdened for their city's spiritual condition. They took off work to pray—no small sacrifice in those hard times. Meeting in the early morning in a farmhouse, they began to pray for revival in their city. As the day passed, their faith grew and they prayed, "Lord, do something in our city that will touch our whole state and nation and even the world!"

Could they possibly have dreamed how their prayers would be answered? The next year they held an evangelistic campaign and one of the farmer's teenage sons came forward and took up the torch of Christ. His name was Billy Graham.

Among Billy Graham's many accomplishments was the formation of the Lausanne Committee in 1974. He recently issued a list of 10 challenges to this organization for the decades ahead. I found them as powerful as they are informative. The following were published in the December 1986 issue of *World Evangelization*:

10–Point Challenge

1. The challenge of reaching the unreached in the next generation.

2. The challenge of creatively using technology to reach the world.

3. The challenge of preserving evangelistic gains by laying a theological base committed to the authority of an infallible Scripture.

4. The challenge of a steadily growing prayer base.

5. The challenge of the bold evangelization of nominal Christians in the West.

6. The challenge of supporting and training Spirit-gifted evangelists.

7. The clear declaration of the evangelistic mission of Lausanne based on the Lausanne Covenant.

8. The challenge of remaining a para-church movement—open to the world but exclusively evangelical.

9. The challenge of building a financial support base founded upon popular prayer support.

10. The challenge of unswerving support of evangelical movements and churches worldwide that lovingly but firmly resist biblical heresy and error.[43]

If met, these challenges could shake the world for good—whether accomplished through the Lausanne Committee for World Evangelization, through a local committee for church missions, or through one's own personal witnessing for Christ. And for those of us who have served the Master for most of our lifetime, such challenges afford an opportunity to pass the torch of God's truth along to a new generation of leaders.

Now you who read this book have the opportunity to do far more than merely look at the torch. You are permitted to seize it and run. Think what a disappointment and tragedy it would have been had the Olympic torch fallen to the ground and gone out. Think how all the world would have gasped if some terrorist had sabotaged the lighting of the torch of liberty at Ellis Island in 1986. How much more of a catastrophe would it be if the next generation God has prepared to bear His torch were to let it fall to the ground, die out or be destroyed by the adversary?

You have a golden opportunity to change this society for good. It's my prayer that through this book you have discovered—or rediscovered—the needed tools and seen them in action.

Review of the Keys to Leadership in the Future

1. Commit yourself to God. He wants to share the privilege and joy of carrying His Word.

2. Set your goal on the next runner. Miraculously we bear not one, but untold thousands of torches. Like feeding the five thousand, the more we hand out, the more we have to share.

3. Be motivated by the things that motivate God.

4. Open your heart to God and He will fill it with genuine enthusiasm.

5. Live in honesty. They who receive the torch from you must be willing to believe you when you speak of its importance.

6. Be strong and of good courage. Though the night be dark, you will always walk in light when bearing this torch.

7. Decide to decide. Indecision is inaction is failure. Hold out your hand and seize the torch.

8. Act responsibly. You are the hope of more people than you know.

9. Keep first things first.

10. Respect the future. He who "inhabits eternity" invites you to share His home there with Him (see Isaiah 57:15).

My final prayer for you, my friend, is: first, submit yourself to God as a willing servant; second, commit yourself to make a difference; and third, never settle for anything mediocre or second best. God is the best and He expects His followers to be the same.

This prayer is not mine alone. It is also the prayer of hundreds of servants who have carried God's torch for many decades. Now the time has come for us to pass it along to you.

Look at the torch. It is yours to carry. Though at times you may stumble and fall, we who hand you this prize are confident you will snap the tape at the finish line with a great and triumphant burst of victory.

May God be with you always.

NOTES

1. Richard Wolfe, *Man at the Top* (Wheaton, IL: Tyndale, 1969), 43.
2. Much of the material in this chapter was adapted from *The Making of a Christian Leader* by Ted Engstrom (Grand Rapids: Zondervan, 1976).
3. Ted W. Engstrom and R. Alec Mackenzie, *Managing Your Time* (Grand Rapids: Zondervan, 1974), 87–89.
4. Ibid., 89–91.
5. A. B. Bruce, *The Training of the Twelve* (New York: Harper, 1886).
6. Kenneth O. Gangel, *Competent to Lead* (Chicago: Moody Press, 1974), 14.
7. (Old Tappan: Fleming H. Revell, 1975).
8. The preceding pages of this chapter are adapted from *Competent to Lead* by Kenneth O. Gangel (Chicago: Moody Press, 1974), 14–17.
9. William Barclay, *The Letters of 1–2 Timothy, Titus, Philemon* (Edinburgh: Saint Andrews Press, 1962), 86–87.
10. Anecdote retold from *What a Day This Can Be*. John Catoir, ed., Director of the Christophers (New York: The Christophers).
11. Og Mandino, *The Greatest Secret in the World* (New York: Frederick Fell, 1972), 30.
12. Ibid., 38–39.
13. John Catoir, ed., *What a Day This Can Be* (New York: The Christophers), 10.
14. Ibid., 10.
15. Alfred J. Kolatch, *Guideposts* (August 1974), 25.
16. John Gardner, *Self Renewal* (New York: W.W. Norton, rev. ed. 1981), 12.
17. From "Creative Thinking" cassette, Earl Nightengale and Whitt Schultz. Quoted in Frank Goble, *Excellence in Leadership* (Aurora, IL: Caroline House, 1972), 21.
18. From the "anonymous" file of my friend and colleague Dr. F. Carlton Booth.
19. Ted Engstrom, *The Making of a Christian Leader* (Grand Rapids: Zondervan, 1976).
20. *U.S. News & World Report*, 6 April 1987, 58.
21. "Urim," from *Unger's Bible Dictionary*, (Chicago: Moody Press, 1966), 1128–29.
22. Robert H. Schuller, "How to Handle Your Foes: Keep on Shining," *Robert H. Schuller Tells You How to Be an Extraordinary Person in an Ordinary World* (Fleming H. Revell, 1985)
23. "Perspectives," *Newsweek*, 24 August 1987, 11.
24. Ted W. Engstrom, *The Making of a Christian Leader* (Grand Rapids: Zondervan, 1976), 191.

25. Ibid., 86.
26. Ibid., 87.
27. Ordway Tead, *The Art of Leadership* (New York: McGraw-Hill, 1963), 289–299.
28. Jim Peterson, *Evangelism As a Life-style* (Colorado Springs, CO: NavPress, 1980).
29. Dale Carnegie, *How to Stop Worrying and Start Living* (New York: Pocket Books, 1984).
30. John Gardner, *Excellence* (New York: W.W. Norton, 1987).
31. Og Mandino, *Og Mandino's University of Success* (New York: Bantam, 1982), xiii.
32. Ordway Tead, *The Art of Leadership* (New York: McGraw-Hill, 1963), 125.
33. Ibid.
34. Frank Goble, *Excellence in Leadership* (Ottawa, IL: Green Hill Publishers, 1978).
35. Gail Sheehy, *Passages* (New York: E.P. Dutton & Co., 1976).
36. Rollo May, *The Courage to Create* (New York: W.W. Norton, 1975).
37. In his book, *The Denial of Death* (New York: Free Press, 1973), Ernest Becker does an excellent job of demonstrating that most of life's actions center around denial of our mortality.
38. C. Peter Wagner, "Confessions of a Workaholic," *Eternity* (August 1975): Vol. XXVI, No. 8.
39. Ibid.
40. Ibid.
41. John R.W. Stott, *Balanced Christianity* (Downers Grove, IL: InterVarsity Press, 1975).
42. Used by permission of Dr. Leighton Ford.
43. Billy Graham, *World Evangelization* (December 1986): 3.

Part One: Leadership Defined

Chapter 1—What Is Leadership?

From *The Making of A Christian Leader* by
Ted Engstrom. *The Making of a Christian Leader* (Grand Rapids: Zondervan, 1976),
19–24.

    1.   What Is Leadership?

Chapter 2—Leadership Style

From *The Art of Management for Christian Leaders* by
Ted Engstrom and Edward R. Dayton. *The Art of Management for Christian Leaders*
(Waco: Word Books, 1976), 29–35.

    3.   Leadership Style

Chapter 3—The Price of Leadership

From *The Christian Executive* by
Ted Engstrom and Edward R. Dayton. *The Christian Executive* (Waco: Word Books,
1979), 70–75.

    9.   The Price of Leadership

Part Two: Leadership and the Bible

Chapters 4—6

From *The Making of A Christian Leader* by
Ted Engstrom. *The Making of a Christian Leader* (Grand Rapids: Zondervan, 1976),
25–50.

    2.   The Old Testament and Leadership
    3.   Christ and Leadership in the Gospels
    4.   The Epistles and Leadership

Chapter 7—"The Pattern We Gave You"

From *60-Second Management Guide* by
Ted Engstrom and Edward R. Dayton. *60-Second Management Guide* (Waco: Word
Books, 1984), 135–138.

    30. The Pattern We Gave You

Part Five: Integrity in Leadership

Chapters 21—22

From *Integrity* by
Ted Engstrom and Robert C. Larson. *Integrity* (Waco: Word Books, 1987), 1–14,
139–156.
1.   Semper Infidelis
9.   A Call to Action

Part Six: Leaders as Managers

Chapters 23—24

From *60-Second Management Guide* by
Ted Engstrom and Edward R. Dayton. *60-Second Management Guide* (Waco: Word
Books, 1984), 15–21.
2. What Good Managers Know
3. What Good Managers Do

Chapter 25—Doing or Being

From *The Art of Management for Christian Leaders* by
Ted Engstrom and Edward R. Dayton. *The Art of Management for Christian Leaders*
(Waco: Word Books, 1976), 99–106.
12. Doing or Being

Chapter 26—Managing Conflict

From *The Christian Executive* by
Ted Engstrom and Edward R. Dayton. *The Christian Executive* (Waco: Word Books,
1979), 177–183.
24. Managing Conflict

Chapters 27—28

From *60-Second Management Guide* by
Ted Engstrom and Edward R. Dayton. *60-Second Management Guide* (Waco: Word
Books, 1984), 77–81, 65–68.
17. The Anguish of Change
14. On Taking Risks

Chapters 29—30

From *The Christian Executive* by
Ted Engstrom and Edward R. Dayton. *The Christian Executive* (Waco: Word Books,
1979), 191–195, 99–105.
26. Dangers
12.   You and Your Board

Chapter 31—Murphy's Law for Managers

From *60-Second Management Guide* by
Ted Engstrom and Edward R. Dayton. *60-Second Management Guide* (Waco: Word

Chapter 40—When Did You Leave Your Family?

From *Seizing the Torch* by

Ted Engstrom and Robert C. Larson. *Seizing the Torch* (Ventura: Regal Books, 1988), 173–192.

9. When Did You Leave Your Family?

Epilogue

From *Seizing the Torch* by

Ted Engstrom and Robert C. Larson. *Seizing the Torch* (Ventura: Regal Books, 1988), 193–213.

10. The Future: A Scenario for the Twenty-First Century

D r. Ted W. Engstrom, president emeritus of World Vision International, past president of Youth for Christ International and an influential American evangelical leader, died July 14, 2006, at his home in Bradbury, California. He was 90.

A gifted preacher, an astute manager and the author of more than 50 books, Dr. Engstrom was a giant in American evangelical circles for more than half a century. As executive vice president and later president and chief executive officer of World Vision, he helped turn a small Christian agency focused on war orphans into one of the world's largest and most extensive relief and development organizations. He served as vice president for 19 years and president for two, retiring in 1987.

Dr. Engstrom was known for being organized, affirming, and decisive. His Christian faith was immediately evident and unwavering. He said he took his life verse from Psalms 32:8: "I will instruct you and teach you in the way you should walk, give you counsel and watch over you."

His considerable organizational skills allowed Dr. Engstrom to crowd an incredible amount of activity into a day. He was a writer, a public speaker, a church official, Bible teacher, business executive, a sports enthusiast and a devoted husband and father of three children. He chaired or was a member of numerous church, educational, and philanthropic boards.

Yet, at the same time, friends and colleagues remember "Dr. Ted" as a gentleman and a scholar who always made time to listen to them. In World Vision's earlier days, he personally interviewed all prospective employees.

---

1.   The following biographical sketch was written and compiled by the staff at World Vision US and posted on www.worldvision.org. Used by permission.

"He valued everyone and made everyone feel valued," said Dean Hirsch, current president and chief executive officer of World Vision International. "And his ability to integrate the Gospel with everyday life was absolutely inspiring. Dr. Ted made work and faith walk together."

Evon Hedley, who first met Dr. Engstrom as a Youth for Christ colleague in 1946 and remained a lifelong friend, said he combined a resolute faith with abundant compassion. Hedley recalled a car trip in which the Hedleys and their children and the Engstroms and their children found themselves caught in a savage windstorm in Hopkinsville, Kentucky. Forced to stop for the night, they were able to find but a single room in a lone motel. They shared it, sleeping on the floor.

Dr. Engstrom is recognized for making two fundamental contributions to American evangelical culture in the 20th century. First, he introduced standard business practices and management principles to churches and other faith-based institutions, which often went awry because they paid too little attention to the bottom line. Second, and more importantly, he combined social outreach with evangelism, contending that service to mankind was as important as preaching salvation in Christ.

"What Ted said was this," said Bill Kliewer, a World Vision marketing executive who first met Dr. Engstrom in 1958: "'Let's give a cup of water in the name of Christ but let's also introduce those who are thirsty to the saving grace of Christ.'"

As an author and editor, Dr. Engstrom combined his business acumen with his passion for Christian service. He co-authored the best-selling *Managing Your Time* and wrote *The Making of a Christian Leader* and *The Fine Art of Mentoring*. Averaging a book a year for 50 years, he also wrote hundreds of magazine articles on subjects ranging from the pursuit of excellence to neighborhood evangelism.

Dr. Engstrom was also an indefatigable correspondent, writing letters and notes to friends, colleagues, and public figures into his nineties. His letters were known equally for their love and their candor.

"Ted is an ideal church member," the Rev. Paul Cedar, former pastor of Lake Avenue Church in Pasadena, California, said at Dr. Ted's 90th birthday party. "He will tell you the truth and love you at the same time."

Dr. Engstrom was born on March 1, 1916 in Cleveland, Ohio. The son of a machine shop supervisor, he grew up the eldest of four children in a humble Christian home. But he didn't share his parents' fervent faith. His biographer, Bob Owen, writes that Dr. Engstrom had a rebellious spirit. He joined a high school fraternity, took up smoking and drinking and played trumpet in a dance band. He kept late hours, distressing his parents, who prayed for him.

"It was my parents' prayers that got to me," Dr. Engstrom explained to Owen. "I'd come home late sometimes, thinking I would sneak into the house unnoticed, only to hear my dad pray, 'Lord, get hold of Ted. Don't let him out of our grasp. Lead and guide him with your Holy Spirit.'"

Their prayers were soon answered. As a freshman student at Taylor University in Upland, Indiana, Dr. Engstrom was moved to walk forward at a Monday morning chapel service and declare himself for Christ. Nearly 70 years later, he remembered it like it was yesterday.

In a 2001 talk to World Vision staff members, Dr. Engstrom recalled, "It was 10:30 in the morning, April 1, 1935, when I responded to the claims of Christ. I was released and rejoiced in the grace that God gave me that day. I walked out and the sky was never bluer; the flowers were never prettier; and the birds never sang better."

Dr. Engstrom earned his way through school by operating a print shop. An English and journalism major, he also edited the campus newspaper and worked as chief cook in the student dining hall. At 6 foot 2 and 200 pounds, he was a natural athlete, lettering in basketball and baseball. In the summer of his senior year, he played catcher and first baseman in the semi-pro Central Indiana League, earning $15 a game.

A year after graduating in 1938, Dr. Engstrom married his college sweetheart, Dorothy Weaver. She was there the morning he committed himself to Christ and she would be at his side for the next 66 years, until her death in 2005.

With his journalism degree and printing experience, Dr. Engstrom took a job with the Higley Press in Butler, Indiana. But within a year, he was back at Taylor University as assistant to the president and director of public relations. While he loved Taylor, which awarded him an honorary doctorate in 1955, he got an offer from Zondervan Publishing House that was too good to refuse. Zondervan, which would become one of the largest Christian publishers in the world, asked Dr. Engstrom to be book editor. The two Dutch founders had been impressed with the writing and editing work he was doing at Taylor.

With the exception of a two-year stint in the US Army, Dr. Engstrom labored at Zondervan as book editor, editorial director and general manager for the next 11 years. He not only edited; he wrote biographies, youth stories, devotionals, and other Christian texts. Among them was a three-volume set of "preacher's helps" entitled *The Treasury of Gospel Gems*. It was filled with poetry, essays, Scripture references, and hundreds of sermon illustrations.

While at Zondervan in Grand Rapids, Michigan, Dr. Engstrom became the local director of Youth for Christ International, an evangelistic ministry to teens. He and Dorothy also started a family, adopting three children between 1945 and 1953.

In 1947 the Grand Rapids chapter of Youth for Christ invited a then little-known evangelist named Billy Graham to do a crusade. Directed by Dr. Engstrom, it was Graham's first city-wide crusade. More than 6,000 people showed up for 10 straight nights. Afterwards, Graham asked Dr. Engstrom to join him. But Dr. Engstrom turned him down, saying he was in the publishing business for life. Nonetheless, he and Graham become lifetime friends.

Publishing, however, was soon pushed aside by Youth for Christ. In 1948, Dr. Engstrom was elected as a delegate to the first World Congress on Evangelism in Switzerland. There he met Bob Pierce, the founder of World Vision, and was excited by the evangelical action that he learned was going on across the globe.

"I'd never even thought of 'world' evangelism before," Dr. Engstrom told Owen, his biographer. "It had never entered my mind."

In 1951, Dr. Engstrom was invited to be executive director of Youth for Christ International. He took a leave of absence from Zondervan and never went back. He moved the family to Youth for Christ headquarters in Wheaton, Illinois, and launched into a hectic schedule of speaking, travelling, and writing the organization's monthly magazine, "Campus Life." In 1957, he was elected president of Youth for Christ and his travel increased dramatically. He visited more than 60 nations and preached at Youth for Christ rallies in most of the world's major cities.

Night after night, Dr. Engstrom returned to the rally podium to issue the closing invitation. "Come to Jesus," he said, "come just as you are. Leave all your sins, all your shortcomings behind and come to Jesus." Hundreds, sometimes thousands, walked forward. Meanwhile, Dr. Engstrom's scrupulously maintained Rolodex began filling up with the names of evangelical leaders: Billy Graham, Leighton Ford, Cliff Barrows, Bill Bright, Robert Schuller, Pat Robertson, James Dobson, and many more.

By 1963, the pace of the Youth for Christ job had exhausted Dr. Engstrom. On the advice of colleagues, he checked into the Mayo Clinic in Rochester, Minnesota. Doctors told him to either change his pace or change his job. He decided to find a new job.

According to Owen, the biographer, Dr. Engstrom's new job came as the result of a chance meeting with World Vision founder Bob Pierce in the lobby of the Mayflower Hotel in Washington, D.C. Pierce told Dr. Engstrom that he needed help at World Vision. "And the Lord laid your name on my heart," said Pierce, who did not know that Dr. Engstrom was planning to resign from Youth for Christ.

Dr. Engstrom told Pierce that he'd consider it. And Pierce, according to Owen, cried. "Oh Buddy," he said, "my prayer has been answered. You've got to come with me to World Vision."

Dr. Engstrom came to World Vision headquarters in Pasadena and signed on as executive vice president, responsible for finance, administration, personnel and promotion. He soon discovered that World Vision was in fiscal straits. Pierce, a dynamic and charismatic leader, had little patience for budgets and bottom-line accounting.

Shortly after arriving at World Vision, Dr. Engstrom began a fiscal austerity program. He introduced standard business practices, trimmed the payroll and closed down the expensive radio ministry.

In his 2001 talk to staff, Dr. Engstrom recalled that era. "In the early days of World Vision," he said, "we were bankrupt. I would call for a prayer meeting and we would pray from 11 pm to 2 am. And then in the morning, God provided the exact amount we needed."

Slowly, World Vision dug its way out of debt. When Pierce, ill in body and spirit, resigned in 1966, the board offered Dr. Engstrom the presidency. He declined. According to Owen's account, he did not want to give any appearance of having forced out Pierce. So for the next 14 years, he continued as executive vice president. In the meantime, he helped recruit Stanley Mooneyham, a former member of Billy Graham's crusade team, as president.

World Vision did not occupy all of Dr. Engstrom's time. He continued to preach, lecture and write. He teamed up with Ed Dayton, another World Vision executive, to conduct more than 100 two-day seminars for pastors, administrators and business executives on "managing your time." He quoted Sir Walter Scott: "Dost thou love life, then do not squander time, for that's the stuff life's made of."

Dr. Engstrom especially emphasized decisiveness. "The longer a decision is delayed," he said, "the more difficult it is to make."

In a biographical note he wrote for World Vision staff, Dr. Engstrom said, "My modus operandi for accomplishing my many hopes, desires and priorities has been years of attempting strong administration, marked by an emphasis on management by objectives, and pursuit of excellence (and a reminder never to surprise me!)."

After Mooneyham retired in 1982, the World Vision board again asked Dr. Engstrom to be president. He served for two years, then became president emeritus in 1984. As president, he continued to stress what he regarded as the essential relationship between social service and evangelism.

"The Bible says that 'to those whom much has been given, much will be required,'" he said. "We minister in the name of the Lord Jesus to a world that is needy and lost."

As president emeritus, Dr. Engstrom continued to work. He came into the office every day and gave his considerable energy to church, Christian education, and world evangelism. In 1989-90, he served as interim president of Azusa Pacific University, the largest evangelical college in the United States.

Even as he celebrated his 90th birthday in 2006, Dr. Ted continued to come into his office at World Vision. He no longer drove and his hearing and vision were fading but his mind was sharp and his spirit strong.

"Whenever the Lord calls, I'm ready," he told friends and World Vision staff who gathered to celebrate his birthday. "I'm not only ready, I'm eager. I'll have all eternity to celebrate God's goodness and grace."

Throughout his long career, Dr. Engstrom received many honors. Five colleges, including Taylor University, his alma mater, awarded him honorary doctorates. He received awards or certificates of honor from the National Association of Evangelicals, the Republic of Korea, the International School of Theology, the Freedoms Foundation at Valley Forge, and the National Religious Broadcasters Association.

Dr. Engstrom chaired or was a member of numerous boards including Youth for Christ International, Focus on the Family, CEO Dialogue, the Asia Center for Theological Studies, the International School of Theology, Azusa Pacific University, the Institute of Christian Organization Development, the Evangelical Council for Financial Accountability, the Institute for American Church Growth, African Enterprise, Taylor University, and World Vision International.

He and his wife, Dorothy, were members of Pasadena's Lake Avenue Congregational Church for more than 40 years, where he also chaired the board.

Dr. Engstrom is survived by his three children, Gordon, Don, and Jo Ann.

Timothy J. Beals is president of Credo Communications, LLC, (www.credo-communications.net) a company that works with Christian ministry leaders and publishers to develop life-changing books, Bible-related products, and other Christian resources.

Prior to starting Credo Communications, LLC, Tim served as founder and publisher of World Vision Press and as associate publisher for the Bible Department at Zondervan. Tim also serves as Adjunct Professor of Writing at Cornerstone University (Grand Rapids, MI) and as Instructor of Publishing at University of the Nations (Kona, HI, and Harpenden, UK).

Tim is co-writer of *On the Side of Angels: A Human Rights Manifesto from a Christian Perspective* (Authentic) and general editor of several Bible editions, including *When You Pray* (Crossway), *The Red Letters* (Crossway), and *The Stewardship Resource Bible* (Crossway).

Tim is the editor of scores of books and Bibles and author of hundreds of local newspaper articles, national magazine features, and devotional pieces.